Palgrave Studies in the History of Economic Thought

Palgrave Studies in the History of Economic Thought publishes contributions by leading scholars, illuminating key events, theories and individuals that have had a lasting impact on the development of modern-day economics. The topics covered include the development of economies, institutions and theories.

The series aims to highlight the academic importance of the history of economic thought, linking it with wider discussions within economics and society more generally. It contains a broad range of titles that illustrate the breath of discussions – from influential economists and schools of thought, through to historical and modern social trends and challenges – within the discipline.

All books in the series undergo a single-blind peer review at both the proposal and manuscript submission stages.

For further information on the series and to submit a proposal for consideration, please contact the Wyndham Hacket Pain (Economics Editor) wyndham.hacketpain@palgrave.com.

Editors
Maria Cristina Marcuzzo • Paolo Paesani

# Richard F. Kahn

Collected Economic Essays

palgrave
macmillan

*Editors*
Maria Cristina Marcuzzo
Department of Statistical Sciences
Sapienza University of Rome
Rome, Italy

Paolo Paesani
Department of Economics and Finance
University of Rome Tor Vergata
Rome, Italy

We are grateful to Palgrave Macmillan, Wiley and The Royal Economic Society, the American Economic Association, the Banca Commerciale Italiana, Europa Publications for the Institute of Bankers, Allen and Unwin, Lloyds Bank Review, and the Scottish Economic Society, for permission to republish these essays.

ISSN 2662-6578 ISSN 2662-6586 (electronic)
Palgrave Studies in the History of Economic Thought
ISBN 978-3-030-98590-5 ISBN 978-3-030-98588-2 (eBook)
https://doi.org/10.1007/978-3-030-98588-2



Cover image: Terry Dean / Alamy Stock Photo

This Palgrave Macmillan imprint is published by the registered company Springer Nature Switzerland AG.
The registered company address is: Gewerbestrasse 11, 6330 Cham, Switzerland

# Praise for *Richard F. Kahn*

"Richard Kahn is of great interest to historians of economics because of his role at the centre of two of the central developments in economics in the 20th century: imperfect competition and the Keynesian revolution. This collection, including an important, previously unpublished paper from 1933, and the very helpful editorial introduction successfully illustrate the evolution of Kahn's thinking from the 1930s to the 1970s."

—Roger E. Backhouse, *University of Birmingham and Erasmus University Rotterdam*

"A long-awaited second collection of Richard Kahn's essays including his later reflections on Keynes and analysis of the postwar international economy and problems of unemployment and inflation – accompanied by an excellent introduction by the editors. An important contribution to the history of economics."

—John B. Davis, *University of Amsterdam and Marquette University*

"This valuable and fascinating collection documents Richard Kahn's central role in the imperfect competition and Keynesian revolutions in economics, making conveniently accessible his articles on imperfect competition, on Keynes, and on inflation and unemployment, including a pathbreaking 1933 paper on imperfect competition previously published only in Italian translation. The helpful and informative editorial introduction provides a useful guide to the nature and importance of Kahn's contributions. Every economist interested in the imperfect competition and Keynesian revolutions should have this book."

—Robert W. Dimand, *Brock University*

# Contents

# Sources

1. (1933). Unpublished.
2. (1937). *Economic Journal*, *47*(185), 1–20.
3. (1952). *Economic Journal*, *62*(245), 119–130.
4. (1985). In G. Harcourt (Ed.), *Keynes and His Contemporaries* (pp. 42–51). London: Macmillan.
5. (1978). *Journal of Economic Literature*, *16*(2), 544–559.
6. (1984). In R. F. Kahn, *The Making of Keynes's General Theory* (pp. 119–168). Cambridge: Cambridge University Press.
7. (1952) In *Banking and Foreign Trade* (pp. 1–18), Lectures delivered at the Fifth International Banking Summer School, Oxford, July. London: Europa Publications for the Institute of Bankers.
8. (1973). *American Economic Review*, *63*(2), 181–188.
9. (1976). In A.P. Thirlwall (Ed.), *Keynes and International Monetary Relations* (pp. 3–35). London: Macmillan.
10. (1976) In G.D.N. Worswick (Ed.), *The Concept and Measurement of Involuntary Unemployment* (pp. 19–33). London: Allen and Unwin.
11. (1976). *Lloyds Bank Review*, 119, 1–11.
12. (1976). *Scottish Journal of Political Economy*, *33*(1), 11–16.

We thank Prof. D. Papineau, Richard Kahn's nephew and literary executor, for granting permission to publish the essay "Imperfect Competition and the Marginal Principle".

The essays of this collection have been reproduced without alteration from the original text, except for few minor corrections of typos and oversights. Spelling, quotation marks, italics, underlines, punctuation and bibliographic reference system have been left as they were in the sources, even if inconsistent among themselves. Only notes have been always reproduced as consecutively numbered footnotes within each essay.

CHAPTER 1

# Introduction

*Maria Cristina Marcuzzo and Paolo Paesani*

The first collection of Richard Kahn's essays was published by Cambridge University Press (Kahn 1972). It contains, among other texts, the article on the multiplier (Kahn 1931), the essay on liquidity preference (Kahn 1954) and the Memorandum to the Radcliffe Committee (Kahn [1958] 1972). Taken together, these essays provide a broad but incomplete picture of Kahn's scientific output. Kahn himself hoped for a second collection of his writings. It is this wish, communicated to Maria Cristina Marcuzzo at the end of the 1980s, that lies behind this volume. The essays

Our heartfelt thanks go to Iolanda Sanfilippo for her excellent editorial assistance in preparing this collection of essays.

M. C. Marcuzzo (✉)
Department of Statistical Sciences, Sapienza University of Rome, Rome, Italy
e-mail: cristina.marcuzzo@uniroma1.it

P. Paesani
Department of Economics and Finance, University of Rome Tor Vergata, Rome, Italy
e-mail: paolo.paesani@uniroma2.it



M. C. Marcuzzo, P. Paesani (eds.), *Richard F. Kahn*, Palgrave Studies in the History of Economic Thought, https://doi.org/10.1007/978-3-030-98588-2_1

collected here, one of which hitherto unpublished in English,[1] represent a selection of those Kahn himself indicated to her and focus on four areas: the theory of imperfect competition, Keynes and the Keynesian revolution, the regulation of international trade and finance and analysis of the link between inflation and unemployment.

Accordingly, the present collection is divided into four parts, as indicated above, within which the essays are generally presented in the chronological order in which they were written; thus the reader is able not only to follow the evolution of Kahn's thinking over time, but also to grasp the overall coherence of his approach. One of the purposes of this introduction is to reconstruct the context in which the articles chosen for this collection came out, bringing to light the network of professional and personal relationships in which Kahn's thought developed and making explicit the problems and questions to which he sought solutions and answers. We have therefore used all those fragments of knowledge, also drawn from unpublished works and correspondence (see Marcuzzo and Rosselli 2005), that were helpful in placing these writings in their context.

The second purpose, in fact, is to show just how relevant these writings are to contemporary economic theory and policy. Nowadays, the focus on power relations and strategic interaction between the actors concerned on the labour market—central to Kahn's thinking about inflation and its nexus with unemployment—is recognized as essential to mainstream and heterodox approaches alike. It is not a matter of re-proposing the Phillips curve, which Kahn refuted together with too sharp a distinction between cost-push and demand-pull inflation (Cristiano and Paesani 2018a), but of drawing attention to the crucial role, in determining inflation and unemployment, played by the institutions that determine nominal wages and regulate conflicts between employers and employees at the sectoral and aggregate level. The sectoral dimension also matters insofar as localized shortages in raw-materials or semi-finished products can trigger cost and price spikes that spill over across the economy. These elements bring attention back to the supply-side causes of inflation and their interaction with demand. Recent debates on the "end of inflation" in connection with globalization, diminished trade union power on wages and the role of

[1] The essay was published in Italian in Kahn (1999) edited by M.C. Marcuzzo in which a selection of Kahn's papers were also translated. For an overall view of Kahn's contribution, see also Marcuzzo (2011).

sectoral demand and supply factors in triggering inflation are all indicative of the relevance of this approach.

A second aspect that makes Kahn's thought topical is the reappraisal of Keynes's contribution to economic theory and policy, with regard both to the employment-wage-price nexus and to the more general issue of uncertainty as an obstacle to maintaining high living standards and full employment. Over the last fifteen years, the global economy has suffered very hard blows, from the global financial crisis in 2007–2009 to the Covid-19 pandemic. Events of such magnitude compel economists and policymakers to forge new models and new tools to deal with the far-reaching and often unforeseen consequences of global shocks. In the current context of high uncertainty, the name of Keynes is again resounding loud and clear thanks to his approach to economic problems with its mixture of creativity, willingness to experiment with new policy instruments and optimistic commitment.

Following in Keynes's footsteps, but bringing his own personal views, Kahn analysed international economic problems in the field of trade and finance. The articles collected here obviously reflect the historical context in which they were produced. Nonetheless, they are worth re-reading today for their constructive spirit, more than fifty years after the end of the Bretton Woods regime, whose origins Kahn recounts, and at a time when the international economic institutions are struggling to maintain an acceptable international economic order.

The economic and financial problems that many economies, at different stages of economic development, face today are partly due to contingent factors and partly to structural reasons. In this context, it is hardly deniable that in many crucial sectors, including information technology, distribution and finance, oligopoly and imperfect competition are the norm rather than the exception. We start from this topic in our exploration of Kahn's thought.

## Competition Theory: Market Imperfections and Entrepreneurial Behaviour

Kahn's role in the elaboration of the theory of imperfect competition, with its development into the theory of oligopoly, is perhaps not sufficiently recognized. Indeed, Sraffa's suggestion in his 1926 article to "abandon the path of competition and turn in the opposite direction, towards monopoly" (Sraffa 1926, p. 542) was initially pursued by the then

23-year-old Kahn, who made it the focus of his first research activity. In the academic year 1928–1929, Kahn had attended Sraffa's lectures ("Advanced Theory of Value"), in which the subject of market imperfection was addressed along very similar lines to the 1926 article.[2] In the same year Kahn took G. Shove's course "Economic Theory",[3] a considerable part of which was devoted to "market imperfections".

It is hardly surprising, therefore, that in the Preface to the Fellowship Dissertation, which Kahn wrote between October 1928 and December 1929, there is ample recognition of these two economists. Nor is it surprising that the Dissertation, because it remained unpublished for almost fifty years[4] and because of its title, *The Economics of the Short Period,* which did not explicitly allude to market imperfection, did not fully reveal the importance of Kahn's contribution to the emergence of the theory of imperfect competition.

In the established textbook tradition, it was the books by Joan Robinson and E. Chamberlin that were indicated as the initiators of that line of analysis. And even Joan Robinson, in spite of her close collaboration with Kahn in writing *The Economics of Imperfect Competition* (Robinson [1933] 1969), did not get round to reading Kahn's Dissertation until January 1933,[5] when her book was in draft form. On the other hand, Kahn had been in correspondence with Chamberlin, to whom he had sent the duopoly part of the dissertation for him to read it, since 1930.[6] The discussion with Kahn resumed in the days when *The Economics of Monopolistic*

[2] Sraffa's Lectures are in the Sraffa papers, Trinity College Library, Cambridge, and are now available online (SRAF/D/2/1). We also have the notes taken by Kahn and his essays written for the course in the Kahn papers, King's College Library, henceforth given with the catalogue reference number (RFK/3/3/359–84).

[3] Of Shove's course, we are left with the notes taken by John Saltmarch in his academic year 1928–1929. See in particular the section entitled "Partial or Conditional Monopoly". For a discussion of Shove's role in the development of the theory of imperfect competition, see Carabelli (2005).

[4] The Dissertation was first published in Italian in 1983, with an Introduction by M. Dardi (Kahn 1983), and then in English in 1989 (Kahn 1989).

[5] See the letter from Joan Robinson (henceforth JVR) to Richard Kahn (henceforth RFK) of 24.1.1933 (RFK papers, 13/90/1/75).

[6] See E. Chamberlin's letters to RFK of 3.8.1930 and 12.9.1930 in RFK papers, 1/13/19–25, and Chamberlin (1961, p. 513n).

*Competition* was about to be published, in February 1933, when Kahn was visiting Harvard.[7]

The main interest of the Dissertation lies in the explanation of why, in a depression, all the firms in an industry work part-time—shutting down their plants for some days and working at full capacity on others—and not the situation predicted by the assumption of perfect competition, i.e. that some firms (the most inefficient) are forced to shut down their plants, while the others (the most efficient) continue to work at full capacity. The key to Kahn's explanation lies in the analysis of quasi-fixed costs and prime costs (i.e. the difference between total and quasi-fixed costs), both being relevant in the short run. If firms work full-time only some days (shutting down plants on the other days), as was the case with the British cotton industry in the depression of the 1920s, it must mean that this method was the most advantageous for maximizing profits or minimizing losses. This means that the average prime cost has a particular pattern, i.e. it is constant up to the point corresponding to full capacity, at which it becomes infinite. But the inverted L-shape of the short-run average (and marginal) prime cost curves means that, if the assumption of perfect competition is maintained, i.e. the assumption of a perfectly elastic demand curve for the firm, the price and quantity produced by the individual firm are determined at the level of full capacity utilization. If, on the other hand, the assumption of imperfect competition is introduced, i.e. each firm faces its own particular market and thus a negatively sloped individual demand curve, the equilibrium level of output may be lower than the level of full capacity utilization.

But in what respects is the contribution of the Dissertation innovative?

In his *Principles*, Marshall had addressed the problem of determining monopoly equilibrium with the concept of the maximum monopoly revenue (Marshall 1964, p. 704), which is the point at which the price difference between the supply and demand curves multiplied by the level of production is maximized. Marshall's solution, although identical to that

[7] RFK to JVR, 9.2.1933 (RFK papers, 13/90/1/100): "I am having lunch with Chamberlin, whose book on Monopolistic Competition is just about to come out, in fact in two days". JVR's letter to RFK, dated 3.3.1933 (RFK papers, 13/90/1/169), is also interesting, concerning the coincidence of the "discoveries" on imperfect competition in those years: "Chamberlin's book has turned up. Very competitively Monopolistic as Piero [Sraffa] says. I find myself enjoying the coincidences without any base emotions, but I must not read it thoroughly or the temptation to put in [i.e. in *The Economics of Imperfect Competition*] footnotes will be too great."

given by the equality of marginal cost and marginal revenue, was not formulated in those terms, and the definition of marginal revenue was only "discovered" in the late 1920s and early 1930s, by more than one author working independently. Moreover, Marshall had not gone into much depth in considering the effects of the behaviour of rival firms on the elasticity of demand of a firm, or the effects of the pricing policy of a single firm on the behaviour of rival firms. Despite Cournot's and Edgeworth's work on duopoly, at the time of the writing of the Dissertation, a determinate solution to the problem and its integration into a general analysis of imperfect competition had yet to be arrived at.

Definition of marginal revenue is also absent from the Dissertation, but there are two aspects of particular interest in comparison with the previous literature on oligopolistic markets. The first is Kahn's invention of a way to measure the degree of market imperfection, under the assumption of linearity of demand curves and average unit cost, through the "annihilation coefficient" which is analytically identical to the measure that would later become known as the "degree of monopoly" (Marcuzzo 1994).

The second aspect of interest is how the effect on the demand curves of firms of a price change by one of them is taken into account. This is the subject of a specific section in which Kahn also criticizes the conclusion reached by Sraffa in his 1926 article, according to which in the case of equilibrium in an imperfect market—i.e. in which there are many firms each with its own individual market and hence a negatively sloped demand curve for its product—the final equilibrium price is the one that would be reached if the market were entirely controlled by a single monopolist. Kahn's position is argued on the basis of the idea that the slope of individual demand curves reflects the assumptions each firm makes about the behaviour of the others. Kahn shows that under any conjecture the relationship between individual and market demand curves is such that it never gives equilibrium at the monopoly price, but at a lower price and consequently at a larger quantity than would be chosen by a monopolist under the same technical conditions (Kahn 1989, p. 117).

The point of contention between Kahn and Sraffa revolves around the different way of conceiving the response of the competing firms in the presence of a price increase by one of them (on this, see Marcuzzo 2001). Kahn focuses on a subjective element, namely the conjectures that each firm makes about what its competitors will do if it decides to raise its price. Sraffa focuses on an objective element, the upward shift in the demand curves of competing firms in the presence of a price increase by one of them (substitution effect). According to Kahn, the fear of losing customers to competitors leads each firm to move along a flatter demand curve than we would observe if the firm operated under pure monopoly conditions. At the market level, this leads to a higher equilibrium quantity than would be the case in a monopoly and a lower price. According to Sraffa, the general increase in prices by all firms leads consumers to reduce their demand (resulting in a reduction of the individual and collective elasticity of demand) without abandoning their trusted supplier. Price increases and quantity reductions stop at the same point where they would stop in the case of a monopoly.

We have focused on the Dissertation because this work clearly identifies the two fundamental questions that arise once the hypothesis of perfect competition is abandoned: (i) if firms no longer take as given the price as they do in perfect competition but decide it, how will they take into account the behaviour (reactions) of other firms? (ii) is pursuit of maximum profit also in this case the best description of the firm's behaviour?

The three articles we have chosen for this part of the collection, "Imperfect Competition and the Marginal Principle" (Chap. 2, Kahn 1933), "The Problem of Duopoly" (Chap. 3, Kahn 1937), and "Oxford Studies in the Price Mechanism" (Chap. 4, Kahn 1952a), represent successive stages in the evolution of Kahn's thought and the literature that developed on the subject at the same time, but they have in common the identical approach to answering these two questions.

Of the first essay we know that Kahn took it with him on his trip to the United States, which began in December 1932 and ended in April 1933. On the evidence of a particular detail we can date the completion of this draft to a few weeks before his departure from England,[8] while it is more difficult to date its beginning. The Dissertation was completed in December 1929 and soon after Kahn began working with Keynes on the *Treatise on Money*, which was published in October 1930 (Keynes [1930] 1971b). In the months immediately following, Kahn was busy discussing and exploring the issues raised by Keynes not only in the *Treatise on Money*, but also in *Can Lloyd George Do It?* (Keynes [1929] 1972). In the same months Kahn began to work on a book he had planned, with the same title as the Dissertation, which remained unfinished.[9]

[8] In the text reference is made to Robinson's book under the title *The Monopoly Analysis of Value*, which was only changed to the definitive one, *The Economics of Imperfect Competition*, in January 1933. See JVR's letter to RFK of 24.1.1933.

[9] This unpublished book can be found in Kahn's archives (RFK papers, 2/8–2/9). On this, see also Marcuzzo and Rosselli (2008).

The article in question was developed from what was to be Ch. VII of the unfinished book and it is certainly the product of discussions in what they jokingly called "The Trumpington Street School", named after the street where Joan and Austin Robinson—returning from India in late 1928—made their home in Cambridge and where Kahn was a frequent visitor.[10] The discussions were certainly provoked by Sraffa's critique of Marshallian theory and also concerned the implications of Keynes's *Treatise on Money*, which was the subject of the "Circus" meetings, as we shall see later.

Kahn sailed on the Majestic to the United States in December 1932, taking with him this article which was to be a summary of some of those discussions. Over the previous two years Kahn had been working intensively with Joan Robinson on solutions to various problems that had arisen during the drafting of the *Economics of Imperfect Competition*.[11] The most important analytical finding presented in this text—the equilibrium "double condition" given by the point of tangency between the average revenue and average cost curves and the point where marginal revenue meets marginal cost—had already appeared in an article by Joan Robinson, "The Diminishing Supply Price", published in the *Economic Journal* of 1932 (Robinson 1932) and later incorporated into the book which was to become known as "Kahn's Theorem".[12]

Kahn presented his article at several conferences in the United States and gave it to Taussig for publication in the *Quarterly Journal of Economics*. However, the article was not accepted. From Kahn's correspondence, which among other things offers a very interesting account of the situation in the country and aspects of American academic life, we know that Kahn reacted with characteristic modesty, and made no further attempts to publish it.[13]

[10] It was about this article that JVR wrote to RFK, in a letter of 11.2.1933: "Austin [Robinson], who has yet only just glanced at it, is very keen that it should be published as the first manifesto of the Trumpington Street School. (After reading it he repeats this view)" (see RFK papers, 13/90/116).

[11] On the cooperation between Kahn and Robinson in drafting Robinson's book, see Rosselli (2005).

[12] "The condition of tangency between the demand curve and the average-cost curve of a profit-maximising firm that just breaks even, Schumpeter in his 1930s Harvard lectures used to refer to as 'Kahn's Theorem'" (Samuelson 1994, p. 54n.).

[13] RFK to JVR, 3.3.1933: "Taussig's refusal of my article on 'Imperfect Competition and the Marginal Principle' was conducted with great candour, which I did all I could to encourage". (RFK papers, 13/90/43).

A few years later, however, he decided to publish an article, "The Theory of Duopoly", which was to become a classic on the subject and which earned Keynes' comment: "Your article is a beautiful piece of work".[14]

In this article, unlike in the Dissertation, there is no room for mathematics and the whole complicated discussion of the effects of the actions of a single duopolist on the behaviour of the other and thus the role of the strategies implicit in each move of each firm, are tackled without any mathematical support.

As we know, Kahn is one of the inventors of the "kinked demand curve" and in general of the introduction of "guesswork" in demand curves, expressed in the value of elasticity, for the analysis of price and quantity produced in a duopoly or in oligopolistic markets in general. The characteristic feature of Kahn's approach to the theory of price formation in imperfect markets is the maintenance of the profit-maximizing assumption as the only certain rule on which to base analysis. Contrary to traditional marginalist analysis, Kahn had always—ever since his first unpublished article—interpreted the hypothesis of pursuit of maximum profit of firms as synonymous with a method "by trial and error", rather than the expression of an optimizing rationality, and even of the entrepreneur's use of marginal calculus. But unlike other alternative approaches to those based on marginal analysis, Kahn never accepted explanations of the price formation mechanism that were descriptive or based on an assumption of non-"rational" behaviour. Without these caveats, Kahn's highly critical stance, in the third essay, towards theories of price formation—based on "what entrepreneurs say they do" (Hall and Hitch 1939)—would indeed be incomprehensible.

From a theoretical point of view, the main proponent of abandoning the theory of perfect competition and the profit-maximizing hypothesis in favour of a theory of price formation on the basis of a (mostly constant) mark-up on (mostly constant) prime costs was Michał Kalecki, who elaborated his theory after a study of prices, revenues and costs in some British industries.

It was Joan Robinson who, impressed by his qualities from their first meeting in the summer of 1936, took it upon herself, in her words, "to blow his trumpet for him" (Robinson [1977] 1979, p. 186). Kalecki then moved to Cambridge at the end of 1937 and the group around Keynes found the necessary funding for his research (Marcuzzo 2020a). At the

[14] J.M. Keynes (henceforth JMK) to RFK of 1.1.1935, in RFK papers, 13/57/122.

end of 1938, "The Cambridge Research Scheme of the National Institute of Economic and Social Research into Prime Costs, Proceeds and Output" was set up and gave Kalecki a job in Cambridge.

At the end of the first year, Kalecki presented the main results of the research in the form of particular reports on the industries concerned (in collaboration with Hsu and Tew) and an Interim Summary of Results of the research in general (RFK 5/1/83–86). These reports were commented on rather critically by J. Robinson (RFK papers, 5/1/163–69) and especially R. Kahn,[15] who objected to the methodology employed by Kalecki. Shortly afterwards Kalecki resigned—although he responded promptly to the criticism that had been levelled at him (RFK papers, 5/1/1963–169)—and left Cambridge in the late summer of 1939.[16]

Kahn's aversion to mark-up pricing—in contrast to Joan Robinson's, who later made it her own—was reiterated by Kahn fifty years later: "I think the concept of a horizontal short-run supply curve is an exaggeration. Nor do I subscribe to the ideas ... of a margin that is fixed. It clearly varies between firms according to how different their first costs are."[17] It is in fact interesting to compare Robinson's later observations on the superiority of Kalecki's theory of price formation over Keynes's (e.g. Robinson [1977] 1979, pp. 188–189) with the position expressed in her Memorandum of July 1939, which was highly critical of the usefulness of Kalecki's degree of monopoly:

> The degree of monopoly is not "a thing in itself". It depends on e.g. 1) Imperfection of the market; 2) Number of Firms in the market, which may alter (a) with technical conditions (probably important in the steel industry); (b) with immediate past history of the industry; 3) Deliberate monopoly agreements; 4) Tacit agreement and custom of the trade, which may alter with boom and slump; 5) Recent wage changes; 6) State of demand for a commodity as a whole. Thus to say that there has been a "change in the degree of monopoly" is never a final account of what has happened, and it is often unreasonable to expect a constant degree of monopoly in face of other changes, e.g. a change in demand. (RFK papers, 5/1)

[15] RFK to M. Kalecki, 10.7.1939 (RFK papers, 5/1/149–58) and 11.7.1939 (RFK papers, 5/1/159–162).

[16] M. Kalecki to RFK, 9.6.1939 in RFK papers, 5/1/146. See also Osiatynski (1991, p. 524).

[17] R.F. Kahn to R. Marris, 2.5.1987 (in Marris 1991, p. 184).

The opposition to the concept of the "degree of monopoly", as developed by Kalecki, confirms Kahn's adherence to the Marshallian approach to price formation, based on equality between marginal revenue and rising marginal cost, the same assumption accepted by Keynes in the *General Theory.*

## Employment Theory: The Keynesian Approach and the Relationship with Keynes

Kahn was the academic economist closest to Keynes from 1930 until Keynes' death in 1946. At first, as Kahn himself told us, he and three other King's students met Keynes once a fortnight for supervision. Soon Kahn proved to be such an outstanding student that he elicited Keynes' enthusiastic comments on the essays he wrote for supervision.

To give a few examples: in the margin of an essay by Kahn of 4 November 1927, Keynes wrote: "You are really good at economics" (RFK papers, 3/3); similarly on 27 April 1928: "Excellent—an almost perfect answer" (RFK papers, 3/3). On one occasion, just before exams, Keynes wrote to his wife: "Yesterday, my favourite pupil, Kahn, wrote the best answer I have ever had from a student; he must absolutely get an A".[18]

And indeed Kahn lived up to expectations, coming top (First Class) in the 1928 Economics Tripos. But when it came to choosing the subject of his thesis to compete for a Fellowship at King's, Keynes suggested a topic (involving the use of the Midland Bank's monetary statistics) that proved impractical (due to the Bank's unwillingness to make them public). So when Kahn, at the suggestion of Shove and Sraffa, proposed to deal with "short run economics", i.e. to explain how firms in a given industry reacted in a depression, with analysis of the type of costs and the type of market in which they operated, Keynes—apart from providing him with the statistics of the cotton industry—did not show much interest in the subject. But in fact, as Kahn wrote almost fifty years later, "my work on the short run was then to influence the development of Keynes' thought" (Kahn 1989, p. 21). Collaboration with Keynes resumed only after Kahn was elected a Fellow of King's in March 1930, again arousing the enthusiasm of Keynes, who wrote in his congratulatory letter to Kahn: "the

[18] JMK to Lydia, 28.4.1928, in JMK papers, PP/45/190.

election went off without a hitch; everyone recognised it as an exceptionally good thesis".[19]

It was in these months that began the exchange of ideas and discussions that, as Kahn tells us in the essay "The Cambridge 'Circus'" (Chap. 5, Kahn 1985), was to lead to the publication of the *General Theory* and in general to the diffusion of the "Keynesian revolution". The question of the role of Kahn and the "Circus"—that is, of the group made up by not only Kahn, but also James Meade, Piero Sraffa, Joan and Austin Robinson—has given rise to very conflicting judgments in the literature. This essay is an important personal testimony to the discussions of those months, during which the so-called "multiplier" article, "The Relation of Home Investment to Employment", was conceived (Kahn 1931).

We know that the multiplier article was written between the summer of 1930—the drafting began in August during a holiday in the Tyrol (Kahn 1984a, p. 91)[20]—and the early months of 1931 and was published in June of that year. The importance of the article on the multiplier lies in the fact that it provided the framework for analysing the conditions under which there is an increase either in the price level or in quantities (or a combination of the two) in aggregate in the face of an increase in demand (in this case public investment in road building). The multiplier remained central in macroeconomic models until monetarism first and subsequently the new classical macroeconomics, emphasizing the link between consumption and permanent income and Ricardian equivalence *à la* Barro, determined its disappearance together with the idea of a constructive role for discretionary fiscal policy (see Marcuzzo 2014).

Kahn always insisted that his role was to help Keynes to free himself definitively from the "stranglehold" of the Quantity Theory of Money, contributing to the alternative approach with a fundamental tool, the aggregate supply curve.[21] However, the limitation of that still immature formulation of an alternative approach to the "classical" one, as Kahn him-

[19] JMK to RFK, 16.3.1930, in RFK papers, 13/57/3.

[20] Among Kahn's papers is an extract from the article, with a dedication to an unidentified Elgar: "With the author's heartful thanks for the cooperation and stimulus received in the Tyrol, August 1930 and Surrey, March 1931" (RFK papers, 13/127).

[21] Letter from RFK to R. Marris, 2.5.1987, in R. Marris 1991, p. 184: "Maynard derived from me the idea of thinking in terms of the supply curves of capital goods and consumption goods". See also Kahn's letter to D. Patinkin, 11.10.1978: "I claim I brought the theory of value into the General Theory in the form of a concept of the supply curve as a whole and that this was a major contribution" (Patinkin 1993, p. 659).

self later acknowledged, was that he had not clarified the fundamental implication of the "multiplier", i.e. the necessary equality of savings and investment. Kahn attributed this difficulty to the fact that the article moved within the definitions of savings and income in the *Treatise on Money*; only after the "discovery" of the principle of effective demand did it become clear that those particular definitions had to be abandoned (Kahn 1984a, pp. 98–100).

In the article on the multiplier Kahn studies the effects of an increase in investment on aggregate output in terms of the demand and supply of consumer goods in aggregate under short-run conditions, which were the appropriate conditions to evaluate the proposal, put forward by Keynes in the pamphlet *Can Lloyd George Do It?* (Keynes [1929] 1972) to implement a public works policy to get out of the economic depression. If the level of demand is high, the productive capacity will already be largely utilized and its greater utilization will call for an increase in costs and therefore in prices. But if the level of demand is low, plant and equipment will be largely unused, so production can be increased without any appreciable increase in unit costs and prices.

The crucial aspect is therefore the shape of the costs of enterprises in the short term. We have seen that study of various types of costs and their development was the focus of analysis in the Dissertation, where Kahn assumed that the average cost curves were shaped like an inverted L. It is natural, therefore, to suppose that Kahn, in writing his article on the multiplier, drew on his prior knowledge to identify the appropriate shape of the cost curves needed to construct an aggregate supply curve for consumer goods. However, in the article on the multiplier, although a wide range within which costs are constant is mentioned, the assumption that they are in the shape of an inverted L is no longer to be found. This was probably influenced by Pigou's criticism of the hypothesis in his Fellowship Committee Report, which Kahn was able to read shortly afterwards: "I think unfortunate that he should assign to [L-shaped supply curves], as he does, a central place in his formal analysis" (RFK papers, 2/8).

The importance of the inverted L-shaped curves lay in the fact that, as we have seen, they forced Kahn to introduce the hypothesis of imperfect competition in his Dissertation. If, on the other hand, the hypothesis of the shape of increasing cost curves is maintained, it is no longer necessary to abandon the hypothesis of perfect competition.

As we know, in the *General Theory* Keynes accepted the traditional assumptions that short run marginal cost curves are increasing[22] and that the degree of competition is given and that firms' behaviour is driven by profit maximization. The most important consequence of application of the Keynesian recipe to unemployment is that any increase in demand—if costs are rising and firms must maximize profits—requires an increase in prices. If money wages are given, the increase in prices leads to a decrease in real wages and thus increase in employment can only be achieved at the expense of a decrease in real wages. In the Keynesian approach the direction of causality goes from increasing employment to decreasing wages and not vice versa. But accepting the existence of an inverse relationship between wages and employment lent itself to misrepresentation of the Keynesian message and its incorporation into a completely different theoretical scheme.

Kahn accepted the responsibility for having suggested to Keynes the idea that "short-period supply curves were rising curves" ("Unemployment as seen by the Keynesians", Kahn 1976c, also Chap. 11, note 14, in this volume) with all the consequences that this entailed. The merit of having induced Keynes to return to the subject of the trend of real wages with respect to employment (Keynes [1939] 1973c), is attributed to the work of two Cambridge Research Students, J. Dunlop and L. Tarshis (Dunlop 1938, 1939 and Tarshis 1938, 1939).

However, there is no evidence that Kahn ever regretted that Keynes had accepted the assumptions of perfect competition and profit maximization. He defended the former on the grounds that it was made "for simplicity" and the latter on the basis of the conviction that alternative assumptions based on the degree of monopoly or a constant mark-up were tautologies or assumptions rather than true theoretical explanations.

The collaboration between Kahn and Keynes was very close in the years leading up to the publication of the *General Theory*. It was Kahn who played the most important role in guiding Keynes' thinking in some relevant respects (Marcuzzo 2002), but in general it was from the discussions within the "Circus" and those of the following months that the *General Theory* took shape.

[22] For the maintenance of this hypothesis, Keynes is known to have attributed the responsibility to Kahn (Keynes 1973a, pp. 399–400).

The voluminous correspondence,[23] in some cases unpublished, between Keynes and Kahn between 1931 and 1935 (the *General Theory* was finished in December of that year) shows Kahn's insistence on the need for definitions to be more precise and demonstrations more stringent. For example, he intervened on the third draft, in September 1935, on the way to demonstrating the necessary equality between savings and investment. In a letter to Keynes in October 1935 (published in Keynes 1973b, p. 637), Kahn wrote:

> I do not like you saying that saving and investment are "different names for the same thing". They are different things (that is the whole point)—they are certainly different acts—but they are equal in magnitude. I still hold that the simple-minded proof that saving = investment, appropriate for those who cannot grapple, with user cost, etc. is called for—not only for the sake of the simple-minded, but to prevent the obvious retort that all your stuff depends on your peculiar definitions. What is wrong with saying that however income is defined,
>
> Income = value of output = consumption + investment
> also income = consumption + saving
> ∴ saving = investment
>
> This truth is far too important (and far seldom recognised) to be concealed in a mist of subtle definition.

Again, Keynes accepted Kahn's suggestion, as can be seen on comparing the final version (Keynes [1936] 1973a, p. 63) with the third draft (Keynes 1973b, p. 424). There is ample evidence that the atmosphere in the months when the *General Theory* was being written was one of expectation of a great theoretical change, of which the then "young Keynesians" were perhaps more convinced than Keynes himself. Joan Robinson even went so far as to say later on: "there were moments when we had some troubles in getting Keynes to see what the point of his revolution really was" (Robinson, [1973] 1979, p. 170).

On the question of the nature of the "Keynesian revolution", which would only come about with the *General Theory*, Keynes was much more cautious and, with regard to the relationship with the *Treatise on Money*, he used expressions on several occasions aiming to recall aspects of continuity as he wrote "Thus the new argument, though (as I now think) much

[23] On this correspondence see Marcuzzo 2005.

more accurate and instructive, is no more than a development of the old" (Keynes [1936] 1973a, pp. 77–78).

Kahn's position is very precise in identifying the points of departure of the *General Theory* from the *Treatise*, which would have consisted above all in the definitive abandonment of the Quantity Theory of Money and in the understanding of the causal link between investments and savings but, unlike Robinson, he seems more inclined to hold that the importance of the Keynesian approach should not be identified solely with the *General Theory*.

As we know, Keynes fell seriously ill in April 1937 and almost immediately after was absorbed by the problems of the imminence and then the outbreak of war. This marked the beginning of a new phase in their collaboration, not least because of the new responsibilities that Keynes's absence from academic life was imposing on Kahn.

In later years, Kahn would return in various contexts to Keynes's ideas, as the two writings that complete this section exemplify: "Some Aspects of the Development of Keynes's Thought" (Chap. 6, Kahn 1978) and the Raffaele Mattioli Lecture (Chap. 7, Kahn 1984b), published here under the title "'The General Theory of Employment, Interest and Money'". By reconstructing what Keynes himself "actually thought and wrote" (Kahn 1978, p. 545), Kahn pursued two related objectives. First, to provide elements useful to clarify some of the controversies between Keynesians and non-Keynesians, particularly severe in the 1970s. Second, to reaffirm the general validity of certain theoretical points which Keynes formulated and which Kahn endorsed and developed. In this respect, Kahn's writings on Keynes are important both as contributions to the history of economic thought and as further developments of the Keynesian approach as an alternative to the neoclassical general equilibrium approach.

As is his custom, Kahn pays great attention to detail, offering a meticulous reconstruction of Keynes' change of mind on the link between money and the price level, from the acceptance of the Cambridge equation in the *Tract on Monetary Reform* (Keynes [1923] 1971a) to the rejection of Quantity Theory in the *General Theory*. Crucial in determining this shift is Keynes's recognition of the role of asset prices and the interest rate in mediating the influence of money on prices, through investment and profits. This recognition allows Keynes, and Kahn with him, to free himself from the "monetary mystique" that posits the existence of a direct causal link between money and prices without explaining what this link derives from. To Keynesians, the link between money and prices is neither direct nor univocal and other forces must be considered, starting with nominal wages as determinants of variable unit costs.

Kahn insists on the influence of contingent conditions in shaping Keynes' ideas on these issues, and indeed on the absence of a systematic and satisfactory treatment of the behaviour of money wages in the *General Theory*, where Keynes focuses on the reluctance of wages to fall in the presence of high unemployment while questioning the idea that if wages fell unemployment would be reabsorbed.

Moreover, the simplification of Keynes's ideas, as in the neoclassical synthesis, opens the way to the possibility of imagining a binary world in which, if there is unemployment, wages do not change and if there is full employment, any increase in aggregate demand has only inflationary consequences. As we will see in greater detail below, Kahn firmly rejects this view in favour of a more complex assessment in which, without ignoring the possible inflationary effects of a sharp increase in aggregate demand, inflation can be triggered by sectoral bottlenecks and/or distributional and inter-union conflicts, even in the presence of high unemployment. Kahn reiterates that full employment and stable prices are compatible with one another, provided policymakers are prepared to use all the available instruments including monetary, fiscal and income policy to foster the appropriate coordination of economic agents' decisions. This attitude is typical of the Keynesian approach to policy problems at both the domestic and international levels, as the writings collected in the third part of this volume evidence.

## International Money and Trade

Britain declared war on Germany on 3 September 1939. Keynes wanted Kahn to be employed by the Treasury as a Civil Servant for the period of the war, but he initially met with considerable resistance because Kahn appeared to be too close to Keynes who was regarded with great suspicion at the time (Marcuzzo 2020b, p. 10). Kahn was eventually given a job at the Board of Trade, where he began work in December 1939. The Board of Trade was in charge of finding ways of reducing the demand for consumer goods, to make room on ships and free up resources for military purposes. It soon became clear that the only solution was to resort to direct rationing of food and clothing. Kahn was one of the architects of the adopted scheme of rationing through a system of points, which was suggested to him by reading the German press (Marcuzzo 2020b, p. 14).

In October 1941, Kahn moved to Cairo to take up a position first as Economic Adviser and then as Deputy Director General of the Middle East Supply Centre. The task of this centre was to gather information and to handle the issue of the priority of imports into the area, in cooperation with some twenty governments in the Middle East that had different administrative structures and independent monetary systems. On his return to London in January 1943, Kahn worked for a year at the Ministry of Supply, with the task of studying the post-war conditions of raw materials, in terms of both price and volume. In the latter period Kahn again worked very closely with Keynes and both worked on a buffer stock scheme for commodities and on problems in the sterling area.

Kahn's return to Cambridge academic life in September 1946 and his growing teaching and administrative commitments did not prevent him from continuing to collaborate with international institutions and to reflect on international monetary and economic issues. Kahn's intellectual contributions in this field, especially between the 1940s and 1960s, can be divided into three distinct although closely related areas: exchange rates and international payments, buffer stocks and commodity price stabilization, economic development and international cooperation.

Regarding the first issue, Kahn devoted particular attention to the problem of the post-war dollar shortages and how different countries could cope with it, as well as the organization of intra-European payments. As Kahn argues, no single one-size-fits-all solution to the problems posed by the shortage of dollars exists and different countries, giving priority to full employment and the improvement of their citizens' living standards, should be left free to adopt the policy mix that best suits their institutional, social and political conditions.

The same spirit pervades Kahn's analysis of buffer stocks and commodity price stabilization, one of the cornerstones of the plans set out by Keynes as early as 1938. Kahn began working on buffer stocks in 1952 as he started cooperating with the Food and Agriculture Organization (FAO). In recent years, this part of Kahn's activity has come under intensive and fruitful research (Fantacci et al. 2012; Paesani and Rosselli 2014; Rosselli 2017). The research has brought to light both the gestation of a book for the FAO—which was never published, and which dealt with fluctuations in the prices of primary products and how best to curb them through the creation of buffer stocks managed by a supranational authority—and Kahn's views on buffer stocks and the context in which those views took shape.

Analysis of Kahn's views on these issues is enhanced with consideration of his contributions as a member of four groups of experts for the United Nation Conference on Trade and Development (UNCTAD) in the course of the years 1965–1969 (Marcuzzo 2020b, pp. 35–36). These reports remain largely unexplored in the literature on Kahn. In the 1965 report, the Group considered the need for reform of the International Monetary System, which would make it responsive to the need for economic growth of both the developed and developing countries, advocating that part of the additional international liquidity created by the International Monetary Fund (IMF), in the form of Special Drawing Rights (SDR), should be placed at the disposal of the International Bank for Reconstruction and Development (on this see also the fourth UNCTAD report). The second and third report dealt respectively with the possibilities of coordinated expansion of trade among the developing countries and with clearing and credit arrangements. In the fourth report (UNCTAD 1969), the group worked on the ideas put forward in the first report and advanced proposals for the shares of SDRs to be assigned to developing countries.

The essays in this section—"The International Regulation of Trade and Exchange" (Chap. 8, Kahn 1952b), "The International Monetary System" (Chap. 9, Kahn 1973) and "The Historical Origins of the International Monetary Fund" (Chap. 10, Kahn 1976b)—reconstruct the design and execution of the new international monetary system that has emerged since the war.

According to Kahn, the primary objective of regulating international trade and exchange rates is to boost employment and improve living standards in all countries, advanced and emerging alike. Free trade and exchange rate liberalization deserve to be pursued only if they are of use in achieving this objective. The possibility that opening up too quickly could make an emerging country poorer, forcing it to export a lot and at decreasing prices in order to pay for essential imports, is real and needs to be taken into account. It follows from all this that the economically and financially weaker countries are entitled to more favourable treatment, in terms of protection from international competition, than the richer and stronger nations.

As far as the system of fixed but adjustable parities is concerned, Kahn warns of the difficulties of managing such a system in the presence of private financial operators driven by short-term speculative objectives and capable of mobilizing huge amounts of capital on the spot and futures markets in pursuit of those objectives. In this context, managing exchange rates rationally—as in the original intentions of Bretton Woods, which Kahn endorses—obliges the monetary authorities and the IMF to equip themselves to counter the destabilizing effects of international financial speculation. The key is to prevent speculation in one direction and the consequent build-up of strong upward or downward pressure on individual currencies. To do so, the monetary authorities must beat the speculators at their own game, catching them by surprise with unexpected changes in official parities of as small a magnitude as possible at frequent but not excessive intervals and without following predetermined time patterns. In this way, they can hope to prevent herd behaviour, making it easier to preserve the official parity system.

In turn, against the idea of a certain superiority of floating versus fixed exchange rates, and the underlying belief in the superior rationality of markets, Kahn reaffirms the merits of adjustable fixed parity policy, provided that it acts in a discretionary, rapid manner and is driven by the primary interest of preserving employment, encouraging productive investment and improving living standards. The same objectives must guide reform of the SDR allocation system, which Kahn discusses in the second part of Chap. 9, focusing on the needs of the emerging countries and the less competitive industrial countries.

The problem of hammering out rules to balance a general need for orderly economic life, prosperity and fairness with the possibility of maintaining temporary forms of discrimination for the benefit of weaker countries and a way out of unexpected situations returns to the centre of Kahn's detailed account of the "Historical Origins of the International Monetary Fund". Kahn's reconstruction is interesting not only as an opportunity to reaffirm the validity of the general principles discussed above, but also for the evidence it offers on Keynes' evolving views on the rules that were being defined at Bretton Woods, as well as the background to the Anglo-American negotiations before and after Bretton Woods and some of the main differences between Keynes's plan for a Clearing Union and the US plan set out by D. White.

Taken together, the three essays collected in this section are an example of how Kahn assesses the capacity of these institutions to perform their task of generating opinions or virtuous behaviour in markets, such as money and foreign exchange (but, as we shall see, also in the labour market), in which we are not faced with optimizing individual behavioural functions. The role of the institutions in these markets should be to create the conditions in which "virtuous" decisions are activated from the collective point of view, given that the individual pursuit of a hypothetical maximum profit or utility is not always capable of generating either a social optimum or, in the long run, an optimum for the individual.

## Unemployment, Wages and Inflation

Kahn's interest in international economic problems was not limited to international trade and exchange rate issues but encompassed other areas, including the problem of inflation, which resurfaced in the developed world in the mid-1950s. His participation, in 1959, in the Group of Experts of the Organization for European Economic Cooperation (OEEC) to study the problem of rising prices marks the high tide of his influence on the theory of inflation.

Besides Kahn, the Group of Experts included W. Fellner (Yale), M. Gilbert (OEEC), B. Hansen (Konjunktur Institutet, Stockholm), F. Lutz (Zurich University) and P. de Wolff (Central Planning Bureau, The Hague). The Report by the Group (Fellner et al. 1961) documents the behaviour of prices between 1953 and 1960 in a selected group of developed countries and analyses the role of demand, wages, monopolistic pricing and external considerations that influence them. In his own recollection of the episode (Marcuzzo 2020b, pp. 30–32), Kahn—who claims to have acted as Chairman *de facto* of the Group—clarifies how the Group introduced the novel concept of wage-wage spiral in opposition to the price-wage spiral notion. As Pasinetti (1991, p. 430) recalls, "It was this Group of Experts that—in the early 1960s, when very few had yet realized the dangers of inflation—introduced the concept of 'wage-wage spiral-leap frogging' connected with the consequences of excessive wage increase".

Kahn's analysis of inflation is based on an articulated theoretical framework, which draws on his reformulation of the liquidity preference theory formulated in Kahn (1954). Here Kahn abandons the idea that there is univocal relationship between the demand for money and interest rate, as represented by a downward sloping function, in favour of a more complex view where money is not taken as exogenous (Cristiano and Paesani 2018a). What is important in determining interest rates is the interaction between different categories of investors, each of them with their expectations and different perception and tolerance of risk and uncertainty. This leads to abandonment of the idea of governing the money supply to achieve price stability and Kahn's recommendation to directly control the entire interest rate term structure.

This recommendation appears in the Memorandum delivered by Kahn to the Radcliffe Committee (Kahn [1958] 1972, pp. 124–152), enriched with his Evidence, which was later published (Radcliffe Committee on the Working of the Monetary System 1960). By controlling the structure of interest rates directly, the monetary authorities can influence domestic investment, exchange rates and international capital movements simultaneously, and so determine both the internal and external equilibrium at the same time. Combining this with control of private consumption through taxation gives full control over aggregate demand and hence over the level and change of output, employment, wages and prices.

During the 1970s, confronted with stagflation, financial instability and social upheaval, during Britain's decade of discontent, Kahn remained faithful to his belief in the close nexus between wage and price inflation and the possibility to reduce both while preserving high employment and external balance through the combination of incomes policy with appropriate fiscal and monetary measures. At the same time, the events of the 1970s forced Kahn to reconsider Keynes's contribution and the characteristics of a Keynesian approach, in order to attempt an all-out defence of them, both against Monetarism and against what we might call the excesses of Keynesianism.

Kahn shared Keynes's belief in the largely political nature of the bargaining processes underlying the determination of wages, and in the difficulty of formulating general theoretical propositions regarding this process. Similarly, Kahn opposed the idea that keeping inflation under control calls for austerity measures designed to increase unemployment and so keep wages and prices under control. This idea had been gaining ground in Britain since the early 1950s, in a context of very low unemployment and rising inflation (see Cristiano and Paesani 2018b, c).

Kahn was dissatisfied with the way Keynes defined involuntary unemployment, even going so far as to say that the second chapter of the *General Theory* always "left him very cold" (Kahn 1976c, p. 23), as he writes in "Unemployment as Seen by the Keynesians", which the present collection contains (Chap. 11). Kahn took issue against both the monetarists and the other anti-Keynesians regarding the explanation of the high inflation rates of the 1970s, based on the expansive fiscal/monetary policies that caused the money supply to grow excessively. For the Keynesians, any possible link between inflation and increasing aggregate demand depends on the level of nominal wages and the response of the trade unions to the economic situation and government measures. For the monetarists, on the other hand, the trade unions have little or nothing to do with inflation, reduction of which requires a squeeze on the growth rate of the money supply, driving unemployment above its natural level, a concept whose soundness Kahn doubted.

It was Kahn's and the Keynesian position not to dispute that persistent inflation is concomitant with parallel increase in the money supply, believing that an increase in the money supply is a necessary condition and not the cause of inflation, the main explanation for which remains the wage-wage spiral. Several factors can exacerbate this spiral. They include a low rate of growth in productivity and living standards, ineffective centralized wage negotiations, and short-sightedness on the part of the trade unions in failing to see the long-term benefits of wage moderation, as Kahn discusses in "Thoughts on the Behaviour of Wages and Monetarism" (1976d, Chap. 12 in this volume). From this perspective, the key to containing inflation and maintaining high employment is to reform wage bargaining and a strong commitment by the State to public investment and programmes to encourage worker mobility and training and improve relations between the social partners within companies.

The reversal in the hegemony of Keynesian thought coincides with the time when the western economies were being hit by levels of inflation unprecedented in the post-war period, and the Cambridge School of economics was gradually falling out of grace. Kahn's retirement in 1972, one year after Joan Robinson, his replacement by Frank Hahn on the Chair of Economics and the failure to appoint lecturers in the Keynesian tradition to Professorial positions represented as many steps in this direction (Saith 2019). In parallel, the Keynesian front, never really united in the first place, became increasingly fractious, as epitomized by the controversy over the relationship between government budget deficits and external balance between Kahn and M. Posner, on the one hand, and the New Cambridge School represented by N. Kaldor and W. Godley, among others, on the other (Kahn and Posner 1974, Shipman 2019).

Kahn's levelled his at times bitter and biting polemic at both politicians and trade unionists, guilty of "irresponsible" behaviour in not curbing the rise in monetary wages, and at the new hegemonic theory—Monetarism—which to all intents and purposes meant restoration of a pre-Keynesian approach. Keynes, too, was accused of not having sufficiently foreseen that, in economies that had experienced high levels of employment for over twenty-five years, money wages would grow in an uncontrollable way and that it would therefore be necessary to design an institutional framework to regulate their upward pressure.

It may be useful to recall here some characteristics of the system that Kahn was facing. In the mid-1960s, the institutional mechanism for determining wages and salaries consisted of three instruments. The first, and most important, was collective bargaining between workers' and employers' representatives, which covered almost all industry and professional organizations. In 1959 there were as many as 651 Trade Unions in Britain, although in the following years the number gradually decreased (in 1976, for example, there were 493 (see Smith 1980, p. 96).

The Congress of Trade Unions (TUC) was the political representative body. The second instrument, established by the Wages Council Acts of 1945, was legislative regulation, which mainly concerned agriculture, the catering industry and a number of particular sectors. The Wages Board or Wages Council was composed of equal numbers of employer and employee representatives and a large number of "impartial", ostensibly independent members (Wootton 1964, p. 82). The third instrument was the arbitration tribunals set up by the Minister of Labour. This instrument provided "arbitration of last resort" when agreement in collective bargaining failed.

By the end of the 1970s collective bargaining covered about 80% of the manual workers and about 50% of the non-manual workers. Wages councils and similar forms of "quasi" collective bargaining covered a substantial part of the remaining non-manual workers. In the non-manual sector, the wages of the non-unionized segment were in fact determined collectively (Nickell and Andres 1983, p. 183). However, the role of national bargaining in determining the wages actually paid by the enterprise, or at the level of the individual department, had been gradually declining throughout the post-war period. Indeed, "wage slippage"—the gap between wages actually paid and nationally negotiated wages—eventually undermined the income policy of Harold Wilson's governments between 1964 and 1970.

When the general election of June 1970 brought the Conservatives back into power, they declared their firm intention not to use an incomes policy; this determination was reiterated by the next Labour government, which, once elected in 1974, declared itself in favour of an incomes policy only as a voluntary response of the social partners (Dawkins 1980, p. 60). This led to the "social contract" of the mid-1970s—to which Kahn refers—which was essentially an agreement between the leaders of the Trade Unions and the Labour government, in which help to moderate the wage squeeze was negotiated in return for social policies acceptable to the Trade Unions.

Those were the years when not only income policy but also full employment policy were disappearing as government objectives. When Margaret Thatcher became Prime Minister in 1979, for the first time since the war the government did not declare full employment as an objective because, according to its monetarist philosophy, it was not an objective that the government could pursue directly through demand-support policies. Rather, the objectives were to reduce public expenditure, taxation, public sector needs and to re-establish market mechanisms. The latter would be directed at indirectly fostering employment. By reducing the growth rate of the money supply, the objective of reducing inflation would also be achieved. To the refutation of the "mystique" of Monetarism and the construction of an alternative institutional framework on Keynesian foundations, Kahn would devote his efforts as a theoretical economist, academic and member of the House of Lords for the rest of his life.

## Conclusions

Kahn's logical abilities were particularly acute in the sense that the mathematician, Felix Klein, distinguished "logicians" from "formalists" and "intuitionists" to explain that "the main strength of the people who belong to this class lies in their logical and critical abilities; in their ability to give precise definitions and to derive from these strict deductions".[24] Unlike Keynes, who knew how to employ rhetoric as a persuasive technique, in Kahn deductive reasoning was always the chosen technique not only for construction of the argument, but also for its defence. It was this obsession with precision in the smallest details that probably prevented Kahn from writing more extensively.

Joan Robinson, who possibly knew Kahn better than anyone else, explained Kahn's "perfectionism" in the preface written in 1976 for the Italian edition of Kahn's collected essays (Kahn 1972, 1976a): "He had great repugnance to the thought that there might be an error attached to his name" (JVR i/8/7). This is also the main reason why Kahn was

[24] "'Formalists' are mathematicians who are exceptionally capable of formally working out a given problem and finding the algorithm. Finally, 'intuitionists' are those who give special importance to geometrical intuition … in all branches of mathematics" (Weintraub 1998, pp. 1841–42).

extraordinarily generous in helping others and equally extraordinarily reluctant to publish. Keynes had intervened in September 1934, in urging Kahn to publish part of the results of the Dissertation, with words that sound prophetic today:

> you must not get into the habit of never doing your own work but always someone else's for them. In the first place you will get subconsciously (or consciously) badly irked by it yourself and in the second place you will end up by getting the credit for everything of any merit published by anyone during your life-time![25]

Two obstacles must be overcome, if one wishes to explore Kahn's individual contribution and originality. The first obstacle lies in his self-effacing nature, his choice frequently to carve out the role of supporting character rather than protagonist, his reluctance to publish works without a very great deal of thought. All the recollections of him concur on these aspects, and on the need to take them into account when fully assessing Richard Kahn's scientific and intellectual contribution. The second obstacle resides in the way of "doing theory" typical of the Cambridge Group of economists—a creative process based on dialogue and continuous exchange of views between professors and young researchers, in written and oral form, before publication. The role of the "Cambridge Circus" in Keynes' transition from the *Treatise on Money* to the *General Theory* is the outstanding example of a creative process that can make it difficult to fully identify the contribution of individuals. Kahn certainly contributed to the work of others while there is less evidence about others playing a direct influence on the development of Kahn's own work, with the exception of Keynes. To summarize the main messages that emerge from reading the twelve essays in this volume, Keynes' strong influence on Kahn is evident, as is Kahn's ability to take up Keynes' legacy and develop it in the face of the contingent problems of the British and international economies.

As far as Kahn's legacy is concerned, we can say that for him the primary objectives of economic policy are to combat unemployment and improve living standards. Both objectives are to be achieved by promoting productive investment and removing obstacles and bottlenecks that can hold back development and trigger inflationary spirals at the sectoral level.

[25] JMK to RFK, 13.8.1934, in RFK papers, 13/57/58.

Price stability and balanced external accounts must be pursued using all possible tools, but without resorting to austerity policies that depress wages and consumption by raising the unemployment rate. Wage developments in relation to productivity are central in determining the link between unemployment and inflation and must be governed by appropriate institutions that foster dialogue and cooperation between the social partners, while respecting the freedom of choice and autonomy of individuals and organizations.

Markets must operate freely, without forgetting that competition is not perfect and that the financial markets are particularly exposed to destabilizing speculation and herd behaviour. This calls for constant vigilance on the part of the relevant authorities and a willingness to act promptly and experiment with innovative regulatory measures, following the logic of trial and error.

In defining growth and development strategies, it is essential to consider the heterogeneity of the actors in the field, the power relations between them, the conjectures that guide their actions, and the possibility of governing those conjectures. This last aspect, perhaps the most important, requires an adequate institutional context, discretion and speed of execution in economic policy choices, as well as a constant effort of persuasion on the part of policymakers and economists in influencing public opinion in the right direction. International cooperation is essential to deal with global problems efficiently. This cooperation must allow for more favourable treatment of the most disadvantaged nations and calls for foresight on the part of the stronger nations and the ability to understand that their own interest in the medium to long term is served by strongly supporting the less favoured nations. The more successful international cooperation is, the less need there will be for individual countries to resort to drastic unilateral measures that are harmful to other countries and counterproductive for those who introduced those measures in the first place.

With this second volume of collected essays, we hope to have contributed to bringing to the attention of contemporary readers these ideas and the man who defended them throughout his life, in academia and in the institutions, Richard Ferdinand Kahn.

## References

Carabelli, A. (2005). A lifelong friendship. The correspondence between Keynes and Shove. In M. C. Marcuzzo and A. Rosselli (Eds.), *Economists in Cambridge: A study through their correspondence, 1907–1946* (pp. 196–215). Abingdon: Routledge.

Chamberlin, E. H. (1961). The origin and early development of monopolistic competition theory. *Quarterly Journal of Economics, 75*(4), 515–543.

Cristiano, C. and Paesani, P. (2018a). Unconventional monetary policy *ante litteram*: Richard Kahn and the monetary policy debate during the works of the Radcliffe Committee. *Cambridge Journal of Economics, 42*(4), 1145–1164.

Cristiano, C. and Paesani, P. (2018b). Price stability and the origins and early influence of the Phillips curve on British policy debates. *History of Political Economy, 50*(3), 483–509.

Cristiano, C. and Paesani, P. (2018c). Monetary policy and price stability in British post-war debate: restatement of evidence from economists' papers presented to the Radcliffe Committee. *European Journal of the History of Economic Thought, 25*(6), 1311–1341.

Dawkins, P. J. (1980). Incomes policy. In W. P. J. Maunder (Ed.), *The British Economy in the 1970s*. London: Heinemann Educational Books.

Dunlop, J. T. (1938). The movement of real and money wages. *Economic Journal, 48*(191), 413–434.

Dunlop, J. T. (1939). Price flexibility and the degree of monopoly. *Quarterly Journal of Economics, 53*(4), 522–534.

Fantacci, L., Marcuzzo, M. C., Rosselli, A. and Sanfilippo, E. (2012). Speculation and buffer stocks: The legacy of Keynes and Kahn. *European Journal of the History of Economic Thought, 19*(3), 453–473.

Fellner, W. J., Gilbert, M., Hansen, B., Kahn, R. F., Lutz, F. and Wolff, P. de (1961). *The Problem of Rising Prices*. Paris: Organisation for European Economic Co-operation.

Hall, R. L. and Hitch, C. J. (1939). Price theory and business behaviour. *Oxford Economic Papers*, 2 (May), 12–45.

Kahn, R. F. (1931). The relation of home investment to employment. *Economic Journal, 41*(161), 173–198.

Kahn, R. F. (1933). Imperfect competition and the marginal principle. Published as Chap. 2 in this volume.

Kahn, R. F. (1937). The problem of duopoly. *Economic Journal, 47*(185), March, 1–20. Reprinted as Chap. 3 in this volume.

Kahn, R. F. (1952a). Oxford studies in the price mechanism. *Economic Journal, 62*(245), March, 119–130. Reprinted as Chap. 4 in this volume.

Kahn, R. F. (1952b). International regulation of trade and exchanges. In *Banking and Foreign Trade* (pp. 1–18), Lectures delivered at the Fifth International

Banking Summer School, Oxford, July. London: Europa Publications for the Institute of Bankers. Reprinted as Chap. 8 in this volume.

Kahn, R. F. (1954). Some notes on liquidity preference. *Manchester School of Economics and Social Studies*, *22*(3), 229–257. Reprinted in R. F. Kahn (1972), *Selected Essays on Employment and Growth* (pp. 72–96). Cambridge: Cambridge University Press.

Kahn, R. F. ([1958] 1972). Memorandum submitted to the Radcliffe Committee on the Working of the Monetary System, May 27. In R. F. Kahn (1972), *Selected Essays on Employment and Growth* (pp. 124–152). Cambridge: Cambridge University Press.

Kahn, R. F. (1972). *Selected Essays on Employment and Growth*. Cambridge: Cambridge University Press.

Kahn, R. F. (1973). The International Monetary System, *American Economic Review*, *63*(2), 181–188. Reprinted as Chap. 9 in this volume.

Kahn, R. F. (1976a). *L'occupazione e la crescita*. Turin: Einaudi.

Kahn, R. F. (1976b). Historical origins of the International Monetary Fund. In A.P. Thirlwall (ed.), *Keynes and International Monetary Relations* (pp. 3–35). London: Macmillan. Reprinted as Chap. 10 in this volume.

Kahn, R. F. (1976c). Unemployment as seen by the Keynesians. In G.D.N. Worswick (Ed.), *The Concept and Measurement of Involuntary Unemployment* (pp. 19–33). London: Allen and Unwin. Reprinted as Chap. 11 in this volume.

Kahn, R. F. (1976d). Thoughts on the behaviour of wages and monetarism. *Lloyds Bank Review*, 119, January, 1–11. Reprinted as Chap. 12 in this volume.

Kahn, R. F. (1978). Some aspects of the development of Keynes's thought. *Journal of Economic Literature*, *16*(2), 544–559. Reprinted as Chap. 6 in this volume.

Kahn, R. F. (1983). *L'economia del breve periodo*. M. Dardi (Ed.). Turin: Boringhieri.

Kahn, R. F. (1984a). *The Making of Keynes' General Theory*. Cambridge: Cambridge University Press.

Kahn, R. F. (1984b). 'The General Theory of Employment, Interest and Money' (Fifth Raffaele Mattioli Lecture). In R. F. Kahn, *The Making of Keynes's General Theory* (pp. 119–168). Reprinted as Chap. 7 in this volume.

Kahn, R. F. (1985). The Cambridge 'Circus'. In G. Harcourt (ed.), *Keynes and His Contemporaries* (pp. 42–51). London: Macmillan. Reprinted as Chap. 5 in this volume.

Kahn, R. F. (1989). *The Economics of the Short Period*. London: Macmillan.

Kahn, R. F. (1999). *Concorrenza, occupazione e moneta*. M. C. Marcuzzo (Transl. and Ed.). Bologna: Il Mulino.

Kahn, R. F. and Posner, M. (1974, April 17). Challenging the "elegant and striking" paradoxes of the New School. *The Times*, p. 19.

Keynes, J. M. ([1923] 1971a). *A Tract on Monetary Reform*. As reprinted in D. E. Moggridge & E. Johnson (Eds.), *The Collected Writings of John Maynard Keynes* (Vol. 4). London: Macmillan for the Royal Economic Society.

Keynes, J. M. ([1930] 1971b). *A Treatise on Money*. As reprinted in D. E. Moggridge & E. Johnson (Eds.), *The Collected Writings of John Maynard Keynes* (Vol. 5 and 6). London: Macmillan for the Royal Economic Society.

Keynes, J. M. ([1929] 1972). *Can Lloyd George Do It?*. As reprinted in D. E. Moggridge & E. Johnson (Eds.), *The Collected Writings of John Maynard Keynes* (Vol. 9: *Essays in Persuasion*, pp. 86–125). London: Macmillan for the Royal Economic Society.

Keynes, J. M. ([1936] 1973a). *The General Theory of Employment, Interest, and Money*. As reprinted in D. E. Moggridge & E. Johnson (Eds.), *The Collected Writings of John Maynard Keynes* (Vol. 7). London: Macmillan for the Royal Economic Society.

Keynes, J. M. (1973b). *The General Theory and After: Part 1*. In D. E. Moggridge & E. Johnson (Eds.), *The Collected Writings of John Maynard Keynes* (Vol. 13). London: Macmillan for the Royal Economic Society.

Keynes, J. M. ([1939] 1973c), Relative movements of real wages and output. *Economic Journal*, *49*(193), 34–51. As reprinted in: D. E. Moggridge & E. Johnson (Eds.), *The Collected Writings of John Maynard Keynes* (Vol. 7: *The General Theory of Employment, Interest, and Money*, pp. 394–412). London: Macmillan for the Royal Economic Society.

Marshall, A. (1964). *Principles of Economics*. London: Macmillan.

Marcuzzo, M. C. (1994). R. F. Kahn and imperfect competition. *Cambridge Journal of Economics*, *18*(1), 25–39.

Marcuzzo, M. C. (2001). Sraffa and Cambridge economics, 1928–1931. In T. Cozzi and R. Marchionatti (Eds.), *Piero Sraffa's Political Economy: A Centenary Estimate* (pp. 81–99). Abingdon: Routledge.

Marcuzzo, M. C. (2002). The Collaboration between J. M. Keynes and R. F. Kahn from the *Treatise* to the *General Theory*. *History of Political Economy*, *34*(2), pp. 421–447.

Marcuzzo, M. C. (2005). Keynes and his favourite pupil. The correspondence between Keynes and Kahn. In M. C. Marcuzzo and A. Rosselli (Eds.), *Economists in Cambridge: A study through their correspondence, 1907–1946* (pp. 21–57). Abingdon: Routledge.

Marcuzzo, M. C. (2011). The "elusive figure who hides in the preface of Cambridge books". An appraisal of Richard Kahn's contributions. In C. Gehrke, N. Salvadori, I. Steedman and R. Sturn (Eds.), *Classical Economics versus Modern Theories. Essays in Honour of Heinz D. Kurz* (Vol. 2, pp. 185–206). Abingdon: Routledge.

Marcuzzo, M. C. (2014). Whatever happened to the Keynesian multiplier?. In R. Baranzini and F. Allisson (Eds.), *Economics and Other Branches: In the Shade of the Oak Tree. Essays in Honour of Pascal Bridel* (pp. 157–168). London: Pickering & Chatto.

Marcuzzo, M. C. (2020a). Kalecki and Cambridge. *Review of Political Economy, 32*(4), 500–510.
Marcuzzo, M. C. (2020b). Richard F. Kahn: A Disciple of Keynes. *History of Economics Review, 76*(1), 2–57.
Marcuzzo, M. C. and Rosselli, A. (2005). *Economists in Cambridge: A study through their correspondence, 1907–1946.* London: Routledge.
Marcuzzo, M. C. and Rosselli, A. (2008). The Cambridge Keynesians: Kahn, J. Robinson and Kaldor. In R. Leeson (Ed.) *Archival Insights into the Evolution of Economics* (Vol. 1, pp. 196–220). London: Palgrave Macmillan.
Marris, R. (1991). *Reconstructing Keynesian Economics with Imperfect Competition: A desk-top simulation.* Aldershot: Elgar.
Nickell, S.J. and Andres, M. (1983). Unions, Real Wages and Employment in Britain 1951–1979. *Oxford Economic Papers, 35* (Supplement: *The Causes of Unemployment,* Nov.), 183–206.
Osiatynski, J. (Ed.) (1991). *Collected Works of Michal Kalecki.* Vol. 2, *Capitalism: Economic Dynamics.* Oxford: Clarendon Press.
Paesani, P. and Rosselli, A. (2014). The Case for a Supra-national Control on Commodities in the post WWII World: Novel Perspectives from FAO and Kaldor Archives. *History of Economic Thought and Policy, 3*(1), 5–30.
Pasinetti, L. (1991). Richard Ferdinand Kahn 1905–1989. *Proceedings of the British Academy, 76,* 423–443. Reprinted in L. Pasinetti (2007). *Keynes and the Cambridge Keynesians* (pp. 65–93). Cambridge: Cambridge University Press.
Patinkin, D. (1993). On the chronology of the *General Theory. Economic Journal,* 103 (418), 647–663.
Radcliffe Committee on the Working of the Monetary System (1960). *Principal Memoranda of Evidence.* Cmnd. 827. London: HMSO.
Robinson, J. V. (1932). Imperfect Competition and Falling Supply Price. *Economic Journal, 42*(168), 544–554.
Robinson, J. V. ([1933] 1969). *The Economics of Imperfect Competition* (2nd ed.). London: Palgrave Macmillan.
Robinson, J. V. ([1973] 1979). What has become of the Keynesian Revolution. Presidential Address presented to the 1972 Annual Meeting of the British Association for the Advancement of Science. In J. V. Robinson (1973), *After Keynes* (pp. 1–11). London: Barnes and Noble. Reprinted in J. V. Robinson (1979), *Collected Economic Papers* (vol. 5, pp. 168–177). Oxford: Blackwell.
Robinson, J. V. ([1977] 1979). Michal Kalecki. *Oxford Bulletin of Economics and Statistics, 39*(1), 7–17. Reprinted in J. V. Robinson (1979), *Collected Economic Papers* (vol. 5, pp. 184–196). Oxford: Blackwell.
Rosselli, A. (2005). An enduring partnership. The correspondence between Kahn and J. Robinson. In M. C. Marcuzzo and A. Rosselli (Eds.), *Economists in Cambridge: A study through their correspondence, 1907–1946* (pp. 259–291). London: Routledge.

Rosselli, A. (2017). Richard Kahn and the stabilization of commodity prices. *Journal of the History of Economic Thought*, *39*(4), 483–501.

Saith, A. (2019). *Ajit Singh of Cambridge and Chandighar*. Basingstoke: Palgrave Macmillan.

Samuelson, P. A. (1994). Richard Kahn: his welfare economics and lifetime achievement, *Cambridge Journal of Economics*, *18*(1), 55–72.

Shipman, A. (2019). *Wynne Godley: A biography*. Basingstoke and London: Palgrave Macmillan.

Smith, D.C. (1980). Trade Unions, growth and industrial disputes. In D. C. Caves and L. B. Krause (Eds.), *Britain's Economic Performance* (pp. 81–134). Washington (DC): Brookings Institutions.

Sraffa, P. (1926). The laws of returns under competitive conditions. *Economic Journal*, *36*(144), 535–550.

Tarshis, L. (1938). Real wages in the United States and Great Britain. *Canadian Journal of Economics*, *4*(3), 362–376.

Tarshis, L. (1939). Changes in Real and Money Wages. *Economic Journal*, *49*(193), pp. 150–154.

UNCTAD (United Nations Conference on Trade and Development) (1969). *International Monetary Reform and Co-operation for Development*. New York: United Nations.

Weintraub, R. (1998). Controversy: Axiomatisches Mißverständnis. *Economic Journal*, *108*(451), 1837–1847.

Wootton, B. (1964). *The Social Foundations of Wage Policy*. London: Allen & Unwin.

PART I

# Imperfect Competition

CHAPTER 2

# Imperfect Competition and the Marginal Principle

*Richard F. Kahn*

## I

So long as the economist had to think of the conditions of demand in terms of price and elasticity, it was difficult to advance the theory of value very far beyond the realm of perfect competition. The maximisation of monopoly net revenue provides but a clumsy tool. Marshall himself must have been well aware of the inadequacy of the construction with which it is usual to associate his name. For in advocating the use of a series of rectangular hyperbolas "made on thin paper", he had to admit that "a careful study of the shapes thus obtained [by drawing diagrams to represent various conditions of demand and of monopoly supply] will give more assistance than any elaborate course of reasoning in the endeavour to realise the multiform action of economic forces in relation to monopolies".[1] It is only recently that the study of monopoly has ceased to be an experimental

Kahn, R. F. (1933). Hitherto unpublished

[1] Principles, p. 483 note.

R. F. Kahn


M. C. Marcuzzo, P. Paesani (eds.), *Richard F. Kahn*, Palgrave Studies in the History of Economic Thought, https://doi.org/10.1007/978-3-030-98588-2_2

branch of economics, dependent on an adequate supply of squared paper, and has become subject to the same simple processes of pictorial reasoning that have long been applied to perfect competition. The change is due to the addition to the economist's apparatus of thought of the marginal revenue curve—a simple device and long overdue—by the hands of a number of independent workers.[2]

Just as marginal cost is the addition to cost of production that results from increasing output by one unit, so marginal revenue is the addition to sale proceeds, or gross revenue, that results from increasing the rate of selling by one unit. And the marginal revenue curve bears the same kind of relationship to the demand curve, which may be regarded as the curve of average revenue, that the marginal cost curve bears to the average cost curve. Now the profit of any individual producer is at a maximum when his marginal revenue is equal to his marginal cost. Thus, instead of having laboriously to discover for what output a certain area is a maximum, we at once get monopoly output as determined by the point of intersection of the marginal revenue curve with the marginal cost curve. If a smaller output than this were produced, more could be added to proceeds than to costs by increasing output; while, if output were greater than that given by the intersection of the marginal revenue and marginal cost curves, a reduction of output would diminish costs more than proceeds. The proposition that the marginal cost of each individual producer is equal to his marginal revenue is fundamental to economic theory.

[2] So far as I can discover, priority is to be attributed to Professor Yntema of the University of Chicago (see Journal of Political Economy, December 1928, p. 687). In Harvard the marginal revenue curve was discovered by Professor Chamberlin (The Theory of Monopolistic Competition, p. 14), by Mr. A. Smithies, of Magdalene College, Oxford, (in an unpublished essay) and, for use at the Harvard Business School, by Professor Philip Cabot and Professor R.S. Meeriam. In Cambridge, England, the idea was introduced independently, in unpublished essays, by Mr. C.H.P. Gifford, of Magdalene College, who was at that time an undergraduate, and by Mr. P.A. Sloan, of Clare College. The term marginal revenue was devised for their conceptions by Mr. Robinson, and it was only on the publication of Professor Viner's article (Zeitschrift für Nationalökonomie, September 1937) that it was realised that, by a coincidence, precisely the same term was in use at Chicago. At Oxford it was Mr. Harrod who invented the curve, again under a different name (Economic Journal, June 1930, p. 238), while mention should also be made of professor Mehta of the University of Allahabad (The Elements of Economics Mathematically Interpreted, p. 252) and of Dr. Schneider of the University of Bonn (Reine Theorie monopolistischer Wirtschaftsformen, p. 14), and probably of several others. The marginal revenue curve forms the basis of Mrs. Robinson's forthcoming book on The Economics of Imperfect Competition, and the substance of this paper is largely derived from her hitherto unpublished work. Professor Chamberlin's treatment of the same subject was not yet available at the time that the paper was prepared.

If competition is perfect, the demand for the individual producer is perfectly elastic. That is a definition of perfect competition. A small reduction in price enables the individual producer to increase his sales by an amount indefinitely large. It follows that when competition is perfect, marginal revenue for the individual producer is equal to the price of the product: when he increases his sales by one unit, he increases his proceeds by the full amount of the price, for there is no appreciable lowering of the price that he charges for the output that he was already selling. Our fundamental proposition then reduces to the well-known rule that if competition is perfect, the marginal cost of each firm is equal to the price that rules in the market. But perfect competition is merely a limiting case. Thanks to the conception of marginal revenue, the marginal principle has now been endowed with university validity. It is no longer necessary to tuck away the treatment of monopoly in a separate water-tight section of our text-books. We can apply the marginal principle to any situation. And if we are interested in perfect competition—it still retains many points of interest, both on practical and on theoretical grounds—we can deduce it as a special case, in fact, as the limiting case.

It must not be supposed that this movement away from the conception of perfect competition is bound up with the growth of trusts and combines. Against the monopolies to which I am referring the Sherman Anti-Trust Law would have nothing to say. The fact significant for the present purpose is that in most industries competition is usually far from perfect, and it follows that if we are to be at all realistic we must turn to the study of monopoly. If competition were perfect any producer could extend his sales to an unlimited extent by an inappreciable cut in his price. But except in the case of certain raw materials the situation in the real world is very different. To quote Mr. Sraffa:

> Business men, who regard themselves as being subject to competitive conditions, would consider absurd the assertion that the limit to their production is to be found in the internal conditions of production in their firms, which do not permit of the production of a greater quantity without an Increase in cost.[3]

In fact every producer must be regarded as a monopolist of his own product, with a definite demand curve for his own product and derived from that demand curve a definite marginal revenue curve. It is this marginal revenue curve which, by its point on of intersection with his marginal cost curve, determines his output.

[3] Economic Journal, December 1926, p. 543.

It will probably be objected by some that it is impossible to speak of the demand curve for an individual firm. They will have in mind the well-known question of duopoly—or of oligopoly, as it may be called for preference. I would reply that the problem of duopoly—the problem of how the other producers will respond when one producer alters his price and output—does not stand in the way of drawing an individual demand curve: what it does is to assist in determining the slope and shape of this demand curve, which is nothing more than the representation of a functional relationship between the individual's sales and the price that he charges. How much will my sales respond if I cut my price ten per cent, having regard to the repercussions of my action on that of my competitors? is the kind of question that the individual asks himself when he is fixing his price. And it is the answer to that kind of question which we find it convenient to represent by the demand curve for his product.

The more imperfect is competition—that is to say, the more imperfect is the market or the smaller is the number of firms in the industry—the less elastic is this individual demand curve. Its slope and shape depend also, as has been said, on the manner in which the other firms react to a change in the particular firm's price and output. That is the problem of duopoly, which it would be going too far afield to discuss. But to those who are interested in the problem of duopoly there is a rather trite suggestion that may be thrown out in passing. It is all a question of assumptions about the behavior of the other firms. It is this question of assumptions which underlies the controversy that began with Cournot and still rages today. Now the most reasonable assumption is that the other firms accommodate themselves to the new situation in such a way as to maximise their profits. In this way we get a perfectly definite position of equilibrium. Or alternatively—it comes, I think, to the same thing—we can suppose that every producer is, quite independently of the other producers, constantly oscillating his price and output in an attempt to hit off the point of maximum profit. For it is only by relying on the persistent adoption by business men of this method of trial and error that the ordinary assumptions of economic theory can really be justified.

## II

This new method of analysis derives its inspiration, so far as English economists are concerned, from an article by Mr. Sraffa, published in the Economic Journal in 1926, though it should be mentioned that Mr. Shove has, by way of oral teaching, long been engaged in following up the same line of thought. Mr. Sraffa, in the course of his article, summed up the traditional treatment in the following words:

> We are thus led to believe that when production is in the hands of a large number of concerns entirely independent of one another as regards control, the conclusions proper to competition may be applied even if the market in which the goods are exchanged is not absolutely perfect, for its imperfections are in general constituted by frictions which may simply retard or slightly modify the effects of the active forces of competition, but which the latter ultimately succeed in substantially overcoming. This view appears to be fundamentally inadmissible. Many of the obstacles which break up that unity of the market which is the essential condition of competition are not of the nature of 'frictions', but are themselves active forces which produce permanent and even cumulative effects. They are frequently, moreover, endowed with sufficient stability to enable them to be made the subject of analysis based on statical assumptions.[4]

That is really the point—the application of statical methods of analysis to the equilibrium of the individual firm. Marshall was, of course, well aware that competition is not perfect in the real world. But he regarded the imperfection of competition as having the nature of a mere friction and was inclined to ignore its importance. "We cannot," he wrote, "regard the conditions of supply by an individual producer as typical of those which govern the general supply in a market".[5] What some economists are doing today is precisely to study the equilibrium of the individual producer in order to obtain a more realistic basis for the conditions determining the output of a whole industry.

Perhaps even more than English economists, American economists are to blame for their failure to come to grips with imperfect competition until recent years. For as much as twenty years before the publication of Mr. Sraffa's article there appeared in this Journal an article on similar lines, from the pen of Professor Moore, in which he attacked the view that "the imperfection of competition is simply a form of friction, producing, for the most part, a negligible variation from the standards that prevail in a

[4] Economic Journal, December 1926, p. 542.
[5] Principles, p. 459.

régime of perfect competition".[6] It is only quite recently that this view has begun to be further questioned.

## III

It is a somewhat insidious domination that the assumption of perfect competition has exerted over economic theory, and is still exerting today. It is the more insidious for being unnoticed—it has operated in hidden channels. Economists are usually aware that competition is seldom perfect, but they less frequently realise that their conclusions only apply to a world of perfect competition. The assumption tacitly made that the demand for the individual firm is perfectly elastic underlies much economic doctrine.

Thus the law that the reward of a factor of production is equal to the value of its marginal physical product only holds if competition is perfect, both in selling the commodity and in buying the factor. Yet even today one sees this law stated without any qualifications whatsoever. The gap that exists in the real world between the wage of labor and the value of its marginal physical product should be of interest both to the economic theorist and to the social reformer.

Again, let us take the view that under ordinary competitive conditions production will be undertaken by optimum firms, each of such a size that its average cost is a minimum. As adopted by many economists this appears to be nothing more than an axiom:—each producer, we are told, will naturally choose that output whose average cost is a minimum. It is seldom realised that what the producer is interested in is not the minimisation of his average cost but the maximisation of his aggregate profit, and that it is only as a result, so to speak, of a mathematical coincidence that if competition is perfect and if profits are normal the maximisation of individual aggregate profit results in each firm being of optimum size. But if competition is not perfect then the equilibrium firm is smaller than the optimum firm: each firm produces under conditions of falling average cost.

The demonstration is very simple. For the individual firm marginal cost is equal to marginal revenue, which is less than price. But if profits are normal, price is equal to average cost, Therefore marginal cost is less than average cost. Therefore the average cost curve must be falling.

Thus in the world as we know it each firm is likely to be producing under conditions of falling long-period cost, and falling supply price can

[6] "Paradoxes of Competition", Quarterly Journal of Economics, Feb. 1906, p. 211.

be regarded as the general rule, arising as a result of the universal prevalence of internal economies.[7] The devices of external economy and of the trees in the forest, which had to be introduced to reconcile the possibility of increasing returns with the existence of perfect competition, can be relegated to the sphere of second-order complications.

In the same way, we are bound to agree with Professor Viner's draftsman[8] that under normal long-period conditions a firm will employ a plant of such a size that average cost would be lower if the firm's output were greater. Just as firms are of less than the long-period optimum size, so plants are worked at less than their optimum level of output.

Let us now turn to the short-period problem presented by a depressed industry. It frequently happens that firms will be working considerably below their capacity levels even though there is a wide margin between the price of their product and their prime costs. Why does not each firm underbid the others in an attempt to secure full-capacity working, until prices are driven down to prime costs? Now Marshall was well aware of the inadequacy of the marginal principle, in the shape in which he applied it to long-period problems, to deal with this kind of question. He was thus led to emphasise what he called the "fear of spoiling the market", which could be held to interfere at a time of depression with the equilisation of price to short-period marginal cost.

But as soon as it is realised that competition is usually rather imperfect and that it is in terms of the equality of marginal cost with the individual firm's marginal revenue that one has to think, the marginal principle appears competent to explain most, if not all, of what the facts reveal; and whatever Marshall really meant by his "fear of spoiling the market", it can be held over for special problems and to attain higher degrees of refinement.

Perhaps sufficient has been said to indicate the absurdity of blaming competition for those inefficiencies which the fashionable policy of "economic planning" is designed to prevent. I come here to a doctrine of Mr. Robinson's, which he conceals in his recent book behind the phrase that "nationalization is often in fact a cure not for an excess of competition, but for a deficiency of it".[9] It is because competition is not perfect that these inefficiencies arise. If only we could reproduce the conditions of

[7] On this point Mrs. Robinson has already published part of her treatment: see Economic Journal, December 1932.

[8] See Zeitschrift für Nationalökonomie, September 1931, p. 36 note.

[9] Structure of Competitive Industry, p. 172.

perfect competition we should have production in the long-period taking place in optimum firms working their plants at the optimum level; and in any given short-period situation output would be distributed among the available plant in the socially most desirable fashion, as provided by the equality of all marginal costs with the price of the product. One method of reproducing the conditions of perfect competition is to set up a co-operative wholesale buying agency to buy the product of each industry by a system of competitive tendering. The demand for each producing unit would then become highly elastic and the organisation of production could be left to look after itself. Moreover, the wastes of competitive advertising would be eliminated. There is no point in spending money on advertising when a very small cut in price is capable of evoking a large response in demand.

## IV

A simple illustration of the application of the marginal principle is provided by the familiar rule that overhead costs do not enter into the determination of price and output in the short period. There are a given number of firms and the output of each firm is determined by the intersection of its marginal cost curve with its marginal revenue curve. Now fixed costs are defined as those costs which do not vary with output in the short period. It follows at once that short-period marginal cost is independent of fixed cost, and consequently that the output and price of a commodity are independent in the short period of the amount of fixed costs.

This is one of the rare occasions on which a major economic doctrine fails to carry conviction to the uninstructed and seems, indeed, to be opposed to ordinary common sense. Outside academic circles it is almost universally believed—and the belief is not usually regarded as one that is open to contradiction—that the business man takes account of his overhead costs when he fixes the price of his product and that a reduction of overhead costs tends to reduce price and increase output. And this overhead costs fallacy lies at the root of an enormous amount of misguided economic policy.

The most notorious example is provided by the prevalent view that a tariff may lower prices as a result of spreading overhead costs over a larger output. To this argument the sophisticated economist has a simple reply, an instance of which may be quoted from a recent publication: "If the circumstances are such that, after the tariff, one of the home manufacturers by enlarging his scale of production could bring prices below those of his foreign rivals, it must have been open to him to do the same thing before the tariff".[10] The answer sounds conclusive. But it proves far too much. It does not confine itself to proving that the price cannot fall as a result of a spreading of overhead costs; it proves that it is quite impossible for a tariff to cause a fall in the price. Now that conclusion, as will be seen later, is not universally valid. What has happened is once again that our sophisticated economist has, quite unknown to himself, taken refuge in the academic realm of perfect competition. But in the world as we know it, a manufacturer has to lower his price in order to sell an increased output and it may not pay him to do so even though his costs would as a result be lowered. It is hopeless to try to meet an argument about the real world by invoking, tacitly or otherwise, the assumption of perfect competition. To meet the overhead costs fallacy on its own ground the marginal principle must be called into play.

This same fallacy underlies the policy of effecting concentration of output by destroying the less efficient plant in an industry. The policy is a popular one in England and is actually in operation in the shipbuilding industry, where it is receiving what amounts in effect to official support: it was through the Bankers' Industrial Development Company, Limited, that an issue of a million pounds' worth of debenture stock was made to the public in order to enable the National Shipbuilders' Security, Limited, to buy up shipyards and destroy them. And it was clear that the favour with which the project was received in official quarters arose out of the belief that the reduction of average costs in the surviving yards, due to a spreading of overhead costs over a larger output, would result in a reduction of prices and an increase of output and employment.

The fallacy involved in such a line of reasoning is scarcely ever pointed out. And small wonder: the application of the marginal principle to the subject of de-rating in a debate in the House of Commons[11] by Lord Passfield (he was then Mr. Sidney Webb) was received with universal scorn, of which the following excerpt provides but one example:

> The right Hon. Gentleman's view of how he conceives a business concern puts forward its tenders is one of the most remarkable I have ever heard. At any rate, it -in down to history as a very good example of the danger of

[10] Tariffs: the Case Examined, by a Committee of Economists, p. 95.
[11] House of Commons, Official Report, 28th Nov., 1928, col. 444-451.

> trusting Socialist statesmen with the management of businesses. If an ex-member of the Socialist Government conceives that he is going to tender without taking into consideration any of his overhead charges, then I think the natural reluctance which has already been shown by business men in this country to confide their destinies to Socialist guidance will be increased end heightened.[12]

That is the normal view. Almost everyone believes that business men take their overhead costs into account in fixing their prices.

## V

What is more serious is that business men themselves believe that they take account of their overhead costs. The economist now finds himself in a serious quandary. The whole of his analysis is based on the assumption that business men behave rationally—that each individual wants to maximise his profit and that he knows how to do it. But the business man's insistence on the part played by overhead costs is quite sufficient evidence for the existence of a strong irrational element, and there is therefore a prima facie case for refusing to admit that what would be true of a rational world is true of this world. Indeed, if men's actions were always to conform to their beliefs, no matter now irrational their beliefs might be, they could never be fallacious. If a business man really believes that overhead costs enter into price, and acts accordingly, then presumably overhead costs do enter into price.

There can be little doubt that he does believe that overhead costs enter into price. But does he act accordingly? If he does, then a large part of economic analysis is valueless; but there is strong reason for thinking otherwise.

For fortunately it is with business men's behavior, not with their thoughts, that we have to reckon. And a general theory that appears so obvious to the business man that to question it seems to him to border on the ridiculous, may fall to obtain any expression whatever in his individual behaviour. The curious gift of being able to follow two conflicting lines of reasoning without suffering the slightest tinge of embarrassment is responsible for much of the difference between what business men say and what

[12] Loc. cit. col. 469.

they do. It is referred to by Mr. E.M. Forster in the following passage from Howard's End:[13]

> The breezy Wilcox manner, though genuine, lacked the clearness of vision that is imperative for truth. When Henry lived in Ducie Street he remembered the mews; when he tried to let he forgot it; and if anyone had remarked that the mews must be either there or not, he would have felt annoyed and afterwards have found some opportunity of stigmatizing the speaker as academic. So does my grocer stigmatize me when I complain of the quality of his sultanas, and he answers in one breath that they are the best sultanas, and how can I expect the best sultanas at that price? It is a flaw inherent in the business mind, and Margaret may do well to be tender to it, considering all that the business mind has done for England.

Most business men believe that overhead costs enter into price and most business men are aware that prices fall just when overhead costs per unit of output are raised through a decline in trade. But very few business men allow this conflict to worry them.

The economic theory of a business man appears to be based on the conception of a fair price, which covers all elements of cost of production. But, this fair price is not deliberately demanded for his product by the seller. The fair price is the price that in the absence of special causes ought, it is believed, to rule in the market. In fact, when the business man starts theorising he is expressing views about ethics rather than about economics. For in this wicked world each individual has to accept the best price that he can obtain. He may find it pleasant to believe that the price that is charged includes a definite allowance for overhead costs, but it is very doubtful whether such a belief represents more than an attempt to sublimate the sordid act of maximising profits. The imaginary allowance for overhead costs is simply the excess of the price that it is most profitable to charge over the prime cost. If it yields a surplus over overhead costs, that is so much the better. Far be it from the individual business man to refuse this unrighteous gain. For vary often the allowance for overhead costs falls considerably short of the actual amount of overhead costs. Exceptional causes are then cited in explanation. Others are always to blame, never the individual whom the economist happens to be addressing.

[13] p. 178.

Competition is unfair, cut-throat, insane—the name is immaterial—or this happens to be an industry, as I am frequently informed by business men, that is subject to the Laws of Supply and Demand. The individual is reluctantly compelled in practice to make the best of the situation in the market, and he never pauses to consider that his theorising can be justified only on the assumption that his competitors do not act as he does. [*hand-written in the margin*: See this passage from Malthus].

This theory is something quite apart from the conduct of his business. But even though it can be maintained that the peculiar economic theory of business men is not directly linked with any similar peculiarity in their economic behavior, the question still remains whether belief in such mis-conceived theory is compatible with success in the attempt to maximise profits. If success depended on a full realisation of the implications of the marginal principle, it would be a bad outlook for economists. But business instinct and intuition will secure some measure of unconscious adherence to the marginal principle and the process of trial and error is likely in most cases to arrive at a fair approximation. It would, however, be absurd to expect the approximation to be exact, particularly in those cases where each order is a subject for a separate bargain or where the firm produces a number of separate varieties.

Here is an unexplored field for the economist to come to the assistance of the individual business man. He can actually offer him a formula to enable him to derive the price that ought to be charged for any individual variety. The formula is a simple one:[14]

$$\text{price} = \text{marginal cost } \times \frac{\text{elasticity of demand}}{\text{elasticity of demand } \textit{minus} \text{ one}}$$

This simple formula can be substituted for that elaborate process of allocating overhead costs, arithmetically so meticulous but economically quite unsound, which provides the livelihood of many cost accountants. If the economist can do nothing more for the business man he can at least save him from a considerable amount of useless expenditure.

[14] It is derived from Mr. Harrod's formula (Economic Journal, December 1931, p. 570 note).

## VI

Turning back from business economics to economic theory we see that the basic factor in the theory of value under imperfect competition is the elasticity of demand for the individual firm's product. This is the case whether the price of an industry's product is arrived at by a process of trial and error or whether it depends on each individual business man's estimate of the responsiveness of the demand, for his product to a change in the price that he charges. If we are inquiring into the effect of any type of change on the price of a commodity, we must discover how this individual elasticity of demand will alter. We must also know how the marginal cost of the firm varies with its output, and then we can determine the effect on the price of the commodity. Let us take, for example, the effect of a tariff in the short period, in which the number of firms is fixed. Under conditions of perfect competition the price must rise (apart from the possibility of external economies, which must be rare in the short period); for in equilibrium price is equal to marginal cost and the marginal cost curve of each firm must be rising. But if competition is not perfect the marginal cost curve of a firm, working considerably below its capacity level of output, may in certain cases be falling. This at once provides the possibility that a tariff may cause a fall in the price of the protected commodity. But on the side of demand the presumption is still in favour of a rise in price; for by curtailing the number of alternative sources from which a customer can satisfy his wants a tariff tends to make the demand for the individual firm more inelastic.[15] On the other hand, if the customers who previously had a particular preference for the foreign firms are fairly neutral in their preferences for the domestic firms—as is likely to be the case, for instance, if their preference for the foreign firms was due to proximity, resulting in low freight rates, and if the domestic industry is highly localized –, then the individual elasticities may be increased, and, apart from the effect of a possible rise in marginal costs, the price will fall.

It will probably be objected that this kind of treatment omits the element of Time, that perpetual bugbear of the economic theorists. Now so far as the adoption of the statistical method of analysis is concerned, it may reasonably be claimed that it does provide a fairly good first approximation, which it would be difficult in purely short-period problems, though

[15] I am grateful to Professor Viner for correcting a misapprehension under which I was laboring in this connection.

certainly not in long-period problems, to improve on. But Time does enter into the individual demand curve for a unit of control in a manner similar in origin though quite different in its effect from that in which it influences the demand curve for the product of a competitive industry. For the individual elasticity of demand represents the responsiveness of an individual's sales to a change in his price, and this responsiveness depends on the period of time for which the new price is maintained. An additional subjective element is thus introduced when competition is imperfect into the conditions determining equilibrium: the position of static equilibrium depends on the foresight of the business man and on the rate at which he discounts the future (in particular on his ability and willingness to forgo immediate profits in the hope of earning greater profits in the future). Now it can be stated as a general proposition that the long-period elasticity of demand is greater than the short-period elasticity of demand. It follows that the shorter the period that business men have in view in framing their policy, the higher will be the price of their product.

Here, I believe, lies the clue to a considerable portion of that problem of time-lags which perplexes economists, particularly in regard to retail prices. A retailer who lowered his prices in response to a fall in wholesale prices might for the moment be earning less than another retailer who kept his prices unchanged. He was formerly in a position of equilibrium dictated by a fairly long-period demand curve but the immediate effect on profits of a change in selling prices is determined by a very short-period demand curve; and the short-period elasticity is much less than the longer-period elasticity. It will only gradually dawn on the seller that he is taking too short-sighted a point of view, end he will only gradually settle down to a position of equilibrium that is similar, in regard to the period that he has in view in picturing his demand curve or in undergoing his trials and errors, to that in which he was found before wholesale prices began to fall. If this theory is correct, retailers should be far readier to raise their prices in response to a rise in wholesale prices than they are to lower their prices in response to a fall; for from the short-sighted point of view it always pays an individual to raise his prices, above the level at which due regard is being paid to the future, even if his coats have not gone up at all—a fortiori therefore if his costs do go up.

## VII

It may finally be of interest to give two special illustrations of the use to which the marginal principle can be put. In the first place we may continue with the problem of retail selling. The magnitude of retailers' margins is usually put down to the high cost of retail selling, and this in its turn is explained by the fact that there are too many shops. It would be natural to deduce that if the number of firms were forcibly reduced, retail margins would fall as a result of the reduction in selling costs. But the deduction would be false. In reality it is not because selling costs are high that retailers' margins are great. It is because the market is so imperfect—because, in other words, the elasticity of demand for the individual shop is so low—that retailers charge such high margins that there are so many shops. The number of shops must be so great that selling costs are equal to the margin that it is profitable to retailers to charge, on the basis of whatever degree of imperfection of the market happens to prevail. A forcible reduction in the number of shops would reduce costs but there is no reason why it should lower margins.

Indeed, if there were less shops the demand for the service of each of them would be less elastic—competition, to put it more crudely, would be less severe—and retail prices would rise. [*handwritten in the margin*: Smith p. 341] That is on the assumption that the marginal cost of retailing does not fall as a shop's turnover expands. The fall in average cost is usually due to the spreading over a larger output of the cost of certain indivisible units—such as human beings and floor space; this does not entail any fall in marginal costs, for it is an economy only from the point of view of the accountant and the entrepreneur, not from the point of view of the technician. But in some cases a shop with larger turnover will be more efficient in a real technical sense: the extra cost of handling an additional customer will actually be less. It may be able to buy its wares more cheaply as a result of buying them in larger quantities; at a certain critical point an increase in size will justify the use of a truck in the place of expensive boy labor; and it may become worthwhile to extend the economies of specialisation. The marginal cost of selling is then reduced as a result of an increase in the size of the individual shop, and there now emerges a tendency for lower prices, as a result of a forcible diminution in the number of shops to set against that tendency for higher prices which is brought about by the reduction in the individual elasticity of demand.

The last illustration is very trivial, and is appended only on account of its neatness. The British shipbuilding industry is exempt from paying the tariff which was recently imposed on imported steel. The question is this: is the effect of the tariff, from which the shipbuilding industry is exempt, to increase or diminish the consumption of British steel by the shipbuilding industry? To answer this question we may assume that shipbuilders provide a market for steel which is entirely separate and independent of the other markets in which steel is sold. Then each individual steel producer equates his marginal revenue from selling steel to shipbuilders with his marginal cost. It follows that if the marginal cost of steel to the individual producer is lowered as a result of the tariff, his marginal revenue from selling steel to shipbuilders is lowered, in other words the price paid for British steel by shipbuilders is lowered, and consequently shipbuilders consume more British steel. On the other hand if marginal costs are raised less British steel is consumed by shipbuilders. The answer to our question is simply that the consumption of British steel by shipbuilders is increased or diminished according as the production of steel takes place under conditions of falling or rising marginal cost to the individual producer.

CHAPTER 3

# The Problem of Duopoly

*Richard F. Kahn*

Whether it pays a firm to raise or to lower its price depends on the effect such action would have on the amount of its sales, and this depends in part on the nature of the reactions of competing firms. The nature of these reactions is the problem of duopoly, or, to speak more properly, of oligopoly.[1] The assumption of perfect competition prevents the problem from arising. With polypoly in an imperfect market (though some would want to deny that that is possible) the problem is not material, for each firm is confronted with a demand curve which depends only on the condition of the market, the reactions of competing firms being negligible in their repercussions on the firm under consideration. But where conditions of polypoly do not prevail, then, whether the market is perfect or imperfect, the problem, is a real one.

Originally publ. in: Kahn, R. F. (1937). The Problem of Duopoly. *The Economic Journal, 47*(185), 1–20. https://doi.org/10.2307/2225275
Reprint by Springer International Publishing 2022 with kind permission

[1] I confine myself in this article entirely to duopoly. But everything that I have to say can be extended to oligopoly. For the sake of brevity, of simplicity and of euphony, I refrain from such extension, the nature of which is usually obvious.

R. F. Kahn



M. C. Marcuzzo, P. Paesani (eds.), *Richard F. Kahn*, Palgrave Studies in the History of Economic Thought, https://doi.org/10.1007/978-3-030-98588-2_3

The solution that I put forward in this article shows considerable resemblance to various solutions which have been published in the last two or three years by some of that vast host who have gathered in this field. The resemblance is, I think, not quite as close as may superficially appear. But in any full-dress treatment I should feel called upon to indicate in what respects my solution was related to, and in what respects it differed from, the work of others. The compass of an article is too limited for such references, and in order to make my meaning as plain as possible, I have sedulously refrained, except in one instance, from weaving into my own exposition threads of discourse concerning contemporary literature. A general acknowledgment must here suffice.[2]

The Cournot–Bertrand difference of opinion provides to-day what is generally considered the easiest route towards a solution of the duopoly problem. Cournot's solution is correct on the assumption that firm A supposes that no matter what its own price and sales[3] may be, firm B will always keep its sales constant; and that firm B makes the same supposition about firm A. The absurdity of this assumption (of the perpetration of which Cournot was doubtless unconscious) is sufficiently evident, and so we come to Bertrand's *objection péremptoire*. But the solution of Bertrand and his successors is itself based on an assumption, once again tacitly. This time the assumption relates to the competitor's price and not to its sales: each firm must be assumed to suppose that, no matter what its own price and sales may be, its competitor will always keep its *price* constant. All this was pointed out by Wicksell and is today familiar. It is embodied in the doctrine that there is no one solution of duopoly, it being all a question of the nature of the assumptions made by each firm about its competitor. And much work has been devoted to the nature of such assumptions and to the consequences which ensue.

It is indeed clear that every position of equilibrium must depend on the nature of the mental processes to which those who control firms are subject. But this is not a peculiarity of duopoly. The ordinary equilibrium of competition demands from business men a compliance with the marginal principle such as even many students of economics find difficult to fulfil. In so far as the thoughts of business men diverge from what is attributed to them, the influence of their thoughts on their actions calls for study. It

[2] I might, however, mention that the characteristic of my solution is asymmetry and that asymmetry has been imported into the theory of duopoly by Professor Pigou (*Economics of Stationary States*, p. 92), by Dr. von Stackelberg (*Marktform und Gleichgewicht*), by Mr. Coase ("The Problem of Duopoly Reconsidered", *Review of Economic Studies*, February 1935), and doubtless by others.

[3] I use the word "sales" in the sense of physical volume.

is, however, usually admitted that a reasonably good approximation to the truth is obtainable by assuming that business men think sensibly, for even if in fact they are not very sensible, they will as a result of trial and error behave in much the same way as though they were.

And so too with duopoly. Instead of attributing to each firm more or less crazy assumptions about the nature of its competitor's behaviour, it is tempting to postulate that the assumptions which it makes are *correct*, being based either on supreme intelligence or on the employment of the method of trial and error. In this way we shall arrive at the *unique* position of duopoly equilibrium, the deviation of any other position from this unique position being a measure of the stupidity of the assumption about his competitor's behaviour with which, rightly or wrongly, the business man is credited.

It was this unique position of equilibrium which Mr. Harrod set out to determine.[4] Each firm works on the basis of a demand curve which makes full allowance for the reactions of its competitor to its own conduct. In order to find the slope of this demand curve, Mr. Harrod assumes that "when the first duopolist increases output by $\Delta x$, the demand curve of the second duopolist moves to the left by an amount equal to $\Delta x$ throughout its range". Mr. Harrod has here failed to avoid the danger which, as Professor Pigou has more recently pointed out,[5] threatens any such attempt to solve the problem. The second duopolist's demand curve has to pay the same attention to the reactions of the first duopolist as does the first duopolist's to those of the second. Every point on the second duopolist's demand curve corresponds to a certain equilibrium state of behaviour of the first duopolist. The second duopolist's demand curve will be moved "to the left by an amount equal to $\Delta x$ throughout its range" if something has happened to increase the first duopolist's *equilibrium* output, above what it would otherwise have been, by a constant amount $\Delta x$. But Mr. Harrod has not postulated any such "something". His increase $\Delta x$ in output does not represent a shift in the first duopolist's position of equilibrium, but a shift *out of equilibrium* undertaken with a view to seeing what will happen. Now the second duopolist's demand curve is drawn on the assumption that, for every point on it, the first duopolist is in equilibrium, and it ceases to have any significance as soon as it is postulated that equilibrium no longer obtains. Mr. Harrod's short cut to a unique solution to the problem of duopoly turns out to be impracticable. But a more devious route remains open.

We are concerned with the effect on firm B's policy of a change in firm A's behaviour (as represented by its sales and price). It is, however,

[4] *Economic Journal*, June 1934, p. 335.
[5] *Economics of Stationary States*, p. 92.

impossible to discuss the nature of a change in policy until we know what is to be implied by the statement that there has been no change in policy. If it is said that firm B has not yet altered its policy, as a result of an increase in A's output and a reduction in A's price, what are we to understand? It cannot be that everything is the same for B as it was before. For if B continues to charge the same price as before, its output must have fallen; while if it maintains its output, it must submit to a lower price. In which case, if either, can B be said to be pursuing the same policy as before, in spite of the cut in A's price?

This is no mere verbal point. "No change in policy" represents a different state of behaviour in one case from what it does in another, and the position of duopoly equilibrium is different accordingly. We have to distinguish the automatic, direct effects on a firm's sales and price from the effects which result from conscious decision, calculation, or the use of trial and error. So long as the effects are confined to the former class no change in policy can be said to have occurred. It is with the development of the latter that a change in policy shows itself. The nature of this change of policy will depend on the nature of the new situation which comes into being when A cuts its price and expands its sales. The nature of this new situation will depend on B's automatic response—on what course its behaviour pursues before the change of policy has become effective. And so the position of duopoly equilibrium depends essentially on what, in the particular case under consideration, "no change of policy" may be said to denote.

If B keeps its price momentarily fixed when A cuts its own price and increases its sales, leaving the full impact of the change to fall on its sales, an immediate situation is set up which is materially different from that which would have been set up if B had kept its sales constant, leaving the full impact to fall momentarily on the price that it receives. And the further repercussions which ensue will be entirely different in the two cases.

It will simplify the argument to confine our treatment to the two extreme cases, leaving it to be understood that any given case may be intermediate in nature.

(*a*) At one extreme we have the case where, in spite of a change in a competitor's price, firms' prices remain constant automatically until they are altered as a result of deliberation or experiment. In view of the nature of the objection advanced by Bertrand against Cournot's solution of the problem of duopoly, it will, on purely mnemonic grounds, be convenient to describe this case as *Bertrandesque*.

(*b*) At the other extreme is the case where it is the volume of sales that automatically remains constant until some other decision is arrived at. This case may no more appropriately be called *Cournotesque.*

In the case of very many commodities a definite and fixed price is announced to the world, and is altered only as a result of a special decision. Here the approximation to the Bertrandesque type is complete. In many other cases the approximation is very close. On the other hand, there are commodities where, owing to the costs or impossibility of storage and to the length of the period of production (in the short-period sense of the life of working capital), it is the volume of sales which continues unaltered until a definite decision is made to alter it. Here, where the price must vary from moment to moment according to the condition of the market, the case is completely Cournotesque. For raw materials which are capable conveniently of being stored no definite rule can be laid down. There are many large producers of such raw materials, and pools dealing with surplus stocks, which operate by announcing to the world a definite price at which they are prepared to deal. Here the tendency is strongly Bertrandesque. More usually the price will be left to the speculators, and policy will be expressed in terms of a definite rate of turnover, to be adhered to until policy is altered. Here the conditions of the Cournotesque type may be fairly closely realised.

It is clear that in practice most cases approximate to the Bertrandesque, and that is the case to which I shall confine myself in the main, leaving the nature of the Cournotesque case to be brought out by analogy rather than by a re-formulation of elaborate analysis.

The duopoly equilibrium that results from the Bertrandesque type of behaviour may be described as *Bertrandesque equilibrium.* Similarly for *Cournotesque equilibrium.* These positions of equilibrium are to be distinguished from the Bertrand and Cournot equilibria. The latter are based on the assumption that each firm *believes* that, in response to a small change in its price and sales, the other firm will make no change, *neither immediately nor at any time in the future,* in its own price or sales (as the case may be). The Bertrandesque and Cournotesque equilibria, on the other hand, are characterised, not by the nature of the firms' beliefs, whether right or wrong, but by what happens *in actual fact.* It is assumed that the firms' beliefs are not erroneous; and, furthermore, it is a question merely of the automatic, immediate impact of a change on the firms' prices and sales, and not of what happens after calculation and deliberation begin to show their influence. The Cournot equilibrium is attained where each firm *thinks* that the other firm will keep its sales unaltered, both now and for ever more. The Cournotesque equilibrium is attained where each firm *knows* how the other firm will react and where the reaction takes the momentary form of keeping sales constant, but probably not for very long.

The absurdity of the Cournot assumption has frequently been pointed out. That a firm should behave as though its competitor's sales cannot be altered is contrary to reason. The Bertrand assumption—that each firm imagines that its competitor's price will never be altered as a result of its own behaviour—has also little to recommend it. The remedy is sometimes thought to lie in adopting some intermediate, and more sensible, assumption. But the solution must still be based on attributing to firms particular beliefs, and these beliefs, though less stupid than those associated with the names of Cournot and Bertrand, cannot be correct, for the correct beliefs are not such as can be expressed in the form: "If I cut my price by a certain amount, he will cut his price by a smaller, but perfectly definite, amount". Such a statement has no meaning. (If it had, Mr. Harrod's solution would be correct.)

My use of the Bertrandesque and Cournotesque types, and of any intermediate type to which a particular case may conform, is not subject to any such difficulty. It is simply a practical question of the nature of the mechanism by which disturbances are in fact propagated from one firm to another. According to the extent to which the immediate impact is confined to the volume of a firm's sales as compared with the extent to which there is an automatic reaction on the firm's price, the ultimate position of equilibrium will be established closer to the Bertrandesque position and farther from the Cournotesque. I contemplate, therefore, a complete range of positions of duopoly equilibrium, varying between the Bertrandesque and the Cournotesque extremes. But every such position is a unique position, in the sense that it is derived on the assumption of rational beliefs. The difference between one such unique position and another is a difference not of belief but of fact, of technical conditions and market practice rather than of psychology—it is a difference in the extent to which the immediate impact of change is distributed between a firm's sales and its price.

I have so far been referring to a firm's sales rather than to its *output*. But as soon as we wish to consider the effect of costs of production, the volume of output has to be brought into the picture. The complications which arise when sales are capable of differing from output, while important, will not be considered here. Henceforth I shall use the word *output* rather than *sales*, leaving it to be understood that the two are kept in equality. It is, however, important that this understanding should not be interpreted too literally. If sales were incapable of differing from output for so much as a single instant, the Bertrandesque case could not possibly be realised. For if a firm's price is momentarily held constant against a change in the price charged by a competitor, the volume of sales must alter before output has time to alter, the difference being reflected in a change in stocks. But we are at liberty to assume that this discrepancy is not maintained for long, that output follows sales with only a short time lag, and that the response of output to sales is *automatic* in the sense that it does not necessitate any *change of policy*, the volume of production being naturally determined by whatever the volume of sales happens for the moment to be.

We may now consider the nature of the duopoly equilibrium which will be established for the Bertrandesque type, the extreme to which in practice most cases approximate. It will, I think, promote the clarity of the exposition if in the first place the case of a perfect market is briefly dealt with, for here the essential nature of the equilibrium is most clearly revealed. It is so revealed, however, only at the expense of some incidental fantasy. I must ask the reader to remember that this fantasy is to be associated with the assumption of a perfect market, not with the duopoly equilibrium which I am describing, and that the fantasy will dissolve as soon as we are at liberty to consider an imperfect market.

It will be convenient to refer to the output which equates a firm's marginal cost to the price in a perfect market, the marginal cost curve being a rising one for this level of output, as the firm's *competitive output*.

We now start with two firms selling their product in the same perfect market, and let us examine the competitive position, in which each firm is producing its competitive output, with marginal cost equated to the price. If one of the firms increases its output the price will clearly fall, the firm's marginal cost will now exceed the price, and its profits will have been reduced. It follows that output will not be increased beyond the competitive point. We now have to consider whether it will pay either firm to reduce its output and raise the price. If firm A reduces its output, firm B will at the most increase its output by the amount required to maintain equality between its marginal cost and the price. Thus the increase in firm B's output will be of no higher order of magnitude than the rise in price itself, being equal to the rise in price divided by the slope of firm B's marginal cost curve. The decrease in the aggregate output of the two firms is of the same order of magnitude as the rise in the price, being equal to the rise in price divided by the slope of the aggregate demand curve. Hence the decrease in output of firm A is also of the same order of magnitude as the rise in the price. Firm A will have attained a small rise in price at the expense of but a small decrease in its output, and since its marginal cost was previously equal to the price, its profits will have increased. It will thus be induced to reduce its output below its competitive output. In more familiar language, the demand for the individual firm is not perfectly elastic at the competitive price, while it is only when demand is perfectly elastic that the competitive output is produced.

We thus conclude that competitive equilibrium is impossible. So long as each firm believes in the Bertrand assumption—that the other firm will keep its price constant—the competitive output will be produced. But one firm will soon discover that by raising its own price it can induce the other firm, which for the moment will be producing in excess of its competitive output, to raise its price too.

Next let us suppose that each firm is producing appreciably less than its competitive output, marginal cost in each case being below the price. The position now is entirely different. If firm A raises its price by a small amount, the immediate effect will be to increase B's output by a large amount, since in the Bertrandesque case which we are considering B does not for the moment alter its price. B's output may now exceed its competitive output, but its reaction to the rise in A's price will be to reduce its output by no more than is required to bring it down to the competitive amount, at which marginal cost and price are equal. Thus a small rise in A's price will result in a *finite* reduction in its output, and it will not pay A to raise its price. B's output no longer rests on the buffer provided by its marginal cost curve, with the result that the demand for A's product is perfectly elastic.

It follows that it does not pay A to raise its price with both firms producing less than their competitive outputs. We now have to consider whether it will pay A to lower its price with the object of expanding its output. At first glance the following argument suggests itself: If A lowers its price, B will lose all, or most of, its output so long as it adheres to the old price. B will therefore be compelled in self-defence to lower its price too, and both firms will be worse off than they were before. Aware that this will be the consequence of a cut in its price, A will refrain from making it.

If this line of argument is correct, equilibrium is indeterminate: it pays neither firm to raise nor to lower the price, and the price (provided that it lies between the competitive price and the monopoly price) is what it is because it happens to be so.

In practice this kind of indeterminacy must often prevail, and in any complete study of duopoly much attention would have properly to be devoted to it. It does, however, imply that each firm can trust the other firm not to initiate a price cut independently, for it is only then that firm A will believe that it can deter firm B from cutting its price by holding its own price constant. Such a belief implies some suspicion of co-operation between the firms—what I shall call the *first degree of collusion* must be said to prevail. It is collusion of a pretty innocent nature, but the backbone of the theory of duopoly must be evolved on the assumption that no firm has any trust whatever in its competitors. This means that from A's point of view any cut in B's price which may happen to follow temporally on a cut in A's price has no *causal* connection with it, and would have taken place anyhow. A small cut in A's price has therefore in itself the effect of increasing A's output by a finite amount, since in itself it transfers all B's customers to A, and it therefore pays A to cut its price. Thus equilibrium cannot rule when both firms are producing less than their competitive outputs.

As long as one adheres to the assumption of a perfect market it is a little difficult to visualise the complete absence of collusion of the first degree. We shall find, however, that in a moderately imperfect market such collusion is far less likely to take place, and since we are merely engaged now in preparing the way for a discussion of an imperfect market, we may proceed on the basis of an assumption which in the ideal case of a perfect market would have little to recommend it. Meanwhile we may take note of a method of analysis which avoids the difficulty. The first degree of collusion is essentially uni-directional in its operation. Under its influence the firms may refrain from cutting the price, but they will not be induced to raise the price. If firm A *raises* its price, firm B will simply take over A's customers, and A will be left with sales reduced to little or nothing. A will not therefore be encouraged to raise its price by the hope that B will then raise its price equally, to the benefit of both the firms. It requires a much higher degree of collusion before such a hope can be supported (a degree of collusion which will in fact result, by the tacit co-operation of the two firms, in the establishment of the monopoly price). So long as we contemplate collusion of no higher degree than the first, it does not interfere with the establishment of the unique position of duopoly equilibrium, provided that we start with the price below the equilibrium price. It is only when the price happens to start above the equilibrium level that this collusion may prevent it from being cut to the equilibrium level. It follows that if we conduct our inquiry by examining the effect produced by a *rise* in a firm's price, concluding that the price exceeds the equilibrium price when the effect is to curtail profits and that it falls short of the equilibrium price when the effect is to increase profits, collusion in the first degree will not appear in the picture. For we shall be considering the establishment of equilibrium from a position in which the price has to rise before it reaches its final value.

In this way we have in effect already shown that if both firms are producing their competitive outputs, the price must be *below* the equilibrium price, for a small rise in the price charged by one of the firms will involve it in but a small decrease in output; while if both firms are producing less than their competitive outputs, the price must be *above* the equilibrium price, for now a small rise in the price charged by one firm will involve it in a large decrease in output. It follows that if there is any unique position of equilibrium at all, it must be one in which one firm is producing its competitive output while the other is producing less than its competitive output.

Asymmetry is the most obvious characteristic of the unique position of duopoly equilibrium to which this article is devoted. Let us now examine such an asymmetrical situation. One firm, say B, is to be supposed to be slightly but continuously undercutting the other firm, A, with the result that B could, if it wanted to, supply the whole market. It does not, however, pay it to produce more than its competitive output, at which its marginal cost is equal to the price, while A is left with that part of the aggregate demand which B does not meet, so that A has to be content with less than its competitive output. It will be convenient to refer to A as the *price leader*[6] and to B as the *price follower*. As the price leader raises its

[6] It might perhaps have been better to devise a new term, for I am anxious to avoid many of the associations with which the concept of *price leadership* is connected. Though the name was suggested to me as a result of reading Mr. A.J. Nichol's *Partial Monopoly and Price Leadership* (published by the author, 1930), I do not desire to abstract more than the purest essence of Mr. Nichol's meaning (if I have interpreted it correctly). In fact I use the term in a purely descriptive sense, in order to distinguish between the two firms (the existence of asymmetry being the essence of my treatment). Still less do I desire to suggest that my price leader is regarded by the rest of the industry as charged with its corporate interests, in the manner hinted at by Professor Chamberlin (*Theory of Monopolistic Competition*, p. 50, note).

price the price follower follows suit, lagging infinitesimally behind. Thus the output of the price leader at any price is equal to the amount demanded by the market at that price *minus* the price follower's competitive output at that price. One particular price, determined by ordinary monopoly principles,[7] will maximise the price leader's profit. At this price the position of *duopoly equilibrium* which corresponds to the Bertrandesque type of behaviour has been reached.

The essential condition of equilibrium is that the price follower always keeps its price just below the price leader's price, no matter what this may be, and produces the maximum output which it is profitable to produce at that price. Thus the position of the price leader, who has to take what is left, is inferior to that of the price follower, at any rate if the two firms are not very dissimilar, and it would pay the price leader to change positions with the price follower, under-cutting instead of being undercut. If an attempt is made in that direction, equilibrium is upset, and is not re-established until either the attempt meets with complete success or has to be given up as a failure. The nature of such disturbances, and the reasons why they are unlikely to be frequent, will be discussed when we come to the more realistic case of an imperfect market. For the present, retaining the assumption of a perfect market, we assume that the leader is prepared, perhaps as a matter of prudence, to accept, for the present at any rate, its position of relative disadvantage.

It should be emphasised—this too will appear clearer when we come to an imperfect market—that the difference between the leader and the follower is a difference of situation rather than of mentality. The belief on the basis of which each firm acts is *correct*, the difference between the natures of the two firms' beliefs being due to the difference between the situations in which they find themselves. This difference may be summed up in the statement that while the price follower's demand curve is perfectly elastic, that of the price leader is a falling one, being obtained by subtracting laterally from the aggregate demand curve the price follower's marginal cost curve.

All this is for the Bertrandesque case. If, to take the other extreme, the Cournotesque case, the firms momentarily keep their outputs rather than their prices constant when the situation alters, a very different position of equilibrium is reached.

[7] Cf. Nichol, *op. cit.*, p. 29.

For the present, however, we continue with the Bertrandesque and turn now to the case of two firms selling in an imperfect market, a case far more congenial to this type of analysis.

The demand curve which *would* govern the behaviour of one firm if, as it altered its price and output, its competitor always adhered to a constant price, may be termed its *Bertrand demand curve*. The slope of this Bertrand demand curve depends on the degree of imperfection of the market and its position depends on the price charged by the other firm. The output at which *Bertrand marginal revenue* (obtained off the Bertrand demand curve) is equal to marginal cost may be described as the firm's *Bertrand output*. In the case of a perfect market the Bertrand demand curve is perfectly elastic and the firm's Bertrand output reduces to its competitive output. But a perfect market is merely the limiting case, and the argument already sketched out is equally applicable to the general case of an imperfect market.

Let us begin by imagining both firms to be producing their Bertrand outputs. If now one firm, say A, raises its price, the immediate effect on the other firm, B, which, in the Bertrandesque case that we are considering, for the moment keeps its price unaltered, is to bring its output to a point at which its Bertrand marginal revenue is less than its marginal cost. It follows that B will respond by raising its price, for it can increase its profits by doing so even on the most unfavourable hypothesis—that A will now keep its price unaltered.

Thus if both firms are producing their Bertrand outputs, a rise in A's price will lead to some rise in B's price. But a rise in A's price would, with A producing its Bertrand output, only just fail to increase A's profit if B were to keep its price unaltered. Thus a rise in A's price will in fact lead to an increase in A's profit. The position in which both firms are producing their Bertrand outputs is, therefore, not one of equilibrium.

Now let us imagine both firms to be producing outputs for which Bertrand marginal revenue exceeds marginal cost. If A raises its price and B for the moment keeps its price unaltered, B's output will be brought closer to its Bertrand level. But so long as the Bertrand output is not actually attained, B will be under no incentive to respond by raising its price, which will remain at the previous level if it is not actually reduced (just as it would have been reduced if A had not raised its price). It follows that A's profit must necessarily decline as a result of A raising its price, and consequently that equilibrium cannot obtain with both firms producing less than their Bertrand outputs.

Consideration of a cut in price, as opposed to a rise, brings us once again up against *collusion in the first degree.* In an imperfect market, however, such collusion turns out to involve something far more in the nature of tacit conspiracy than was the case in a perfect market and the assumption that it is not in operation now offers no difficulty. Whereas in a perfect market an infinitesimal cut in price by one firm deprives the other firm of a finite part of its output, the effect now is only infinitesimal. It is the less likely that, with both firms producing below their Bertrand outputs, one firm will be restrained from cutting its own price by the belief that the other firm is not doing likewise, but that it will be instigated to follow suit as soon as, though no sooner than, a cut is initiated. If we imagine the cuts in price to be infinitesimal but numerous, so that at one moment of time neither firm can be conscious whether its competitor is cutting its price or not, it seems in general unlikely that collusion of the first degree will be in evidence. If both firms are producing less than their Bertrand outputs, B will be cutting its price whether A cuts its price or not, so that a cut in A's price has the effect *per se* of increasing A's profit. Collusion of the first degree is not an impossibility in an imperfect market, but the possibility will not here be pursued.

And so again we arrive at the conclusion that the position of equilibrium is one of asymmetry. One firm, the price follower, produces its Bertrand output, for the price leader's price does not alter with its own, while the other firm, the price leader, produces less than its Bertrand output, since a change in its price brings about a change in the same direction in the price follower's price such as to maintain equality of Bertrand marginal revenue with marginal cost.

For every price that the price leader might charge there is a certain Bertrand demand curve for the price follower. From this Bertrand demand curve the follower's marginal revenue curve can be derived, and the follower's output and price, corresponding to the particular price charged by the leader, are given by the intersection of this Bertrand marginal revenue curve with the follower's marginal cost curve. The leader's output, corresponding to this particular price, can then be derived, and so we obtain the leader's demand curve, which is steeper than its Bertrand demand curve because a change in the leader's price brings about a change in the same direction in the follower's price. From the leader's demand curve its equilibrium output and price, and so those of the follower, can be derived.

So long as the follower keeps its price constant, as it will at first in the Bertrandesque case that we are considering, the leader can increase its profit by cutting its own price below the equilibrium level. But the follower's output will now begin to fall short of its Bertrand output, and it will find that, for every value of the leader's price, it can increase its own profit by cutting its price in turn. This it will do, with the result that the leader's profit will be rapidly brought down below the original amount that it was earning in the equilibrium position. Profiting by this experience, the leader will return to the equilibrium position, and stay there, for in this way it can induce the follower to maintain its own price. The follower, on the other hand, cannot by raising its price above the equilibrium level induce the leader to raise its price too. For with the follower's price held constant even at the equilibrium level it will pay the leader to *lower* its price—*a fortiori* if the follower holds its price constant *above* the equilibrium level. It is the correlation that exists between the follower's price and its own which causes the leader to maintain its price. Only by an alteration in the complete correlation, not merely by an alteration of its price, could the follower influence the leader's price.[8]

Thus the difference between the behaviour of the two firms is the result of the difference in their situations. One firm's output is resting on the impenetrable barrier provided by the equality of Bertrand marginal revenue with marginal cost, and a rise in its competitor's price has the effect, so long as it keeps its own price constant, of raising its actual output above its Bertrand output, so that a reduction of output is now profitable. But the leader's output is less than its Bertrand output, so that a rise in *its* competitor's price does not necessitate any response on the part of its own price. Not only does the follower behave *as though* the leader's price were independent of its own, but this is in fact the case; while the leader takes such account of the reactions of the follower's price to a change in its own as do in fact occur. There are thus two, and only two, unique positions of equilibrium, according to which of the two firms happens to be in the position of the price leader and which in the position of the price follower.

In many cases it will be a matter of historical accident which of these two positions of equilibrium is set up. But if the firms are sufficiently

[8] Thus if the follower were to simulate the conduct which would be appropriate if its marginal cost were higher than it actually is, lowering its price with the leader's, but maintaining a narrower gap between them, a more profitable situation might result in equilibrium. Such conduct would necessitate a higher degree of intelligence than I am prepared to concede. I imagine my firms to be searching, by means of experiment or of trial and error, for the most profitable price and output—but not for more than that, not for the most profitable line of reaction to a change in a competitor's behaviour.

dissimilar, in regard to size, costs and the nature of the market's preferences for their products, one of the two positions will be more profitable *for both the firms* than the other, and that one will then be selected. It is only if the two firms are rather alike that both firms would be better off as follower rather than leader, and in a fairly imperfect market it does not require a very high degree of dissimilarity to pre-destine one firm for the position of follower and the other for the position of leader.

To establish my claim that the position of equilibrium that I am describing is, in a certain sense, *unique*, it may be helpful to demonstrate in mechanistic terms how it might be established. So long as it is maintained that the position of equilibrium depends on what each firm *believes* about the other firm's behaviour, a mechanical model is obviously impossible. It is of the essence of my way of thinking that the *ultimate* position of equilibrium does not depend on the nature of firm's beliefs, which can be supposed to become rapidly revised if they start by being erroneous, but on what in fact happens. It depends in particular on whether the immediate reaction on one firm of a change in the policy of the other firm is confined to its sales, its price for the moment remaining unaltered—the Bertrandesque case—or whether it is confined to its price, its sales for the moment remaining unaltered—the Cournotesque case—or whether some intermediate assumption is appropriate.

Our mechanical model is one in which each firm, independently of the other, is constantly engaged in making small random shifts in its policy, with a consequent effect on its profits. The mechanism is such that the policy is gradually modified in the direction in which a small shift shows itself to have the effect of increasing profits and away from the direction in which a small shift diminishes its profits.

In the Bertrandesque case it is the price which has to be supposed to shift up and down, searching for higher profits, while in the Cournotesque case it is the output; in an intermediate case it is an appropriate conjunction of price and output. Whether the shifting is by way of occasional discontinuous steps, each followed by a period of rest, or whether it takes the form of a continual fluctuating movement, makes no difference. This is not obvious at first sight, for in the case of a continual fluctuating movement it might well be asked what difference it makes whether it is the price (the Bertrandesque case) or the output (the Cournotesque case) which is deemed to fluctuate; for in fact they both fluctuate in contrary motion. The answer is that although the price and output are both continually fluctuating, their fluctuations cannot *both* be independent of the fluctuations of the other firm. In the Bertrandesque case the *price* fluctuates about a mean level which is independent of the phase of its fluctuations which the other firm happens to have attained, while the output, on the other hand, is *ceteris paribus* smaller if the other firm's price happens to have reached the lower region of its cycle than if it is negotiating the upper region. In the Cournotesque case the rôles are reversed : the *output's* fluctuation is an independent one, while the course of the *price* is governed by the fluctuations of *both* firms.

It need scarcely be pointed out that there must be nothing in the way of synchronisation. The fluctuations must either be quite irregular or, if they are regular, the periods of fluctuation of the two firms must neither be equal nor bear to one another the ratio of any two whole numbers.

We continue now to confine ourselves to the Bertrandesque case. The mechanism, as so far described, will not establish my unique position of duopoly equilibrium. The equilibrium that it will establish—for equilibrium it is—has an interest of its own, but it cannot be discussed in this place. In order to secure my duopoly equilibrium we must endow the mechanism with memory. Let us suppose a situation in which every downward fluctuation of the price of one of the firms, below a momentarily constant mean, has the effect of increasing its profit, and that every upward fluctuation of its price has the effect of diminishing its profit. Then, as we have so far described the mechanism, the mean about which the price fluctuates will be lowered, under the downward drag of increasing profit. But now let us suppose that as the reactions on the behaviour of the other firm have time to develop, the profit of the firm which is under consideration, averaged over a large number of fluctuations, becomes gradually reduced *below what it previously was*. The situation is one, in other words, in which a lowering of the mean price has the *momentary* effect of increasing profits, but *ultimately* leads to a reduction of profits. In such a case it is to be supposed that the mechanism, being endowed with memory, gradually raises the mean level about which the price fluctuates in spite of the fact that every downward fluctuation of the price increases profit and every upward fluctuation diminishes profit; and that it continues to raise the mean level in this way until the profit, averaged over a large number of fluctuations, just begins to decline.

Such a mechanism will settle down in one or other of the two unique positions of duopoly equilibrium. No other position is possible. In an equilibrium position the price leader's fluctuations will suggest that a downward movement of its mean price would increase its profit. Its mean price may therefore begin to fall, but after a short lapse of time—sufficient to cause the price follower to lower the mean about which its own price is fluctuating—the leader's profit, though still increased by every downward fluctuation of its price, will have become less than it previously was. As a result of memory, the mean price will then be restored to its former level.

In the case of the follower, memory has no part to play. Both upward and downward fluctuations of its price have the effect of reducing its profits, and there is therefore no incentive to alter its mean price. If it were to raise its mean price above the Bertrand level (at which marginal cost is equal to Bertrand marginal revenue), and keep it there for some length of time, not only would it suffer an immediate reduction in its profits, but with the lapse of time its profits would progressively decline, for the follower would now start lowering its mean price, being no longer restrained from doing so by the lowering of the follower's price which would be the normal response to such a movement.

A possible objection may here arise. If each firm is charging a price higher than its Bertrandesque price (but lower than the monopoly price), and each firm is in consequence engaged in progressively lowering its mean price, it will find that, with the lapse of time, owing to the fall in the other firm's price, its own profit is not increasing but diminishing. It might be held that the kind of memory with which we are endowing the system would thus result in each firm *raising* its price (since a fall in the price is accompanied by falling profit)—until the monopoly price is reached. This would be a false inference. The fall in firm A's profit is not *due* to the lowering of its price: it will occur equally if its mean price is kept constant, for the lowering of B's price is not in this case the result of the lowering of A's price. Memory serves to raise a firm's price only if, with the lapse of time, its profit falls with a lowering of its own mean price. But if its profits fall whether it lowers its mean price or holds it constant, there is no part for memory to play. A rise in the firm's mean price will fail to counteract the progressive decline in its profits—unless the other firm happened to choose the same moment for raising its own mean price, which would be a pure coincidence.

Our mechanical model finds a close analogy in real life. When firms pursue the methods of "trial and error" they are in fact complying with the conditions laid down for the operation of our model. The attribute of "memory" is a plausible one to ascribe to such firms. A firm may find that every time it makes a small cut in its price its profits momentarily increase. But if a permanent lowering of the price range over which it operates in its search for the most profitable price results, with the lapse of time, in profits which are less than it was previously earning, and if experiment indicates that this falling off in profits is the *effect* of the lowering of price, the firm will once again raise its range of prices.

Where prices are less subject to variation, being announced by each firm and then adhered to for a long period of time, it is frequently the case that one particular firm is year after year the first to come out with its price list, which is carefully scrutinised by its competitors before they announce their prices. Here price leadership and price followership are clearly in evidence. There are retail stores which employ agents who, disguised as potential customers, enter their rivals' establishments and inquire what the goods are priced at. Here again asymmetry shows itself.

The equilibrium remains subject to one possibility of disturbance. If the two firms are not markedly dissimilar, it will pay the price leader to change positions with the price follower, the larger output being desirable at the expense of the lower price. It may therefore cut its price, and a process of competitive price-cutting will then ensue, each firm cutting its price in an attempt to force the onus of price leadership on its competitor. Sooner or later a point will be reached at which the firm that happens for the moment to be charging the higher price decides that the probability of securing release from its disadvantageous position is insufficient compensation for the sacrifices involved in the contest. It will then push the price back to the duopoly point, its competitor following in its wake.

We have seen that the firms will often in practice be sufficiently dissimilar, in regard to size, costs and the attitude of the market to their products, for the distribution of the rôles between them to be effected without conflict, a reversal leading to an actual reduction of the profits of both the firms. The dissimilarity will often fail to be as great as this, but it may still be so great that the advantage that one firm could gain by forcing the rôle of price leadership on to the other will be outweighed by the perils and the risks of the contest.

The asymmetry of the duopoly equilibrium will itself enforce dissimilarity on the firms. They may have been similar by origin, but plant, organisation and the nature of the product will gradually become adapted to the situation, and the firms will become so much differentiated that the leader would gain little or would actually lose by changing positions with the follower.

Even if for the moment the firms remain similar, it will be only on rare occasions that the price leader will venture to issue a challenge. Having been once defeated, it will have no reason to suppose that another attempt will be more successful, and it will wait for some propitious circumstance before embarking on it. For instance, a sudden change in demand which in any case necessitates a complete revision of the scale of prices may be regarded as providing a suitable opportunity for another attempt to become rid of the incubus of price leadership. But so long as conditions remain fairly stable, the position of duopoly equilibrium is likely to be sustained for long periods, and such disturbances as occur will occupy a relatively short space of time.

If we appear to have lingered too long over the Bertrandesque type, it must be remembered that this is the extreme to which reality usually approximates. A summary indication of the solution of the Cournotesque type must suffice, and then any intermediate type can be fitted in by analogy. It will be convenient this time to proceed straight to an imperfect market. With the Cournotesque type of behaviour each firm keeps its *output* constant, until it may decide to alter it. This time we have an *output leader* and an *output follower*. The output leader keeps its output constant, no matter what course the output follower pursues, so that the latter's output and price are determined by its *Cournot demand curve*, drawn on the assumption that its competitor's output is a constant. The output follower always produces its *Cournot output*, and the output leader, which produces more than its Cournot output because an increase in its output induces the output follower to reduce its output, chooses such an output and price as to maximise its profit. Once again we have asymmetry, but this time, if the two firms are similar, the leader produces a bigger output and charges a smaller price than the follower. Equilibrium in the Cournotesque case is less monopolistic (the prices are lower) than the Cournot equilibrium, while it is clear that it is more monopolistic than equilibrium in the Bertrandesque case, which in its turn is more monopolistic than the Bertrand equilibrium.

Since the asymmetry of the Cournotesque case is opposite to the asymmetry of the Bertrandesque case, the leader, if the firms are similar, producing a bigger instead of a smaller output than the follower, it follows that there must be one particular type of behaviour, intermediate between the Bertrandesque and the Cournotesque, for which the unique position of duopoly equilibrium happens to be symmetrical. It is worth inquiring into the nature of the behaviour which results in a symmetrical position of equilibrium. Let us consider what happens to the follower when the leader lowers its price and increases its output. Where behaviour verges on the

Bertrandesque, the automatic effect is a small fall in the follower's price and a considerable fall in its output, and the follower than proceeds to *lower its price* further and to *raise its output,* though not back to the previous level. Where, on the other hand, behaviour verges on the Cournotesque, the automatic effect is a considerable fall in the follower's price and a small fall in output, while the follower then proceeds to *raise its price,* though not back to the previous level, and to *lower its output* still further. There is an intermediate type of behaviour for which no further reactions ensue on the automatic effects, the automatic changes being exactly such as to maximise the follower's profit on the basis of the new policy of the leader, and there is no further change for conscious policy to bring about. This is the type of behaviour which results in a symmetrical solution. There is no difference between follower and leader because "no change of policy" does everything which a change of policy would aim at. This, perhaps, is what many workers on the problem of duopoly have in a sense been searching for. But it is merely a very particular type of behaviour (varying in its nature according to the inter-relationships between the firms' marginal cost curves, the demand curve for the product, and the imperfection, if any, of the market), which would be found to operate in practice only as the result of coincidence; it is of no assistance to those who seek a solution of the problem of duopoly.

CHAPTER 4

# Oxford Studies in the Price Mechanism

*Richard F. Kahn*

In its early days there appeared in *Oxford Economic Papers* a number of important articles dealing with aspects of the price-system. An invidious task of selection has been undertaken by Mr. T. Wilson (General Editor of *Oxford Economic Papers)* and Mr. P.W.S. Andrews (Honorary Secretary to the Editorial Board), editors of *Oxford Studies in the Price Mechanism*,[1] which also includes a number of hitherto unpublished essays and a general introduction by Mr. Wilson.

It is impossible to deal adequately, or even inadequately, with all contributions to a volume which covers such a wide range. Two chapters

Originally publ. in: Kahn, R. F. (1952). Oxford Studies in the Price Mechanism. *The Economic Journal, 62*(245), 119–130. https://doi.org/10.2307/2227177
Reprint by Springer International Publishing 2022 with kind permission

[1]Oxford University Press. 1951. Pp. xv+274. 21*s*. The first two numbers of *Oxford Economic Papers* were reviewed by Professor Austin Robinson (*Economic Journal*, September 1939, pp. 538–43). A large part of the present review is devoted to the same two articles on which Professor Robinson then concentrated, and many of Professor Robinson's criticisms, which have never been answered, are here repeated.

R. F. Kahn



M. C. Marcuzzo, P. Paesani (eds.), *Richard F. Kahn*, Palgrave Studies in the History of Economic Thought, https://doi.org/10.1007/978-3-030-98588-2_4

perhaps stand out as inviting a reviewer's comments. They both take their origin in the pre-war Oxford Economists' Research Group. The one is the famous Hall-Hitch exposition of the "'full-cost' principle"—"Price Theory and Business Behaviour," by Mr. R.L. Hall and Mr. C.J. Hitch, published in May 1939. The other is a new essay by Mr. Andrews, who was secretary of the Oxford Group, on "Industrial Analysis in Economics." Mr. Andrews has, of course, built extensively on the "full-cost" principle,[2] but in many important respects he deviates from the explanations provided by Mr. Hall and Mr. Hitch, and his essay is an interesting postscript to his book on *Manufacturing Business.*[3]

The Hall-Hitch "'full-cost' principle" has become heralded by some as a veritable Law of Economics. Mr. Andrews states, in the course of his own contribution to the *Oxford Studies*, that "realistic enquiries at Oxford had elucidated ... that a general method of pricing was to add a margin as for net profit to average short-run costs" and that "business men appeared to adhere firmly to this method." In the light of such very categoric statements of the Hall-Hitch principle, it is refreshing and salutary to take advantage of the opportunity now presented of reconsidering the original Hall-Hitch article. The enunciation of the "principle" was much more tentative than the manifestos of its more recent upholders would suggest. It was directed as much to the relatively easy task of destroying the faith of anybody who really did believe that business men thought in terms of marginal cost and marginal revenue as to the more difficult task of providing a guide to business men's behaviour. "A large majority of entrepreneurs explained that they did not actually charge the 'full cost' price, a few admitting that they might charge more in periods of exceptionally high demand, and a greater number that they might charge less in periods of exceptionally depressed demand."

Mr. Hall and Mr. Hitch were "acutely conscious of the shortcomings of an enquiry of this kind." Of the entrepreneurs interviewed, after submission of a questionnaire, the evidence of only thirty-eight was considered—"far too small a sample to warrant any final conclusions." Of the thirty-eight, the behaviour of eight was "clearly not explicable in terms of

[2] It is a pity that Mr. Andrews has not made use of this opportunity of commenting on the criticisms of the original Hall-Hitch article by Professor Robinson, *loc. cit.*, and by Professor F. Machlup, "Marginal Analysis and Empirical Research," *American Economic Review*, September 1946 (reproduced in R.V. Clemence's *Readings in Economic Analysis*, Vol. 2).

[3] See Professor Austin Robinson's review article, *Economic Journal*, December 1950 (and his contribution to a discussion in the June 1951 number). I have tried to avoid undue duplication of Professor Robinson's comments, with which I find myself almost entirely in agreement. But some duplication has proved inevitable; and I have borrowed from Professor Robinson without specific reference to his article.

full cost" (according to their statements price "might not be related to cost at all"; "what the market will bear is the only consideration"; "any price which will make some contribution to overheads is better than nothing "; and so on). The views of the remaining thirty entrepreneurs are tabulated. Strong deviationist tendencies are exhibited by at least seven of them ("the proper price is equal to full cost, but they cannot get this at present "; "full cost ought to be charged, but they could not get the business if they did "; "when trade is depressed competition makes it impossible as a rule to raise allocation per unit"; "in a weak market it is necessary to quote a price which will get the order"; 10% is added for profit "if possible"; allowance is made for a "reasonable profit"; "the margin added for profit is naturally smaller on competitive lines"; and "they produce at prices consumers want and reduce costs to make this possible)." Not all of the twenty-three which remain out of the original thirty-eight could be regarded, even on their own showing, as adhering "firmly" (Mr. Andrews's word) to the "full-cost" principle, and Mr. Hall and Mr. Hitch did not claim "rigid" adherence for more than twelve, of whom two (if not three) appear to be disqualified, as they were members of price-fixing trade associations. This leaves ten (or nine) survivors.

Of these a high proportion appear to state that the average amount of overhead costs per unit of output, employed in calculating full cost, is worked out on the basis of actual or forecast output. We are, therefore, required to believe that these firms would raise their prices in a depression, relatively to wages and the prices of their raw materials. We may take this at its face value if we choose, but it cannot be generally typical of business behaviour. Even Mr. Andrews recognises that it would be "absurd" to suppose "the charging of a higher price in a falling market," and he takes refuge in a "budgeted" or "notional output" (perhaps "the last output achieved in relatively prosperous conditions") or an "average, taking the good years with the bad."[4] Mr. Andrews has told us that "it was the work of this Research Group that developed so strongly the conviction that the behaviour of the business men was consistent,"[5] and he appears to forget that, according to Mr. Hall and Mr. Hitch, "somewhat more than half the firms used figures of actual or estimated output."

The one quite certain conclusion to which the Hall-Hitch article drives the reader is that far too elaborate a theoretical edifice has, in the twelve years which have elapsed since its publication, been built on a very slender

[4] *Manufacturing Business*, pp. 164, 165.

[5] *Ibid.*, p. xv.

factual basis.[6] The pioneer effort of the Oxford Economists' Research Group should by now have been taken much farther.[7]

The field is of outstanding importance, and justifies a critical approach. Those who are studying business men's behaviour in the matter of prices would do well to keep a number of fundamental questions in the forefront of their minds. The most important question, on which light is normally shed only by implication by workers in this field, is whether the business man is being revealed as a man who knows his job better than the economist or whether the upshot is that an individual business man could increase his profits if he employed on his staff graduates in economics (so long as his competitors did not do likewise).[8] A clearer view on this fundamental issue can reasonably be demanded (and, incidentally, it is vital if one is to assess the implications to the presumption in favour of *laisser-faire* of any failure of business men to understand how to maximise their profits). So long as the reason given for the business man's reluctance to alter his prices is his knowledge that if he cuts his price his competitors will be instigated to cut their prices too, whereas if he raises his price his competitors will simply take away most of his trade, it is compatible with the traditional hypothesis of profit maximisation, as modified by the theory of oligopoly. This was fully recognised by Mr. Hall and Mr. Hitch, who devoted considerable attention to the "kinked demand curve." But all that the kinked demand curve explains is why the price remains where it is (for no other reason than that it happens to be there) until something happens

[6] See also Professor Machlup's comments on the evidence of the thirty-eight entrepreneurs, *loc. cit.*, p. 545.

[7] Mr. D. C. Hague has made a start: "Economic Theory and Business Behaviour," *Review of Economic Studies*, 1949–50, No. 41. His general conclusion is (p. 154): "Profit maximisation by balancing cost against revenue was ... carried out, but only on a long-term and unscientific basis. Short-run profit-maximisation is usually unacceptable in practice. ... The main occupation of most entrepreneurs is keeping the margin between [average cost and average revenue] as wide as possible at any given level of output."

In his chapter on "Price and Production Policies" in *A Survey of Contemporary Economics* (1948, edited by Howard S. Ellis), Professor Joe S. Bain says : "Empirical research ... has left open the possibility that flexible application of such formulae may give results roughly equivalent to marginal calculations, and it has suggested many alternatives to straightforward 'full cost' pricing. The facts here, and their interpretation, are still largely to be discovered" (p. 155). Later in his chapter Professor Bain expresses doubt as to the value of "broad and superficial questionnaire investigations into pricing methods" (p. 165).

[8] See R.F. Harrod, "Price and Cost in Entrepreneurs' Policy," *Oxford Economic Papers*, May 1939, p. 2. This introduction by Mr. Harrod to the Hall-Hitch paper is not reprinted in the *Oxford Studies.*

to cause it to alter. As Mr. Andrews complains, "the reason why the 'kink' should occur at the full-cost … level of price was not adduced. If anything the determination of prices appeared even less rational than before." The important, and interesting, question is not why prices are not altered when they are not altered but *how much they are altered by* when they do alter. A general upheaval in the price structure takes place from time to time as a result of a breakdown of what elsewhere I have called the *first degree of collusion*,[9] on which depends the belief that a cut in price will be the actual cause of a firm's competitors cutting their prices too, so that probably all will be worse off. Apart from a severe fall in demand, when Mr. Hall and Mr. Hitch admit "usually one entrepreneur is overcome by panic: 'there is always one fool who cuts,'" it is usually a general change in costs which provides the signal that such a breakdown is about to occur. The statements of business men suggest *prima facie* that while each is usually sensible in not altering his price so long as the price structure in his industry remains rigid, he has something to learn about the principles on which, looking at it from his own individual point of view, he should adjust his prices on the occasion of one of these periodical *bouleversements* of the price structure. This Mr. Hall and Mr. Hitch seem to accept when they suggest in one passage "that maximum profits, if they result at all from the application of [the 'full-cost'] rule, do so as an accidental (or possibly evolutionary) by-product."

But if a considerable number of business men in the same industry all took advice on how to maximise their profits they would, at a time of subnormal demand, all be worse off. The "full-cost" principle, in so far as it operates, acts as a self-defence mechanism, protecting business men against the disastrous effects on profits produced by the existence of surplus capacity in an industry which is fairly competitive and homogeneous. The second important question, therefore, to bear in mind in examining business men's behaviour is how far it is a matter of what I would call the *second degree of collusion*—of Professor Fellner's *esprit de corps*, which it would *pay* the individual to ignore but which "yet he does not violate because he places above individual advantage good standing in the group, or the interests of the group."[10] In the words of Mr. Hall and Mr. Hitch, a price is reached "by what was in effect an agreement, though an unconscious one, in which all the firms in the group, acting on the same principle

[9] "The Problem of Duopoly," *Economic Journal*, March 1937, p. 9.
[10] W. Fellner, *Competition among the Few*, p. 43.

of 'full cost,' sought independently to reach a similar result"—the outcome of "the community of outlook of business men."[11] Such community of outlook need not be confined to the group which is normally described as an "industry." When it takes the form of a moral principle, expressed in the idea of what Mr. Hall and Mr. Hitch call "the 'right' price, the one which 'ought' to be charged," it goes deeper and wider than community of outlook, and plays the canonical role of keeping prices down at times of scarcity as well as keeping them up at times of abundance. These are the considerations which Mr. Hall and Mr. Hitch were induced by their investigations to put in the forefront. The other factors—kinked demand curves and all that—were subsidiary. This is one of the points about the Hall-Hitch inquiry which appears to be overlooked by Mr. Andrews and others.

This leads us to the question on whose "full costs" an individual producer will base his prices. The replies given by business men usually suggest that they base their prices on their own costs rather than on those of somebody else—imaginary or real. On the whole, Mr. Hall and Mr. Hitch appear to accept this, but they refer to a common case in which the price is set by one strong firm at its own "full-cost" level, and it is then accepted by other firms in the "group." More generally, "where costs do not differ widely within an industry" "the nearest that we can get to an exact statement is that the price ruling … is likely to approximate to the full cost of the representative firm." The "principle" is getting pretty amorphous at this point. In Mr. Andrews's hands, despite the lip-service which he pays to it, it becomes yet more amorphous. A business will not raise its prices as a result "of a rise in its costs due to a decrease in the productive efficiency of the business." On the other hand, businesses "will reduce prices fairly promptly" as a result of improved efficiency—provided that they are "relatively stronger businesses" rather than "weak businesses which are only just holding on." It is high time that Mr. Andrews published the empirical studies which have led him to these opinions. While the kinked demand curve seems to lurk behind Mr. Andrews's analysis, he places a great deal of weight on "the experience of a business man in an established business" giving him "a fair idea of what level of price is likely to be dangerous" by

[11] Mr. Harrod (*loc. cit.*, pp. 9, 10) asks himself the question "why do not the primary producers … fall victim to this morality?" and provides an answer supplied to him by Mr. Hitch: "in the case of the primary producers there is no unique rule available which is capable of elevation to moral status." I would add that it is a matter also of the ***number*** of competing producers, and not only of the output rather than the price being the subject of entrepreneurs' decision.

attracting competition. In so far as the danger consists of the setting up of new businesses, or the diversion of existing businesses from the production of other commodities, one might imagine that the "principle"—which incidentally would then operate only in keeping prices down in a sellers' market and not in keeping them up in a buyers' market—would consist of charging not much more than the "full cost" of the potential competitor. Mr. Andrews tries to base a firm's price on its own costs. However, a firm's "gross profit that it can get will seem to be limited by the competition which is actually or potentially present in its market," which sounds like a roundabout way of saying that to the extent that the costs of a potential competitor are judged to be higher than a firm's own costs (normally the gap will surely be considerable), the firm will estimate the maximum price which it is safe to charge by reference to the potential competitor's "full cost" rather than its own. If, on the other hand, a business man regards his own efficiency as an indication of the efficiency of potential competitors, why should he bother about his costs at all in deciding how high a price it is safe to charge? His *profits* will tell him all that he needs to know: good profits, on this theory, are the sign, *and the only necessary sign*, that prices are dangerously high, and average costs need not be calculated at all (they may be necessary to decide on *relative* prices of different products, but that is another story, though, as Professor Robinson has pointed out, there is a "superficial similarity"[12]).

It would be wrong to infer that Mr. Andrews's conclusion boils down to the familiar case of imperfect competition with free entry. Nothing could be more different.[13] In terms of the jargon and the analysis of the school for which Mr. Andrews has no sympathy, the upshot of Mr. Andrews's analysis in this section of his treatment, although Mr. Andrews does not carry his argument to its logical conclusion, is that the demand curve for each individual firm is rendered so elastic by the *potentiality* of new entry into the industry that it is only in very exceptional cases that the price will be sufficiently high *actually* to attract new firms in. The number, and therefore the size, of the firms in an industry would then (and should according to Mr. Andrews but he does not say so) be a matter of historical accident, and so, therefore, would be the average cost of production, and hence the price of the product, in so far as these depend on the internal economies of large-scale production. This is the case in which, but for the

[12] Austin Robinson, *loc. cit.*, p. 776.

[13] See F. Machlup, *loc. cit.*, p. 538, note 24, and p. 544.

fear of new entries, the price would be so high, and profits so attractive, as to increase the number of competing firms. In the opposite case, in which there is no question of new firms coming in, Mr. Andrews gives reasons why prices are not cut in such a way as to drive some of the existing firms out (with the result, which he does not state, that potential economies of large scale fail to be exploited and that *laisser-faire* fails to establish the maximum possible efficiency). Mr. Andrews explains how the development of his own ideas on this subject threw light on the meaning of Marshall's. He suggests that "we should presume Marshall's competitive analysis for manufacturing industry to imply identical prices for identical commodities, but not individual demands of infinitely large extent at those prices," and he stresses the idea that "personal contact and familiarity with conditions and requirements on both sides of the bargain will produce the individual business's 'share' of the market." Mr. Andrews is plaintive about "the inter-war rejection of Marshall." The reasons for his affinity with Marshall are clear, but in the course of a very interesting development of the case for Marshall, which is not perhaps helped by his decision to abandon the concept of the "representative firm," Mr. Andrews does not gloss over Marshall's unhappiness in dealing with internal economies : "at the back of his mind there was always the concept of an individual business taking all decisions and deciding its whole position—in such a way as to maximise its profits. His ultimate refusal to persist with this view arose from difficulties which he encountered when trying to apply it to manufacturing industries."

One wishes that the Hall–Hitch article had included a specimen of the actual questionnaire presented to the victims of the inquiry. In its absence gnawing doubts as to possible tendentiousness in its presentation find easy prey.[14] But the fundamental doubt is whether these business men, and other business men in similar predicaments, did not feel called upon to devise, and present to the Oxford intellectuals, a theory of business behaviour which is primarily a rationalisation and, in considerable measure, a false rationalisation of behaviour based on instinct rather than reasoning.[15] It is with business men's behaviour, not with their thoughts, that we have to reckon. The economic *theory* of a business man may be based on the concept of a *fair price*, which is the price which, it is believed, in the

[14] But Mr. Harrod assures us that "the members of the group had completely open minds as to what the result would be" (*loc. cit.*, p. 2).

[15] See F. Machlup, *loc. cit.*, p. 537.

absence of special circumstances, *ought* to rule. But very often this theory is a theory of ethics rather than of economics, and the business man takes the best price that he can get (though if this is higher than the fair price he may be reluctant to extort it to the full). This facility of the business mind to follow simultaneously two inconsistent lines is referred to by Mr. E.M. Forster in the following passage from *Howard's End*:

> "The breezy Wilcox manner, though genuine, lacked the clearness of vision that is imperative for truth. When Henry lived in Ducie Street, he remembered the mews; when he tried to let he forgot it; and if anyone had remarked that the mews must be either there or not, he would have felt annoyed, and afterwards have found some opportunity of stigmatizing the speaker as academic. So does my grocer stigmatize me when I complain of the quality of his sultanas, and he answers in one breath that they are the best sultanas, and how can I expect the best sultanas at that price? It is a flaw inherent in the business mind, and Margaret may do well to be tender to it, considering all that the business mind has done for England."

The conflict between what business men say and prevalent academic doctrine on price and output policy arises partly from the habit of expressing this doctrine in terms of a tendency for marginal revenue to be equated to marginal cost. Such phrases mean nothing to the business man. But the essence of this doctrine does not lie in the use of marginal concepts.[16] It could be equally well, if less elegantly, expressed in terms of each individual firm maximising its profits. Put in that more homely form, the concept does readily lend itself to the operation of the forces of trial and error,[17] and to the display of *flair*—the success of which by no means depends upon the manner in which it is rationalised.

It seems clear enough that the "full-cost" principle does not operate rigorously, in the manner often attributed to it—though not by Mr. Hall and Mr. Hitch. It would be quite wrong to go to the opposite extreme and infer that, regarded as one of many factors, it does not operate at all. One cannot disregard altogether the views expressed by business men about their own behaviour. And many of them do in fact employ cost accountants to make the calculations which the "full-cost" principle demands, and the results of these calculations must clearly have some effect on their behaviour, even though their attitude towards their cost

[16] See F. Machlup, *loc. cit.*, pp. 537, 540; D.C. Hague, *loc. cit.*, p. 146.

[17] But see R.F. Harrod, *loc. cit.*, p. 5.

accountants is as healthy as that of Mr. Mark Spade, the author of *How to Run a Bassoon Factory*,[18] who asks the business man to "accept the fact that a thing which cost you seven and six in materials and labour was a dead loss when sold for twenty five pounds, gracefully. If you have that sort of accountant you will probably find that it all works out right in the end."

The actual behaviour of prices and profits—as revealed by comparisons of different firms and products and of different points of time—fails to support the "full-cost" principle in its undiluted form. But it fails equally to support, in its undiluted form, a narrow interpretation of the operation of the profit motive. Mr. Andrews is clearly right that in the upward direction prices are limited by the danger of attracting new competition into the industry, and not merely by such new competition after it has materialised, and this idea is perhaps as important as the idea that it is *esprit de corps* which limits price-cutting in the downward direction. Our understanding of these matters is likely to become greater when the forces determining prices are treated quite separately for buyers' markets and for sellers' markets.

The Oxford Economists' Research Group also investigated, by similar methods, the influence of the rate of interest on business men's behaviour, and in the *Studies* are now reprinted the original presentation of the Group's results by Professor Meade and Mr. Andrews, whose paper was first published in October 1938. The inquiry was again directed to a very small number of cases—thirty-seven in all—which were investigated by personal interview following on the submission of a questionnaire. In February 1940 Mr. Andrews published the results of a later inquiry conducted on a much wider, but necessarily more mechanical, basis, and his paper also is now reprinted. Sir Hubert Henderson's original introductory article is also now reprinted, with the conclusion that the majority of the business men denied "that their activities have been, or are likely to be, directly affected in any way by changes in interest rates."

Here again the Oxford economists are inclined to leave us to decide for ourselves whether the business men knew their own job or whether their

[18] Published in 1934: see especially Chapter X on "Time-Study and Costing." (This important work was republished in 1950 with *Business for Pleasure*, introduced by an incriminating foreword by Mr. Nigel Balchin.)

conduct, at least as revealed by their answers, showed lack of rationality.[19] The Oxford Group were obviously surprised by the results of their inquiries. But ought they to have been surprised? Sir Hubert Henderson, at any rate, seems to think not, in view of the operation of wear and tear, obsolescence, and risk and uncertainty. He went on, by way of concession to the conventional view, to point out that "a very high proportion of our aggregate capital expenditure" probably consists of "durable consumers' goods" (especially houses) and "the assets of public bodies and public utilities," which, as he pointed out, is just where one would expect the rate of interest to be important. But the last word in that phase of the discussion was with Professor Sayers, who in his summing-up, published in February 1940 and also now reprinted, thought that "the potency of that weapon [the rate of interest] in a constantly changing world must ... be described as very low." The editors have given Professor Sayers the opportunity of thinking again, and we now have a fresh appraisal, written early in 1949. Professor Sayers is now "inclined to the view that changes in the interest rate may have considerable effect on business activity through their effects on both capital outlay and consumption outlay." In a footnote he quotes Professor Meade, 'looking back, after eleven years': "What seems to have been overlooked is the extent to which our interviews were confined to risky manufacturing or commercial business." Professor Sayers himself mentions that business men who in the thirties were pooh-poohing the significance of low interest rates had in the twenties been emphasising loudly the depressive effects of dear money. There are other reasons too—some more reputable than others—for viewing a change in the rate of interest under a different aspect according to whether it is expansion or restriction which the economy calls for. But topical allusions are not allowed by Professor Sayers to reach the surface (which is perhaps as well at a time when building is subject to a stringent direct control and the aim is to expand rather than contract the building of houses). His survey of the development of thought on this question is sedulously academic in tone and contains much interesting matter.

[19] For a close examination it is desirable to refer to the details of individual cases which, running into many pages in the original articles (*Oxford Economic Papers*, October 1938, pp. 15–28, and February 1940, pp. 46–70), have been omitted from the reprinted versions. The omission of the following comment is particularly regrettable: "The business is conducted on a basis of sound common sense, and is free from idiotic word-spinning theorists whose intervention invariably leads to Carey Street. There is no need to treat the above information as strictly confidential" (*ibid.*, p. 48).

One of the surprising results of these inquiries is that most of the business men appeared to deny that the expansion of their businesses was in any way hampered by difficulties of finance. It is true that it was the rate of interest as such which dominated the inquiry. But the original thirty-seven were asked in the course of discussion about the effect of abundance or scarcity of liquid resources, and Mr. Andrews's later questionnaire made specific reference to "the facility with which you can raise new capital from the public." Less emphasis on the "rate of interest" (carrying with it a suggestion of bank loans, debentures and preference shares) and more on the terms on which ordinary shares could be issued would be helpful in future inquiries of this kind. How far do managements launch their new issues with a view to exploiting a favourable market position in the shares in their companies rather than to financing new investment which they want immediately to undertake? Any correlation which may exist between the expected return on the shares and a firm's investment in plant, and buildings is likely to be pretty long-term in character, the timing of the execution of investment plans in any short period being then dependent, and only very slightly, on the yield earned on the firm's surplus liquid resources. The widening of the ambit of the inquiry in this way would lead on to the question whether the management have a sense of loyalty only to the existing shareholders or also to the potential shareholders who would take up a new issue if it was made, and might as a result be led to disappointment.

The same section of the *Studies* reproduces Professor A.J. Brown's pioneering and courageous attack on the statistical relationship between the rate of interest and the demand for idle money. He regarded the latter as partly dependent on "the rate at which the general price-level has lately been changing," being "a measure of the expectations of appreciation or depreciation of money," but he failed to note that fixed-interest securities would be subject to the same expectations of appreciation or depreciation. Professor Brown's attempt to provide a basis for a correlation, without a direct causal relationship, between the rate of interest and "business enterprise" is open to Professor Sayers's objection that we have to "assume that somehow or other the idle funds can be pumped into the ownership of firms," but both here and elsewhere in the essay there is much to ponder over.

Professor Brown is responsible also for the whole of the section devoted to the Rate of Exchange. In April 1942 he published his important article on the conditions which must be fulfilled if there is to be exchange stability under a free system. This is reprinted, together with a new essay, in which Professor Brown provides a very useful appraisal of the work which has been done in recent years on the measurement of the fundamental elasticities of international demand and supply.

The remaining two chapters of the *Studies* open up fresh subjects, discussion of which would take us too far afield. Mr. B.D. Giles, in a hitherto unpublished essay, surveys the whole field of "Agriculture and the Price Mechanism." Dr. H.W. Robinson summarises the results, published at the time in various articles, of the work of another Oxford group (at the Institute of Statistics) which in the years 1936–39 made a statistical study of mobility of labour. In a new essay he deals also with "The Experience and Lessons of the Past Ten Years" on the response of labour to economic incentives. Writing at the end of 1949 (*i.e.,* before the policy of rearmament was adopted), Dr. Robinson felt that, thanks to other means of control over production, the Government's reluctance to make use of power of control over labour "had not had many far-reaching effects" on the distribution of manpower. But, even then, he was worried about the future, if the normal economic incentives were to remain inoperative. It is appropriate that the final page of these *Oxford Studies* should include a comment on "allergy to economic risk-taking" and refer to "the danger that stern realities will be overlooked or ignored on the grounds of humanitarianism," but give the reader no clear idea what Dr. Robinson wants to do about it.

# PART II

# Keynes

CHAPTER 5

# The Cambridge 'Circus'

*Richard F. Kahn*

Chairman, once again I feel very honoured to have been invited to one of these fascinating seminars. Geoff Harcourt has delivered a brilliant paper, with a great deal of which I agree. I only wish that time would enable me to make some contribution to the discussion on the paper, as I am strongly tempted to deal with the wide range covered by him. But Austin Robinson and I have been asked to talk about the 'Circus' which covers a far narrower range of time than the whole period covered so brilliantly by Geoff.

By way of preamble I shall mention that, although I am speaking before Austin Robinson, in a good deal of what I am going to say, I am giving you Austin's ideas, based on his notes with which he kindly provided me and on suggestions made by him to me.

There exist a number of published accounts of the Cambridge Circus of November 1930 to May 1931. Many members of my audience will be familiar with at least some of them. I attach a list at the end of my contribution to this discussion.

---

Originally publ. in: Kahn, R. F. (1985). The Cambridge 'Circus.' In G. Harcourt (Ed.) *Keynes and His Contemporaries* (pp. 42–51). Palgrave Macmillan.
Reprint by Springer International Publishing 2022 with kind permission

---

R. F. Kahn



M. C. Marcuzzo, P. Paesani (eds.), *Richard F. Kahn*,
Palgrave Studies in the History of Economic Thought,
https://doi.org/10.1007/978-3-030-98588-2_5

They all, apart from an article by Joan Robinson, rely on human memory, looking back forty years. Human memory is fallible. But agreement between Austin and Joan Robinson, Piero Sraffa, James Meade and myself carries some weight.

The absence of any documentary records is regrettable. For this I carry a full load of responsibility.

A glance at the relevant chronology is useful. In March of 1929 the Liberal Party published *We Can Conquer Unemployment: Lloyd George's Pledge*. In May 1929 there were published both *Can Lloyd George Do It?*[1] by Keynes and Hubert Henderson, and the notorious Government White Paper,[2] embodying the Treasury's refutation of the Liberal Party's proposals, based largely on the notorious 'Treasury view'.

Keynes's membership of the Macmillan Committee, which sat from November 1929 to June 1931,[3] provided him with an opportunity for arguing his case for an increase of public expenditure as a means of reducing unemployment, which was accepted in a Supplementary Report[4] signed by six, out of fourteen, members of the Committee (including, in addition to Keynes, Ernest Bevin and Reginald McKenna, Chairman of the Midland Bank). Keynes took full advantage of his opportunity for cross-examining both Governor Norman and Richard Hopkins, the senior Treasury official responsible for the 'Treasury view' (together with Otto Niemeyer).

The Committee of Economists of the Economic Advisory Council, of which I was one of the Secretaries, was appointed at the end of July 1930 and reported at the end of October 1930.[5] It provided a battle-ground between Keynes and Pigou, Josiah Stamp, Hubert Henderson and Lionel Robbins. Keynes had some success in obtaining agreement with his view that higher public expenditure was the way to reduce unemployment.

The *Treatise on Money*[6] was finished in September 1930 and published at the end of October. Keynes's liberation from the fetters of the *Treatise* to the freedom of the *General Theory* can to a considerable degree be attributed to his collaborative work on these Committees and to his propagandist activities. He was far happier writing for a non-academic audience – whether

[1] *The Collected Writings of John Maynard Keynes*, Vol. IX (*Essays in Persuasion*) pp. 86–125.

[2] *Memoranda to Ministers on Certain Proposals Relating to Unemployment.* Cmd 3331 (HMSO, 1929).

[3] *Report*, Cmd. 3897 (HMSO, 1931).

[4] *Ibid.*, pp. 190–209.

[5] *The Economic Advisory Council, 1930–39*, by Susan Howson and Donald Winch (1977) pp. 180–243.

[6] *Collected Writings*, Vols V and VI.

members of the intelligent public, politicians or bankers. His popular and other non-academic writings were unrestrained in contrast to the elements of strain and torture which entered into his academic writings.

To secure conviction, he relied on sincerity and commonsense. He could display his skill at advocacy without arousing the resentment displayed by many of his academic colleagues. When it came to the more precise logic of the *General Theory* he had to demand from his readers the abandonment of firmly ingrained theoretical ideas. Keynes, the propagandist, was always forging ahead of the author of theoretical works. Indeed it was his zest as a reformer that set the pace for the writing of the *General Theory*.

The knowledge that the *Treatise* would be published at the end of October 1930 led to a group of five young Cambridge economists getting together to discuss the basic issues, stimulated by my knowledge that Keynes was already dissatisfied with the *Treatise*. (I was in a strong position because since January 1930 I had been discussing the proofs with Keynes – too late to contribute much more than the corrections of misprints.)

The Group consisted of Joan and Austin Robinson, Piero Sraffa, James Meade (of Oxford), who was spending the academic year with us in Cambridge, and myself. In addition to discussions among ourselves from October 1930 to March 1931, in the Summer Term of 1931 we held a seminar, with other members of the Faculty and the best of the third-year students (in their final year).

Don Patinkin[7] has expressed doubt as to the importance of the Circus as an influence on the development of Keynes's thought. In so far as he relies on documents, he is fully entitled to make his case. Others can then judge. For my own part I feel unable to arouse any feeling of passion over an operation which took place fifty-three years ago. In fact no documents have survived from the Circus itself, but when some years ago the five of us met to prepare the account printed in Volume XIII of the *Writings of John Maynard Keynes*[8] our memories were in complete agreement.

To anybody who did not know Keynes, it is astonishing that he was willing to have discussions with me, week after week; I acting as the Group's spokesman and as the link between Keynes and the Group. We discussed the problems which had arisen and their implications. I then informed the Group of Keynes's reactions and of questions which he wished us to consider. As week followed week, this procedure resulted in

[7] Don Patinkin, *Keynes' Monetary Thought. A Study of its Development.* (Duke University Press, 1976).

[8] *Collected Writings*, Vol. XIII, pp. 337–42.

considerable progress in modifying both Keynes's and our minds. Keynes could easily have asked us to submit a comprehensive memorandum for his consideration.

Austin Robinson, in the course of his *Economic Journal* Obituary, wrote:

> At no moment of his life did Keynes'[s] greatness of character appear more strongly than at this time. He had just completed what he might reasonably have considered as his *magnum opus*. There are few authors who would not have been strongly tempted to take up a position and to use their authority and reputation to maintain it until dislodged by sheer weight of opposition. Keynes never even appeared to hesitate. He was off with the rest of us in pursuit of truth with an enthusiasm and zest as if he were demolishing the work of his worst enemy.[9]

Whenever I took to Keynes (in his rooms in College) the latest thoughts of the Circus, he listened very objectively. Rather than defend the *Treatise* against our criticisms, we would discuss together what modifications were called for – for me to take back for consideration by the Circus. Keynes was as objective over this as though we were discussing someone else's text.

I do not recall that I made available to the Group advance copies of my 'multiplier' article, published in the *Economic Journal* in June 1931. But James Meade, who was closely associated with me in the drafting of the article, and I were able to give an exposition of the article.

The *Treatise* represented a considerable challenge. In its time it was a pioneer path-breaking work in the development of Keynes's thought. But it lagged well behind the progress of Keynes's thinking in the world of practical affairs – of *Can Lloyd George Do It?*, the Macmillan Committee and the Committee of Economists.

Already by June 1931, in his three Harris Foundation lectures,[10] delivered in the University of Chicago, Keynes had made an enormous advance. For this the Circus may claim some credit. They were written in fairly popular language and, in their analysis of the causes of fluctuations, display a marked advance towards the *General Theory* (not published until 1936).

A serious obstacle to understanding the *Treatise* was the definition of income, and hence of saving, as excluding 'abnormal' profits and losses.

[9] *Economic Journal*, p. 40, March 1947.

[10] *Collected Writings*, Vol. XIII, pp. 343–67.

The exposition of my 'multiplier' article was complicated as a result of being written in *Treatise* language. Both James Meade and I failed to appreciate that his complicated relationship boiled down to the identical equality of the aggregate rate of saving and the aggregate rate of investment once income and saving were defined so as to include actual entrepreneurs' profits and not confined to normal profits.

Keynes's Fundamental Equations in his *Treatise* expressed the price-levels of consumption-goods and investment-goods in terms of costs of production. This in itself was an important break-through and prepared the way for the emphasis placed in the *General Theory* on the determination of prices by costs of production.

In formulating the equations Keynes did not discuss what determined these two outputs; they represent a snapshot photograph of one arbitrary position. As Donald Moggridge has written:

> The Fundamental Equations did not strictly speaking assume that a potential difference between [saving as defined in the *Treatise* and investment] would be adjusted otherwise than through a change in the prices of investment-goods and/or consumption-goods with consequential effects on profits.[11]

Part of the criticism to which Keynes was subject arose from the fact that the Fundamental Equations determined prices rather than output. Looking back, it now seems to me a virtue that these equations, though so much criticised, showed price-levels to be determined by costs of production, adjusted by the extent to which profits were abnormal or subnormal. The major criticism of the Circus was crystallised by picking up the famous passage, christened by Austin Robinson as the Widow's Cruse:

> However much of their profits entrepreneurs spend on consumption, the increment of wealth belonging to entrepreneurs remains the same as before. Thus profits as a source of capital investment for entrepreneurs are a widow's cruse which remains undepleted however much of them may be devoted to riotous living.[12]

[11] *Collected Writings*, Vol. XIII, p. 339.

[12] *Collected Writings*, Vol. V, p. 125.

It is to be noted that:

1. The result of greater expenditure by entrepreneurs is to raise the prices of consumption-goods and thus to diminish real wages. In so far as wage-earners save, they diminish their consumption, with the result that the benefits to entrepreneurs of an increase in their consumption is all the greater. But for the sake of simplicity of exposition, it is convenient to assume that wage-earners do not save, spending the whole of their wages on consumption.
2. Austin Robinson's phrase 'widow's cruse' was used by the Circus as shorthand for the criticism that in evolving his Fundamental Equations Keynes appeared to be assuming that the outputs both of consumption-goods and of capital-goods were fixed. But over any period of time the increment of wealth belonging to entrepreneurs is equal to the rate of investment whether outputs are fixed or not.

Keynes did in fact add that 'profits (or losses) having once come into existence become, as we shall see (for this will be the main topic of several succeeding chapters), a cause of what subsequently ensues; indeed the mainspring of change in the existing economic system. This is the essential reason why it is useful to segregate them in our Fundamental Equation'.[13]

The fact is that considerable parts of the two Volumes of the *Treatise* – especially of the second Volume – are devoted to fluctuations in the rate of investment and to the Credit Cycle.

Looking back I am puzzled because I cannot recall such a rejoinder from Keynes to the unanimous Circus criticism that in the *Treatise* outputs of consumption-goods and of investment-goods are arbitrarily taken as given.

Important light is thrown by Donald Moggridge's discovery of a memorandum enclosed in a letter from Keynes to Hawtrey in November 1930, less than a month after publication of the *Treatise*. Keynes was dealing with a large number of criticisms by Hawtrey of the proofs of the *Treatise* which he had not had time to deal with before publication. Keynes wrote:

> The question *how much* reduction of output is caused, whether by a realised fall of price or an anticipated fall of prices, is important but not strictly a monetary phenomenon. I have not attempted to deal with it in my book

[13] *Ibid.*, p. 126.

> though I have done a great deal of work on it. I am primarily concerned with what governs *prices*.[14]

And finally the even more astonishing passage:

> I repeat that I am not dealing with the complete set of causes which determine volume of output. For this would have led me on an endlessly long journey into the theory of short-period supply prices and a long way from monetary theory; though I agree that it will probably be difficult in the future to prevent monetary theory and the theory of short-period supply prices from running together.[15]

In discussing fluctuations of output in the *Treatise*, especially in Volume 2, Keynes was unable to estimate the extent of an increase of output caused by, say, a given rise in the rate of investment. There is nothing in the *Treatise* to explain why even a relatively small increase in the rate of investment should not push output right up to full utilisation of available equipment and labour.

The reason is that Keynes did not in the *Treatise* introduce the Propensity to Consume (based on my 'multiplier'), which is determined by the proportion of an increase in income which is saved (although the concept is implicit in *Can Lloyd George Do It?*, published a year earlier in 1929).

The Circus were working on fertile ground. It is my strong belief – based on our several and joint memories – that the Circus encouraged the development indicated by Keynes to Hawtrey.

There is one piece of written evidence. During the summer of 1931 Joan Robinson wrote 'A Parable of Saving and Investment'. It was shown to Keynes, and approved by him in April 1932. It was not published (in *Economica)* until February 1933.[16] She recorded that, as regards the Widow's Cruse:

> Mr. Keynes has now admitted that in that passage[17] he was tacitly assuming that output was unchanged although the price-level was falling. Evidently,

[14] *Collected Writings*, Vol. XIII, p. 145.

[15] *Ibid.*, pp. 145–6.

[16] *Collected Writings*, Vol. XIII, pp. 268 and 342.

[17] *Collected Writings*, Vol. V, p. 139.

he, like the rest of us, had been misled by his upbringing to keeping his eye on demand and forgetting supply.

In the course of her article Joan indicated the extent of the Circus's movement away from the framework of *Treatise* thinking.

Keynes normally lectured in only one term each academic year. Those advertised for the Summer Term of 1931 were cancelled – because under Circus influence he wanted to do some rethinking. The Lectures delivered in the Summer Term of 1932 were still entitled 'The Pure Theory of Money', but by the Autumn Term of 1932 the title had been changed to the 'Monetary Theory of Production'.

I repeat that to anybody who did not know Keynes well it must seem astonishing how readily he received my regular reports on our discussions, doubts, new ideas and tentative conclusions. As Austin Robinson indicated in the passage which I have quoted from his *Obituary*, see above, to those, having just completed a *magnum opus*, Keynes might well, had he been a lesser man, have been unreceptive. He was in fact the very opposite. He picked up our ideas, incorporated them in his own thinking and went ahead. And he asked me to take suggestions for further discussion back to the Circus. But it did not occur to any of us that we were doing more than adding glosses and embroideries to Keynes's work. Any further advance was made by Keynes.

With the disbanding of the Circus in June 1931, discussions continued – until the completion of the *General Theory* (in 1936) – between Keynes, Joan Robinson and myself and, in addition, with Dennis Robertson and others.

It began carrying forward from the Circus, with a series of letters between Keynes, Joan Robinson and me between September 1931 and May 1932.[18] That was the beginning of the long process of argument at long last embodied in the publication of the *General Theory* in 1936. For such part as I played in these discussions, I am deeply indebted to the experience which I gained as a member of the Circus and as its 'messenger boy.'

[18] *Collected Writings*, Vol. XIII, pp. 373–80.

## PUBLISHED ACCOUNTS OF THE CIRCUS

1. Keynes, *Collected Writings,* Vol. XIII, pp. 337–42 and 202–213
2. Austin Robinson, 'Obituary of Keynes', *Economic Journal,* pp. 39–40, March 1947.
3. Donald Moggridge, 'From the *Treatise* to *The General Theory*', *History of Political Economy,* Vol. 5, No. 1 pp. 75–79, (Spring 1973).
4. *Keynes, Cambridge and the General Theory,* edited by Don Patinkin and J. Clark Leith (1977), pp. 6, 33–6, 66, 146–8.
5. Don Patinkin, *Keynes' Monetary Thought,* (Duke University Press, 1976).
6. Richard Kahn, *The Making of Keynes' General Theory* (Cambridge University Press, 1984) pp. 103–11.

[All these accounts originate from Austin Robinson.- R.F.K.]

CHAPTER 6

# Some Aspects of the Development of Keynes's Thought

*Richard F. Kahn*

In this brief essay I have picked out certain particular strands of thought, on the basis partly of theoretical significance and partly of relationship to economic policy.

Originally publ. in: Kahn, R. F. (1978). Some Aspects of the Development of Keynes's Thought. *Journal of Economic Literature, 16*(2), 545–559. http://www.jstor.org/stable/2722880
Reprint by Springer International Publishing 2022 with kind permission

This article incorporates—either literally or by way of substance—considerable portions of a lecture delivered on 6 November 1974 to the British Academy on "Re-reading Keynes" [8, 1974]. I am indebted to the British Academy for permission to make use of this material. I owe much to Professor Donald Moggridge of the University of Toronto.
My references to Keynes's writings are to the Royal Economic Society edition of *The Collected Writings of John Maynard Keynes*, edited by Professor Sir Austin Robinson and Professor Donald Moggridge. Volumes XIII and XIV in the series, entitled *The General Theory and After*, comprise, with considerable editorial comment hitherto unpublished, memoranda and letters, and some of Keynes's articles.

R. F. Kahn



M. C. Marcuzzo, P. Paesani (eds.), *Richard F. Kahn*, Palgrave Studies in the History of Economic Thought, https://doi.org/10.1007/978-3-030-98588-2_6

Monetary economics is in a state of shameful confusion. One example is the common failure to distinguish between "crowding out" in a physical sense and in a financial sense. At a time when labor bottlenecks and scarcity of productive equipment are wide-spread, the doctrine is a matter of common sense. In the financial sense it takes us back to the notorious "Treasury view" of 1929—that if more saving is devoted to one purpose, less is available for other purposes, so that it is impossible to reduce unemployment by trying to increase investment. What is completely overlooked is Keynes's discovery that—when, as at the present time, there is plenty of surplus labor and equipment—an increase of investment results in an equal increase in saving.

Then there is the severe controversy between monetarists and Keynesians; likewise there is the controversy whether a reduction in real wages is required to reduce unemployment.

The word "Keynes" has become a term of abuse. It seems worthwhile to go back and enquire what Keynes actually thought and wrote, at the expense of adding yet one more (necessarily brief) to the many published surveys, of which Professor Don Patinkin's is a good example [25, 1976].

Keynes was born on 5 June 1883. He published *The Tract on Monetary Reform* [10, IV, 1971] in 1923 at the age of 40; the *Treatise on Money* in 1930 at the age of 47 [11, V, 1971; 12, VI, 1971]; and the *General Theory of Employment, Interest and Money* [13, VII, (1936) 1973] at the age of 50. It had been a long and painful process of escape from traditional economics.

In his popular writings Keynes was well ahead of his serious books. *Can Lloyd George Do It?* [14, IX, 1972, pp. 86–125], by Keynes and Hubert Henderson, published in 1929, is based, in essence, on Keynes's ideas about the main cause of unemployment and the character of the remedy. But it lacked a complete theoretical foundation. For example, he noted that one of the resources that can enable new investment to provide a net addition to the amount of employment "comes from the savings which now run to waste through lack of adequate credit." Some years were to elapse before Keynes realized that in this sense savings do not "run to waste," but are not made.

The gradual change in Keynes's attitude towards the Quantity Theory of Money illustrates the development of his thought. Irving Fisher is regarded as the great codifier of the Theory, in his *Purchasing Power of Money* [2, 1913]. He did not however, do more than express the truism in its well-known algebraic form. The character of any causation is not apparent. Keynes, in his *Tract,* states that "his exposition follows the general lines of Professor Pigou and Dr. Marshall rather than the perhaps more familiar analysis of Professor Irving Fisher" [10, IV, (1923) 1971, p. 63, fn.]. There is more in this than the formal difference between expressing the theory in terms of the velocity of circulation of money and the value of the transactions that take place in the course, say, of a year, and in terms of the stock of money and the stock of money expressed in real value.

> Marshall had pointed out that [19, 1923, p. 43]: changes in the rapidity of circulation of money are themselves incidental to changes in the amount of ready purchasing power which the people of a country find it advantageous to keep in their own holding. This amount is governed by causes, the chief of which can be seen with but little trouble.

But

> This "Quantity doctrine" is helpful as far as it goes: but it does not indicate what are the "other things" which must be assumed to be equal in order to justify the proposition: and it does not explain the causes which govern "rapidity of circulation." It is almost a truism. [19, 1923, p. 48.]

Pigou codified Marshall in the form of his "Cambridge equation," which expresses the relation between the stock of money and the stock of money expressed in real terms. He emphasized at the outset that there was no "fundamental disagreement [between him and Irving Fisher] about the real causes at work" [26, 1917, p. 39]. Later in the article, however, he wrote of his presentation [26, 1917, p. 54]:

> It focusses attention on the proportion of their resources that people choose to keep in the form of titles to legal tender instead of focussing it on "velocity of circulation." This fact gives it, as I think, a real advantage, because it brings us at once into relation with volition—an ultimate cause of demand—instead of with something that seems at first sight accidental and arbitrary.

According to this view, the causative process takes the form of decisions as to the amount of wealth that individuals, as a whole, wish to hold in the form of money. Given the quantity of money, the price-level has to accommodate these decisions.

In the *Tract,* Keynes is at one point as orthodox on the subject of the Quantity Theory as an earlier economist, and more orthodox than many. He had been encouraged to become an economist by Alfred Marshall, whom he knew well, as a result of Marshall's friendship with his father, the Cambridge logician and economist who wrote the *Scope and Method of Political Economy* [18, 1891]. But Keynes was far more strictly monetarist than Marshall and Pigou.

The Quantity Theory he said was "fundamental. Its correspondence with fact is not open to question." He quoted a saying of Goschen's, of sixty years earlier—it could with much more justification be repeated today—that "there are many persons who cannot bear the relation of the level of prices to the volume of currency affirmed without a feeling akin to irritation." Keynes in 1923 shared Goschen's contempt for such Philistines.

And yet a few pages further on Keynes denied the validity of the Quantity Theory, in the form in which it is normally presented, except "in *the long run,* in which we are all dead." A change in the quantity of money, in a period shorter than that long run, is itself the cause of a change in the ratio of the quantity of money to the price-level. [10, IV, (1923) 1971, pp. 61, 65].

Six months after the *Tract* was published, Keynes started work in July 1924 on a new book, which six years later was to be published in two volumes under the title of *A Treatise on Money* [11, V, (1930) 1971; 12, VI, (1930) 1971]. The Quantity Theory of Money continued for a time to dominate his thinking, although the part played by investment in working capital began to assume an important role.

It was at this stage that Dennis Robertson was working on his *Banking Policy and the Price Level* [30, 1926]. Already in November 1915, in his preface to his book on *Industrial Fluctuations,* Robertson wrote that the war had "compelled clear thinking on the real nature of saving and investment in the most unlikely quarters" [29, 1915].

In a letter addressed to Robertson after the publication of his *General Theory,* Keynes wrote: "I certainly date all my emancipation from the discussions between us which preceded your *Banking Policy and the Price Level*" [16, XIV, (1936) 1973, p. 94].[1] As Professor Sir Austin Robinson put it in his obituary of Keynes, *Banking Policy and the Price Level* was the first book "to bring home to us in Cambridge ... the essential distinction between the act of saving and the act of investment" [31, 1947, p. 36]. In his introduction Robertson wrote of his discussions with Keynes: "Neither of us now know how much of the ideas contained [in chapters V and VI] is his and how much is mine." Keynes, in his preface to his *Treatise,* refers to the "penetrating light cast by Mr. D. H. Robertson on certain fundamental matters."

In 1926 Keynes was hoping that his new book would be published in 1927. It was not published until 1930.

Keynes's long struggle over a period of six years to produce a version of the *Treatise* worthy of publication was directed partly to an escape from the stranglehold of the Quantity Theory of Money in its crude form. In

[1] See also Vol. XIII, p. 1 [15, 1973].

the end Keynes was able to write that "the forms of the quantity theory ... on which we have all been brought up ... are but ill adapted" for the purpose of exhibiting "the causal process by which the price level is determined. ... They do not, any of them, have the advantage of separating out those factors through which ... the causal process actually operates during a period of change" [11, V, (1930) 1971, p. 120].

Five pages further on, Keynes wrote that the conclusions that he drew from his Fundamental Equations

> are, of course, obvious and may serve to remind us that all these equations are purely formal; they are mere identities; truisms which tell us nothing in themselves. In this respect they resemble *all other versions of the quantity theory of money*. Their only point is to analyse and arrange our material in what will turn out to be a useful way for tracing cause and effect, when we have vitalised them by the introduction of extraneous facts from the actual world. [11, V, (1930) 1971, p. 125, italics added.]

Keynes seems to have been so much under the spell of the Quantity Theory that he could write about his Fundamental Equations as though they were "versions" of the Quantity Theory; although, up to this point in his book, the quantity of money does not figure in them in any sense.

Seven pages further on, Keynes attempted a reconciliation with the Quantity Theory. It was not successful. But in it can be seen the seed of what in the *General Theory* was to flourish under the name of the Liquidity Preference Theory. This Theory explained how the quantity of money exercises a causative influence by helping to determine the rate of interest—or more generally, as we would put it now, the state of credit and the price levels of securities, both fixed-interest and equities.

And yet, another three pages on, Keynes insisted on a symbolic presentation, which must to most readers of the time have appeared to have been a reaffirmation of the Quantity Theory in its simple form.

Later on in the book, Keynes was more explicit. He wrote that under equilibrium conditions "the quantity of money available for the Industrial Circulation *does* (if habits and methods are unchanged) rule the situation. Equilibrium conditions prevail '*when the price-level is in equilibrium with the cost of production*'" [12, VI, (1930) 1971, p. 4]. In the section of the book from which I am now quoting, the *modus operandi* of price determination ceases to be the conventional determination by the quantity of money only when equilibrium is disturbed as a result of the rate of physical investment failing to match thriftiness. And yet much earlier in the book, the Fundamental Equations indicated that the price level under conditions of equilibrium is determined by money costs of production per unit of output [11, V, (1930) 1971, pp. 122–24]. There is a serious internal inconsistency in the *Treatise*.

The baby had been born but the umbilical cord had not yet been cut.

Keynes's insight grew immediately after he had completed the *Treatise* in September 1930. A year later, in the course of a special preface to the German edition, he criticized the well-known concept of forced saving. It was often supposed to be the result of, and equal to, an expansion of bank credit. This "forced" saving was regarded as supplementing "voluntary" saving—the value of an economy's physical investment being equal to the sum of the two. This doctrine, together with the concept itself of "forced" saving, Keynes completely rejected [11, V, (1930) 1971, p. xxiv]. Investment creates the necessary "voluntary" saving, quite irrespective of the extent to which it is financed by the banks.

Later in 1931 and early in 1932, Keynes was making rapid progress towards a completely new formulation. The *General Theory* [13, VII, 1973] was finished at the end of 1935 and published early in 1936, five years after the *Treatise*.

Towards the end of his *General Theory*, Keynes did provide a symbolic expression, involving four elasticities of response, which he wrote "can be regarded as a generalised statement of the Quantity Theory of Money." He added: "I do not myself attach much value to manipulations of this kind ... I doubt if they carry us any further than ordinary discourse can" [13, VII, (1936) 1973, p. 305]. He referred to a warning he had given a few pages back [13, VII, (1936) 1973, p. 297–98]:

> It is a great fault of symbolic pseudo-mathematical methods of formalising a system of economic analysis ... that they expressly assume strict independence between the factors involved. ...; whereas, in ordinary discourse, ... we can keep "at the back of our heads" the necessary reserves and qualifications. ... Too large a proportion of recent "mathematical" economics are merely concoctions, as imprecise as the initial assumptions they rest on, which allow the author to lose sight of the complexities and interdependencies of the real world in a maze of pretentious and unhelpful symbols.

The equation that presents the so-called Quantity Theory is, of course, correct. But it is not an equation. It is an identity, like so many so-called equations in economics. An identity may be a useful means of avoiding error, but it cannot, taken by itself, prove anything about causation.

A large volume of literature now exists comparing the *Treatise* with the *General Theory*, commenting on the transition. To discuss the subject—still more the commentators—would require several articles. I confine myself to some personal comments.

Looking back, I find astonishing the confusion of thought of those of us, who, directly or indirectly, were in close touch with Keynes in Cambridge. Donald Moggridge describes it in Volumes XIII and XIV of the Royal Economic Society edition of *The Collected Writings of John Maynard Keynes* [15, 1973; 16, 1973].[2]

In the *Treatise* Keynes concentrated on the determination of the prices of consumption-goods and capital-goods rather than on their outputs. This seemed to us to be made by an entirely different Keynes from the co-author of *Can Lloyd George Do It?* [14, IX, 1972, pp. 86–125], published in 1929, a year earlier than the *Treatise*. Actually, Keynes devoted a considerable part of the practical second volume of the *Treatise* to fluctuations and unemployment.

When I re-read my own letters to Keynes [15, XIII, (1931) 1973, pp. 373–75], I found them so confused that I had difficulty in believing that they were written by the author of my article, written nine months earlier [7, 1931]. In our discussions of the price level of capital goods, we seem to have failed to appreciate how Keynes brought in expectations. In developing his Fundamental Equation, Keynes took the price level of new investment goods simply as given, reserving its examination to a later part of the chapter.

When he got on to the subject, he began with the prices of securities, explaining their determination by expectations of the returns likely to be received on securities in the future and by the quantity of savings deposits (and the rate of interest paid on them). He wrote in terms of "bullishness" and "bearishness" of the public, and of "two opinions." The actual price level of investments he regarded as the resultant of the sentiment of the public and the behavior of the banking system. But he then allowed himself to become completely confused by the two quite different meanings of the word "investment"—in securities and in new capital goods. (This is one of the rare occasions on which the French vocabulary is richer than

[2] See especially Vol. XIII, pp. 337–43.

the English. Joan Robinson, taking a hint from John Hicks, has established the word *placement* for investment in securities.)

Keynes wrote [11, V, (1930) 1971, p. 129]:

> The price level of investments as a whole, and hence of new investments, is that price level at which the desire of the public to hold savings deposits is equal to the amount of savings deposits which the banking system is willing and able to create.

He got himself involved in confusion between securities and capital goods. The prices of capital goods, of course, depend on expectations about their future earnings, not on the future earnings of the equities which they underlie. There is some relation between the two. There is also, quite obviously, a relation between the prices of equities and the prices of the capital goods that underlie them. But the former are subject to fluctuations larger, and different in character, from the latter [11, V, (1930) 1971, pp. 127, 130].

Here, despite its faults, are to be found the germs of the Liquidity Preference Theory of the *General Theory.* The Liquidity Preference Theory of the *General Theory* also involves a serious fault. The expectations relate to fixed-interest securities—to "the complex of rates of interest for varying maturities which will rule at future dates." In Chapter 13 there is no place for equities as part of a man's wealth. Keynes's failure to present his theory of determination of the rate of interest in terms of "portfolio analysis" can be explained by his ardent desire to make his presentation as simple as possible, in the hope of carrying conviction to those unwilling to be convinced. But he should have explained—both in this and in other contexts—the character of his simplifying assumptions.

The following passage is significant [13, VII, (1936) 1973, pp. 173–74]:

> Whilst liquidity-preference due to the speculative-motive corresponds to what is my *Treatise on Money* I called "the state of bearishness," it is by no means the same thing. For "bearishness" is there defined as the functional relationship, not between the rate of interest (or price of debts) and the quantity of money, but between the price of assets and debts, taken together, and the quantity of money. This treatment, however, involved a confusion between results due to a change in the rate of interest and those due to a change in the schedule of the marginal efficiency of capital, which I hope I have here avoided.

Keynes's chapter on the marginal efficiency of capital is based on the prospective future yield of a capital asset which, together with the rate of interest, determines the price of the asset.

Keynes was not a man who easily got worried or lacked confidence in himself. But without allowing his spirits, which were normally buoyant, to be affected, he was at no stage satisfied with his accomplishment. On the evening on which he finished the *Treatise*, he wrote to his mother: "Artistically it is a failure—I have changed my mind too much ... for it to be a proper unity" [15, XIII, (1930) 1973, p. 176].

Five months before he completely finished the *General Theory*, Keynes wrote to me: "I am in the stage of not liking my book very much" [15, XIII, (1935) 1973, p. 634]. Joan Robinson recalls that in reply to a note from her: "I hope you are not suffering from author's melancholy," Keynes replied: "Author's melancholy did set in at the end. I feel I have not been worthy of my task."

Eight months after he had finished the *General Theory*, Keynes wrote to Sir Ralph Hawtrey [16, XIV, (1936) 1973, p. 47]:

> I may mention that I am thinking of producing in the course of the next year or so what might be called *footnotes* to my previous book. ... Of course, in fact, the whole book needs rewriting and re-casting.

It would have given Keynes intense pleasure had he lived to hear Pigou, in November 1949, partially renounce his review of the *General Theory* [27, 1936]. It was a moving occasion. It took the form of two lectures delivered to a large audience of Cambridge dons and undergraduates. Referring to "the kernel of Keynes' contribution," as set out on page 246 of the *General Theory*, Pigou said [28, 1950, p. 65]:

> Whatever imperfection there may be in his working out of the fundamental conception embodied there, the conception itself is an extremely fruitful germinal idea. In my original review article on the *General Theory* I failed to grasp its significance and did not assign to Keynes the credit due for it. Nobody before him, so far as I know, had brought all the relevant factors, real and monetary at once, together in a single formal scheme, through which their interplay could be coherently investigated.

I turn now to Keynes's treatment of the behavior of money wages. It will serve to illustrate the attitude towards the Quantity Theory of Money of the Keynes of the *General Theory* if I begin by outlining the attitude of many Keynesians to the extremely serious problem presented today by inflation. According to the monetarist school of thought, the remedy is to prevent the supply of money from increasing faster than the rate of increase of the national product added to such modest rate of rise of the price level as appears acceptable. We are assured that, after a period of some years, the economy will settle down in a happy state of tranquil growth, with the price level rising at a modest rate.

Part of the Keynesian comment about such a policy is that a decline in the ratio of the supply of money to the value of output would mean rising rates of interest, and a progressive failure of the supply of credit to meet the needs of industry, falling prices on the Stock Exchange, and bankruptcies at an increasing rate. Unemployment would grow progressively and would reach a level which was politically unacceptable, before it had an appreciable influence, if any at all, on the outcome of wage bargaining.

Already in his *Treatise on Money,* Keynes had drawn the fundamental distinction between cost inflation and the kind of inflation that shows itself in profits being abnormally high. The distinction is brought out sharply in his Fundamental Equations [11, V, (1930) 1971]. Underlying a rising price level are two elements. The first is a rising rate of efficiency-earnings—the rate of money earnings per unit of output. This Keynes called *income inflation*. The second element Keynes called *profit inflation*. It is the result of the level of demand being such as to push prices above earnings per unit of output, resulting in profits being abnormal.

In so far as the abnormal profits are earned in the production of consumption goods, they are earned at the expense of real wages. Incidentally, here we can trace the seed of what was, over 20 years later, to become the post-Keynesian theory of the distribution of income. In so far as the abnormal profits are earned in the production of capital goods, real wages are not directly affected. But such profits encourage an increase in the rate of investment—the output of capital goods—and this results in abnormal profits being earned in the production of consumption goods as well.

As I have already indicated, Keynes had not, when he completed the *Treatise*, broken entirely loose from the trammels of the Quantity Theory of Money. But here we have a theory of determination of the price level in which the Quantity Theory plays no explicit part. Implicitly it appears through monetary influences on the output of capital goods. In this particular part of the *Treatise*, monetary influences appear in the form of the market rate of interest. Following Wicksell, the great Swedish economist [36, 1898], Keynes described as the natural rate of interest that rate of interest which would result in such an output of capital goods— such a rate of investment—as would entail no profit inflation. But inflation could still take the form of income inflation, as a result of money wages rising faster than productivity.

By introducing income inflation as a possibility consistent with the absence of profit inflation, Keynes improved on Wicksell. Keynes has been accused of either failing adequately to acknowledge his debt to Swedish economists or of failing to profit from their pioneer work. Professor Gunnar Myrdal, in his rightly famous book on *Monetary Equilibrium*, published in German in 1933,[3] wrote [23, 1939, pp. 8–9]:

> The English school of theorists has only slowly arrived at Wicksell's statement of the problem.
>
> ... J. M. Keynes' new, brilliant, though not always clear, work, *A Treatise on Money*, is completely permeated by Wicksell's influence. Nevertheless Keynes' work, too, suffers somewhat from the attractive Anglo-Saxon kind of unnecessary originality, which has its roots in certain systematic gaps in the knowledge of the German language on the part of the majority of English economists.

Keynes did, in fact, admit in the *Treatise*—referring to books by Ludwig von Mises, Professor Hans Neisser, and Professor Friedrich Hayek—that he would have made more references to them if his knowledge of German had not been so poor. "In German I can only clearly understand what I know already."

Wicksell was available to Keynes only in German. Keynes certainly derived the phrase "natural rate of interest" from Wicksell. And he regarded Wicksell's book as sufficiently important for me to translate. Sir Roy Harrod's view is that "the process of thought by which Keynes reached his conclusions was independent, and not derived from the study of Wicksell" [4, 1951, p. 409].

[3] A shorter version of Professor Myrdal's book was originally published in Swedish [21, 1931]. Three introductory chapters were added in the German version, from the first of which the passage quoted in the text is taken. The German version was published in 1933 as part of *Beiträge zur Geldtheorie*, edited by Professor Hayek [22]. An English translation of the German version was published in 1939 [23].

The truth seems to lie closer to the implications of Professor Gunnar Myrdal's phrase "systematic gaps in the knowledge of the German language" than to that of his phrase "completely permeated."

On this issue we have Keynes's own testimony, in an article published in 1937, replying to an article by Professor Bertil Ohlin. Keynes wrote that Sir Ralph Hawtrey and Dennis Robertson had "strayed from the fold" of classical economics sooner than he had. He regarded Sir Ralph Hawtrey "as [his] grandparent and Mr. Robertson as [his] parent in the paths of errancy," and he had "been greatly influenced by them." Keynes might have adopted "Wicksell as [his] great-grandparent, if [he] had known his works in more detail at an earlier stage in [his] own thought and also if [he] did not have the feeling that Wicksell was trying to be 'classical'" [16, XIV, (1937) 1973, p. 202, fn. 2].

Professor Myrdal, in his recent book of essays, called *Against the Stream,* does actually praise Wicksell because he "was always eager to root his new ideas in thoughts which, after laborious study, he had found expressed somewhere in the great literature, in part from the beginning of the nineteenth century" [24, 1972, p. 59]. This view, taken by Professor Myrdal, confirms Keynes's complaint that Wicksell was *trying* to be classical.

In fact, Professor Myrdal's own book, *Monetary Equilibrium,* is strongly based on classical thought as the following quotation indicates: "The 'natural' or, as Wicksell sometimes says, the 'real,' rate of interest is defined as the marginal increment in 'physical productivity' of the services of land and labour when they are saved" [23, 1939, p. 49].

That is by the way. I was saying that Keynes improved on Wicksell by demonstrating the compatibility of income inflation, due to money wages rising faster than productivity, with the market rate of interest being equal to the natural rate; and so he demonstrated the compatibility of income inflation with profit inflation: whereas Wicksell defined the natural rate as the rate of interest that would result in stability of the price level.

The fact that later on, in his *General Theory,* Keynes abandoned the use of Wicksell's term "natural rate of interest" is irrelevant to the issue of the degree of Wicksell's influence on Keynes [13, VII, (1936) 1973, pp. 242–43].

It is unfortunate that Keynes failed in his *General Theory* to refer to Professor Myrdal's book. But although it was published in German in 1933, the English translation was not published until 1939.

Keynes's concept of income inflation, published 44 years ago, fits in with much modern thinking about the causes of inflation. Although

Keynes abandoned the actual phrase in his *General Theory*, he strengthened the logical basis of the concept. One of the important contributions of the *General Theory* is what Sir John Hicks, in his recent book on *The Crisis in Keynesian Economics*, calls the "*wage theorem*" [6, 1974, p. 59]. Keynes had already in his *Treatise* enunciated the doctrine, which emerged logically from his discovery of income inflation [11, V, (1930) 1973, p. 150]. The money wage is the fulcrum on which rests the whole structure of everything expressed in terms of money—all prices, incomes of every kind, and all money values. A higher level of money wages means that everything expressed in terms of money is higher in the same proportion. The one important exception is the quantity of money. If it is held constant, a higher money wage means that in real value—in terms of its purchasing power over labor and goods—the quantity of money is reduced. The only important influence on the real state of the economy of a higher money wage takes the form of the higher rates of interest, and the general tightening of credit, which result from a reduction in the real value of the quantity of money.

In addition, all incomes and debts fixed contractually in terms of money are smaller in real value as a result of the money-wage being higher. I am, of course, abstracting from effects on exports and imports.

The basis of the fundamental role of the money wage in determining all prices, money incomes, and money values is that money wages not only form part of costs of production but, because they are to a large extent spent, they form part of total purchasing power expressed in terms of money. The higher costs resulting from a higher level of money wages are met by the resultant addition to demand in terms of money; while in real terms demand is unaltered.

Keynes's analysis of the behavior of money wages is unsystematic and unsatisfactory. His failure to consider adequately how wages would, or might, behave under conditions of fairly full employment is attributable to the high level of unemployment with which he was faced and to his belief that, apart from war, unemployment would never fall to a really low level. His main concern was not with rising wages but with certain aspects of falling wages. First of all, he stressed the extreme reluctance of money wages to fall even under the pressure of severe unemployment. Sir John Hicks points out that in 1933 in this country, "the wage-index had fallen no more than 5 per cent below its level in the mid-twenties" [6, 1974, p. 67]. In the early 1930's the number of unemployed rose above 2 million—above a percentage of 20—and in 1932 was about 2,800,000—a percentage of 28. During the last stages of Keynes's completion of his *General Theory,* in 1934 and 1935, unemployment was falling, but it remained over 1,200,000.

The difficulty of securing a fall of wages had been the basis of the argument used by Keynes in *The Economic Consequences of Mr. Winston Churchill.* Even if severe unemployment in the unsheltered industries did result in some fall of wages, "wages will not fall in the sheltered industries, merely because there is unemployment in the unsheltered industries. Therefore, you will have to see to it that there is unemployment in the sheltered industries also" [14, IX, (1925) 1972, p. 215].

Keynes had to contest the very widely held view that, quite apart from favorable effects on exports, if only wages fell more heavily, unemployment would be reduced. He argued emphatically that lower wages simply meant lower purchasing power and that far from unemployment being reduced, it would be increased if a fall of wages resulted in an expectation of further falls of wages and prices.

Furthermore, a really heavy cut in wages, resulting in a heavy fall of prices, would seriously endanger the financial position of companies that were partly financed by loans and debentures. As a result, the financial position of banks would be threatened. Although their assets would rise in real value to the same extent as the deposits held with them, some of their borrowers would become bankrupt. The solidarity of the whole financial system would be threatened [14, IX, (1931) 1972, pp. 150–58].

Keynes was mainly concerned, in the *General Theory,* with the failure of economists and others to appreciate the reluctance of money wages to fall and to realize that even if they did fall, unemployment would not be diminished, except in industries subject to competition with overseas suppliers.

However, he did write something about the relationship between the behavior of money wages and the level of demand as reflected in the level of employment. He expressed such a relationship in what would today be regarded as the wrong form. He referred to a rise of the level of money wages in response to a rise of demand and employment, whereas today we would refer to the relationship between the rate of increase of money wages and the level of employment. This is just one aspect of the fact that Keynes's concepts were designed for an economy in a state of depression. Similarly, he would discuss the influence of a change in the actual quantity of money as opposed to a change in its rate of growth.

Among the forces responsible for the behavior of money-wages, Keynes mentioned "the power of trade unions" [11, V, (1930) 1971, p. 152], the greater readiness of entrepreneurs to give way to pressure "when they are doing better business," and "the psychology of the workers and the policies of employers and trade unions" [13, VII, (1936) 1973, pp. 300–301]. However, there is no analysis of the problem. The only reasoned statement that I have been able to find either in the *Treatise* or in the *General Theory* is the following in the *General Theory* [13, VII, (1936) 1973, pp. 252–53]:

> ... [this] accords with our experience of human nature. For although the struggle for money-wages is ... essentially a struggle to maintain a high *relative* wage, this struggle is likely, as employment increases, to be intensified in each individual case both because the bargaining position of the worker is improved.

So we find that, as long ago as 1936, Keynes regarded what is now called the "leap-frogging effect"—or the wage-wage spiral as opposed to the wage-price spiral—as the main cause of rising wages. This is the view many of us have held for some years.

Keynes added that "these motives will operate within limits," and that the level of money wages in practice fluctuated very little. His belief was dominated not only by contemporary experience, with heavy unemployment, but also by the "fair measure of stability of prices" between 1820 and 1914, which he attributed to "a balance of forces in an age when individual groups of employers were strong" [13, VII, (1936) 1973, p. 308].

As to full employment, Keynes wrote that "when a further increase in the quantity of effective demand produces no further increase in output ... we have reached a condition which might be appropriately designated as one of true inflation" [13, VII, (1936) 1973, p. 303]. But he had written earlier, "full, or even approximately full, employment is of rare and short-lived occurrence" [13, VII, (1936) 1973, p. 250].

There are passages in the *General Theory* that seem to suggest that there is one quite definite level of demand, resulting in a level of employment which can be described as a "state of full employment." As Sir John Hicks, in his recent book, remarks,

> when the Keynes theory is set out in this textbook manner ... it is bound to give the impression that there are just two 'states' of the economy: a 'state of unemployment' in which money wages are constant, and a 'state of full employment' in which pressure of demand causes wages to rise. [6, 1974, p. 60.]

Some of the gross over-simplifications of Keynes's analysis of which the textbooks are shamefully guilty are attributable to Keynes's burning desire to be understood. To clarify his presentation, he was apt to give a misleading impression of believing in a number of simple relationships. Many of his readers have failed to realize that the simplifying assumptions made for the sake of clarity are not to be taken literally.

But actually, in the relationship between the behavior of money wages and the level of employment, no such excuse is admissible. Keynes stated clearly in a number of passages that, to quote one of them, "the wage-unit may tend to rise before full employment has been reached." On the previous page he had recognized that, in general, the demand for some services and commodities will reach a level beyond which their supply is, for the time being, perfectly inelastic, while in other directions there is still substantial surplus of resources without employment [13, VII, (1936) 1973, p. 30].

It seems odd that, in the passages I have quoted, Keynes seemed to regard the behavior of the level of money-wages as though it was open to a choice of policy. That was not his view at all. Already in the *Treatise* he had written:

> It is more important to have a system which avoids, so far as possible, the necessity for *induced* changes [in the behavior of moneywages], than it is to attempt to stabilise the price level according to any precise principle, *provided always that the rate of change in the price level is kept within narrow limits.* [11, V, (1930) 1971, p. 153, italics added.]

Of course, it always was Keynes's view that, to quote from *The Economic Consequences of Mr. Winston Churchill,* a policy of trying to reduce wages and prices "by intensifying unemployment without limit ... is a policy ... from which any humane or judicious person must shrink" [14, IX, (1925) 1972, p. 218].

In the middle of the Second World War, an article in the *Economic Journal* by Professor Hayek, on "A Commodity Reserve Currency" [5,

1943], gave Keynes an opportunity, at a time when in the Treasury he was deeply involved in postwar problems, to air his views in public in the today more relevant context of coping with an upward surge of money wages as opposed to reluctance of money wages to fall. In a *Rejoinder* to Professor Hayek's article, Keynes mentioned "attempts to confine the natural tendency of wages to rise beyond the limits set by the volume of money" [17, 1943, p. 185], which rely on "the weapon of deliberately creating unemployment. This weapon the world, after a good try, has decided to discard."

> Keynes referred to the view that in a capitalist country this policy is doomed to failure because it will be found impossible in conditions of full employment to prevent a progressive increase of wages. According to this view severe slumps and recurrent periods of unemployment have been hitherto the only effective means of holding efficiency wages within a reasonably stable range. Whether this is so remains to be seen. The more conscious we are of this problem, the likelier shall we be to surmount it. [17, 1943, p. 187.]

So Keynes foresaw that there would be a problem. He did not foresee that nothing would be done about the problem until it had gotten out of hand. He did not foresee the order of magnitude of the problem. The terrifying size of the problem is today attributable in the United Kingdom partly to the failure of all governments before July 1961 to be fully conscious of the existence of the problem, still more of its potential order of magnitude.

A note by Frank Graham [3, 1944], the Princeton Professor, on the Keynes versus Hayek controversy, refers to correspondence that had passed a year earlier between himself and Keynes. In a letter to Graham, Keynes had asked:

> How much otherwise avoidable unemployment do you propose to bring about in order to keep the Trade Unions in order? Do you think it will be politically possible when they understand what you are up to? My own preliminary view is that other, more reasonable, less punitive means must be found.

Keynes was also corresponding in 1943 on the same subject with Benjamin Graham, the famous advocate of an international composite buffer stock. Keynes explained his view that:

> If money-wages rise faster than efficiency, this aggravates the difficulty of maintaining full employment ... and is one of the main obstacles which a full employment policy has to overcome.
>
> ... The more aware we were of the risk, the more likely we should be to find a way round other than totalitarianism. But I recognized the reality of the risk.

Keynes failed to foresee that, 29 years after the end of the war, the percentage rate of increase of money costs of production in a number of industrial countries would have reached double figures.

Keynes was essentially a man of moderation. He would have had difficulty in accepting as a possibility the degree of stupidity in advanced countries indicated in such figures.

Keynes's unawareness of the magnitude of the problem with which industrial countries generally, and ours in particular, were to be faced is echoed in various documents written towards the end of the war. Keynes, preoccupied with various talks with the Americans, could devote little time to the drafting of the Coalition Government's White Paper on *Employment Policy* [35, 1944]. But there is no evidence that he wanted more emphasis to be given to the problem of curbing the upward tendency of wages, to which one perfunctory page is devoted.

Beveridge quotes from an article published anonymously in *The Times,* a warning by Professor Joan Robinson. "In peacetime the vicious spiral of wages and prices might become chronic" [34, 1943].[4] He took the problem somewhat more seriously than the Government and devoted two and a half pages to it, in the course of which he wrote [1, 1944, pp. 200–201]:

> The primary responsibility of preventing a full employment policy from coming to grief in a vicious spiral of wages and prices will rest on those who conduct the bargaining on behalf of labour. The more explicitly that responsibility is stated, the greater can be the confidence that it will be accepted. ... Wages ought to be determined by reason, not by the methods of strike and lock-out. Ordeal by battle has for centuries been rejected as a means of settling legal disputes between citizens.

Keynes had, in *The Economic Consequences of the Peace*, expressed his horror of inflation. There we find the famous statement that "Lenin is said to have declared that the best way to destroy the capitalist system was to

[4] Joan Robinson's article received Keynes's approval after it had been published.

debauch the currency." Keynes added that "Lenin was certainly right" [9, (1919) 1971, pp. 148–49]. In the first chapter of his *Tract on Monetary Reform,* published in 1923, he analyzed the great injuries inflicted both by heavy inflation and by heavy deflation, and expressed himself on balance in favor of stability of the price level. "Inflation is unjust and deflation is inexpedient," he wrote. "Of the two perhaps deflation is, if we rule out exaggerated inflations such as that of Germany, the worse" [10, IV, (1923) 1971, p. 36].

Keynes obviously regarded the upward and downward movements of the price level both between 1914 and 1922 and during and after the Napoleonic Wars as altogether exceptional. He believed himself to be living in a country in which, as in other advanced industrial countries, the price level was quite remarkably stable. In the *Treatise,* Keynes referred to "the sensational rise of prices" in Britain between 1550 and 1650. The price level rose by 200 percent between 1500 and 1650. The average annual rate at which it rose was 0.75 percent. That is the degree of inflation which Keynes regarded as abnormal. Even more exceptional was the fall of prices in 1930 to which Keynes referred as he was completing the *Treatise* [12, VI, (1930) 1971, pp. 137, 338].

During the Second World War, the official cost-of-living index rose at an average annual rate of about 6 percent—a remarkable achievement, part of the credit for which is due, not only to Keynes, but also to those civil servants, many of them economists, who gladly followed his lead. It was quite largely due to cooperation between the Government and the Trade Union Council (TUC).

There is nothing in the *General Theory*—rather the contrary—that anticipates Keynes's growing awareness that if unemployment ceased to be a serious problem, it would be replaced by the problem of pressure to raise money wages faster than productivity. But while the *General Theory* was going through the press, it continued to be discussed with Keynes by his disciples, particularly by Professor Joan Robinson, who included an essay on the subject in a book published in 1937, which Keynes read in draft and approved in its final form [33, 1937].

In a comment on the *Australian Full Employment White Paper,* Keynes wrote in June 1945: "One is also, simply because one knows no solution, inclined to turn a blind eye to the wages problem in a full employment economy" (quoted in Moggridge and Howson [20, 1974, p. 244, fn. 1]).

At this point I shall go back for a moment to Keynes's letter to Benjamin Graham of December 1943. Keynes wrote:

> The task of keeping efficiency-wages reasonably stable (I am sure they will creep up steadily in spite of our best efforts) is a *political* rather than an economic problem. [Quoted in 20, 1974, p. 244, fn. 1, italics added.]

In the course of his "Inaugural Keynes Lecture" delivered three years ago, Austin Robinson quoted the following passage from a letter written by Keynes in 1944, as editor of the *Economic Journal,* to an author who had submitted an over-formalistic analysis of the problem of inflation:

> I do not doubt that a serious problem will arise as to how wages are to be restrained when we have a combination of collective bargaining and full employment. But I am not sure how much light the kind of analytical method you apply can throw on this essentially *political problem.* [32, 1971, p. 208, italics added.]

It is clear to me that these references to the problem of rapidly rising wages as being political point to incomes policy. But Keynes had absolutely no idea of the terrifying orders of magnitude which recent years have displayed.

## References

1. Beveridge, William. *Full employment in a free society.* London: Allen and Unwin, 1944.
2. Fisher, Irving. *The purchasing power of money.* New York: Macmillan, 1913.
3. Graham, Frank D. "Keynes vs. Hayek on a Commodity Reserve Currency," *Econ. J.*, Dec. 1944, *54*, pp. 422–29.
4. Harrod, Roy. *The life of John Maynard Keynes.* London: Macmillan, 1951.
5. von Hayek, Friedrich. "A Commodity Reserve Currency," *Econ. J.*, June–Sept. 1943, *53*, pp. 176–84.
6. Hicks, John. *The crisis in Keynesian economics.* Oxford: Basil Blackwell, 1974.
7. Kahn, Richard. "The Relation of Home Investment to Unemployment," *Econ. J.*, June 1931, *41*, pp. 173–98; reprinted in *Selected essays on employment and growth.* Cambridge: Cambridge University Press, 1972, pp. 1–27.
8. ———. "On Re-reading Keynes," in *Proceedings of the British Academy.* Vol. LX. London: Oxford University Press, 1974, pp. 361–91.
9. Keynes, John Maynard. *The collected writings of John Maynard Keynes.* Vol. II. *The economic consequences of the peace.* London: Macmillan; New York: St. Martin's; for the Royal Economic Society, [1919] 1971.
10. ———. Vol. IV. *A tract on monetary reform.* [1923] 1971 (see [9, 1971] for full citation).

11. ———. Vol. V. *A treatise on money, 1. The pure theory of money.* [1930] 1971 (see [9, 1971]).
12. ———. Vol. VI. *A treatise on money, 2. The applied theory of money.* [1930] 1971 (see [9, 1971]).
13. ———. Vol. VII. *The general theory of employment, interest and money.* [1936] 1973 (see [9, 1971]).
14. ———. Vol. IX. *Essays in persuasion.* [1931] 1972 (see [9, 1971]).
15. ———. Vol. XIII. *The general theory and after. Part I: Preparation.* Edited by DONALD MOGGRIDGE. 1973 (see [9, 1971]).
16. ———. Vol. XIV. *The general theory and after. Part II: Defence and Development.* Edited by DONALD MOGGRIDGE. 1973 (see [9, 1971]).
17. ———. "The Objective of International Price Stability [Rejoinder to Hayek]," *Econ. J.*, June–Sept. 1943, *53*, pp. 185–87.
18. KEYNES, JOHN NEVILLE. *The scope and method of political economy.* London: Macmillan, 1891.
19. MARSHALL, ALFRED. *Money, credit and commerce.* London: Macmillan, 1923.
20. MOGGRIDGE, DONALD E. AND HOWSON, SUSAN. "Keynes on Monetary Policy, 1910–1946," *Oxford Econ. Pap.*, July 1974, *26*(2), pp. 226–47.
21. MYRDAL, GUNNAR. "Om penningteoretisk jämvikt," *Ekonomisk Tidskr.*, 1931.
22. ———. "Der Gleichgewichtsbegriff als Instrument der geldtheoretischen Analyse," in *Beiträge zur Geldtheorie.* Edited by Friedrich A. von Hayek. Vienna, 1933.
23. ———. *Monetary equilibrium.* London: W. Hodge, 1939.
24. ———. *Against the stream: Critical essays on economics.* New York: Pantheon Books, 1972.
25. PATINKIN, DON. *Keynes' monetary thought: A study of its development.* Durham, N.C.: Duke University Press, 1976.
26. PIGOU, A. C. "The Value of Money," *Quart. J. Econ.*, Nov. 1917, *32*, pp. 38–65.
27. ———. "Mr. J. M. Keynes' *General Theory of Employment, Interest, and* Money," *Economica*, May 1936, *3*, pp. 115–32.
28. ———. *Keynes' "General Theory": A retrospective view.* London: Macmillan, 1950.
29. ROBERTSON, DENNIS. *A study of industrial fluctuation.* London: P. S. King, 1915; reprinted by the London School of Economics, 1948.
30. ———. *Banking policy and the price level.* London: P. S. King, 1926; reprinted New York: Kelley, 1949.
31. ROBINSON, AUSTIN. "John Maynard Keynes, 1883–1946," *Econ. J.*, March 1947, *57*, pp. 1–68.
32. ———. "John Maynard Keynes: Economist, Author, Statesman," Lecture, April 22, 1971, in *Proceedings of the British Academy.* Vol. LVII. London: Oxford University Press, 1971, pp. 197–214; *Econ. J.* ["J. M. Keynes: Economist, Author, Statesman,"], June 1972, *82*(326), pp. 531–46.

33. ROBINSON, JOAN. "Full Employment," in *Essays in the theory of employment.* London: Macmillan, 1937; Oxford: Basil Blackwell, 1947, pp. 3–39; reprinted in *Collected economic papers.* Vol. IV. Oxford: Basil Blackwell, 1973, pp. 176–98.
34. ———. "Planning Full Employment," *The Times*, Jan. 22 and 23, 1943, pp. 18 and 19; reprinted in *Collected economic papers.* Vol. I. Oxford: Basil Blackwell, 1951, pp. 81–88.
35. U.K. GOVERNMENT WHITE PAPER. *Employment Policy.* Cmd. 6527. London: H. M. Stationery Office, May 1944.
36. WICKSELL, KNUT. *Geldzins und Güterpreise.* Jena: Gustav Fischer, 1898; translated into English by RICHARD KAHN as *Interest and prices.* London: Macmillan, 1936.

CHAPTER 7

# 'The General Theory of Employment, Interest and Money'

*Richard F. Kahn*

## Introduction

The Preface to the *General Theory* ends with the words:

> The composition of this book has been for the author a long struggle of escape, and so must the reading of it be for most readers if the author's assault upon them is to be successful, – a struggle of escape from habitual modes of thought and expression. The ideas which are here expressed so laboriously are extremely simple and should be obvious. The difficulty lies,

Originally publ. in: Kahn, R. F. (1984). 'The General Theory of Employment, Interest and Money'. In R. Kahn, *The Making of Keynes's General Theory* (pp. 119–168). Cambridge University Press.
Reprint by Springer International Publishing 2022 with kind permission.
Reproduced with permission of the Licensor through PLSclear

This is the fifth of six Raffaele Mattioli Lectures, delivered by Kahn in June 1978 at the Luigi Bocconi University and later published as *The Making of Keynes's General Theory*, Cambridge University Press, 1984 (*editors' note*).

R. F. Kahn



M. C. Marcuzzo, P. Paesani (eds.), *Richard F. Kahn*, Palgrave Studies in the History of Economic Thought,
https://doi.org/10.1007/978-3-030-98588-2_7

not in the new ideas, but in escaping from the old ones, which ramify, for those brought up as most of us have been, into every corner of our minds.[1]

The Preface opens with the words:

This book is chiefly addressed to my fellow economists. I hope that it will be intelligible to others. But its main purpose is to deal with difficult questions of theory, and only in the second place with the applications of this theory to practice.[2]

## THE WORD 'GENERAL'

The book opens as follows:

I have called this book the *General Theory of Employment, Interest and Money*, placing the emphasis on the prefix *general*. The object of such a title is to contrast the character of my arguments and conclusions with those of the *classical* theory of the subject, upon which I was brought up and which dominates the economic thought, both practical and theoretical, of the governing and academic classes of this generation, as it has for a hundred years past. I shall argue that the postulates of the classical theory arc applicable to a special case only and not to the general case, the situation which it assumes being a limiting point of the possible positions of equilibrium. Moreover, the characteristics of the special case assumed by the classical theory happen not to be those of the economic society in which we actually live, with the result that its teaching is misleading and disastrous if we attempt to apply it to the facts of experience.[3]

In Chapter 2 Keynes discussed the *Postulates of the Classical Economics* in unnecessarily complex fashion, as Keynes admitted in his article in the *Quarterly Journal of Economics* of February 1937.[4] The relevant postulate is

[1] KEYNES, vol. VII, p. xxiii.

[2] *Ibid.*, p. xxi.

[3] KEYNES, vol. VII, p. 3.

[4] KEYNES, "The General Theory of Employment', *Quarterly Journal of Economics*, February 1937, pp. 209–23; reprinted in KEYNES, vol. XIV, pp. 209–23. See in particular on p. 110 the opening of Keynes' reply to JACOB VINER's article 'Mr. Keynes on the Causes of Unemployment. A Review', *Quarterly Journal of Economics*, November 1936, pp. 147–67.

In a contribution to a Conference organised by the Royal Economic Society held at Durham in March 1974, referring to Keynes' complicated definition of '*involuntary*' *unemployment* of the *General Theory* (KEYNES, vol. VII, p. 15), I said:

'I am today unable to see why it was necessary to be so complicated [...] there is involuntary unemployment to the extent that, at the current money-wage and with the current price-level, the number of men desiring to work exceeds the number of men for whose labour there is a demand ('Unemployment as seen by the Keynesians', in GEORGE DAVID N. WORSWICK (ed.), *The Concept and Measurement of Involuntary Unemployment*. London: George Allen and Unwin; Boulder, Colorado: Westview Press, 1976, p. 21).

in effect that there is no 'involuntary unemployment'. Keynes regarded the classical position of the economy as the limiting position of 'full employment'.

Keynes' Preface to the French edition was signed on 20 February 1939 – more than three years after the signature of the Preface to the English edition. The following is a long extract:

> my readers will sometimes wonder what I am talking about when I speak, with what some of my English critics consider a misuse of language, of the 'classical' school of thought and 'classical' economists. It may, therefore, be helpful to my French readers if I attempt to indicate very briefly what I regard as the main *differentiae* of my approach.
>
> I have called my theory a *general* theory. I mean by this that I am chiefly concerned with the behaviour of the economic system as a whole [...].
>
> I argue that important mistakes have been made through extending to the system as a whole conclusions which have been correctly arrived at in respect of a part of it taken in isolation.
>
> Let me give examples of what I mean. My contention that for the system as a whole the amount of income which is saved, in the sense that it is not spent on current consumption, is and must necessarily be exactly equal to the amount of net new investment has been considered a paradox and has been the occasion of widespread controversy. The explanation of this is undoubtedly to be found in the fact that this relationship of equality between saving and investment, which necessarily holds good for the system as a whole, does not hold good at all for a particular individual.[5]

This is a far more fruitful exposition of the meaning of the word 'general' – the result of three years of discussion and thought.

## The character of the achievement

A good account of the character, in Keynes' own mind, of the achievement of the *General Theory* is provided by an extract from a letter written to Roy Harrod on 30 August 1936, in commenting on a draft article by Harrod. It is reproduced by the Royal Economic Society Edition Editors in their own Introduction to Vol. VII of Keynes' *Collected Writings* (*The General Theory*):[6]

> You don't mention *effective demand* or, more precisely, the demand schedule for output as a whole, except in so far as it is implicit in the multiplier.

[5] Keynes, vol. VII, pp. xxxii.

[6] It is a part of an encouraging letter to Roy F. Harrod about a draft of his article on 'Mr. Keynes and Traditional Theory' (*Econometrica*, January 1937, pp. 74–86).

> To me the most extraordinary thing, regarded historically, is the complete disappearance of the theory of demand and supply for output as a whole, *i. e.* the theory of employment, *after* it had been for a quarter of a century the most discussed thing in economics. One of the most important transitions for me, after my *Treatise on Money* had been published, was suddenly realising this. It only came after I had enunciated to myself the psychological law that, when income increases, the gap between income and consumption will increase, – a conclusion of vast importance to my own thinking but not apparently, expressed just like that, to anyone else's. Then, appreciably later, came the notion of interest being the measure of liquidity preference, which became quite clear in my mind the moment I thought of it. And last of all, after an immense amount of muddling and many drafts, the proper definition of the marginal efficiency of capital linked up one thing with another.[7]

The *General Theory* is short-period in the Marshallian sense:

> We take as given the existing skill and quantity of available labour, the existing quality and quantity of available equipment, the existing technique, the degree of competition, the tastes and habits of the consumer, the disutility of different intensities of labour and of the activities of supervision and organisation, as well as the social structure including the forces, other than our variables set forth below, which determine the distribution of the national income. This does not mean that we assume these factors to be constant; but merely that, in this place and context, we are not considering or taking into account the effects and consequences of changes in them.[8]

Most of the exposition is based on the assumption of given stocks of equipment at a moment of time and given technical knowledge. The subject of investigation is the degree of utilisation of the equipment and the labour supply.

There is little study of the effects of accumulation with the passage of time as the result of investment.

However, this subject does enter in a fundamental sense into the very important chapters on 'The Marginal Efficiency of Capital', 'The State of Long Term Expectations', 'Sundry Observations on the Nature of Capital' and 'Concluding Notes on the Social Philosophy to which the General Theory might Lead'.

Keynes set out, and then elaborated, those factors knowledge of which is sufficient, and of which knowledge is necessary, to determine the position of an economy. Under the term 'position' is to be included not only

[7] KEYNES, vol. VII, p. XV. This letter appears in full in vol. XIV, pp. 84–6.
[8] KEYNES, vol. VII, p. 245.

such physical entities as rates of investment, consumption, output, and employment, but also rates of interest, and in addition the price-level of consumption-goods in terms of money-wage units (the real wage) and the prices of capital-assets.

The chapters on 'The Principle of Effective Demand' and 'Expectation as Determining Output and Employment', 'The Marginal Efficiency of Capital' and 'The State of Long-Term Expectations', 'The General Theory of the Rate of Interest' together with 'The Psychological and Business Incentives to Liquidity', and the three chapters on the 'Propensity to Consume', constitute the real kernel of the book (amounting to 117 pages out of the total of 382), together with the discussions of the influence of the money-wage and the behaviour of money-wages and prices. In these chapters the factors causatively responsible for the state of the economy are elaborated.

There is no separate compartment labelled 'monetary theory'. The Quantity Theory of Money had finally been abandoned.

But, as the full title of the book indicates, money plays a vital role, and the behaviour of the system is influenced by the behaviour of the quantity of money.

Although Keynes was not interested in the actual process of movement from one position to another, he did in fact devote three pages to the lag in the response of the output of consumption-goods to an unforeseen increase in the output of capital-goods. He emphasised that this did not detract from 'the logical theory of the multiplier, which holds good continuously, without time-lag, at all moments of time'.[9]

He wrote:

> The fact that an unforeseen change only exercises its full effect on employment over a period of time is important in certain contexts; in particular it plays a part in the analysis of the trade cycle (on lines such as I followed in my *Treatise on Money*). But it does not in any way affect the significance of the theory of the multiplier as set forth in this chapter; nor render it inapplicable as an indicator of the total benefit to employment to be expected from an expansion in the capital goods industries. Moreover, except in conditions where the consumption industries are already working almost at capacity so that an expansion of output requires an expansion of plant and not merely the more intensive employment of the existing plant, there is no reason to suppose that more than a brief interval of time need elapse before

[9] KEYNES, vol. VII, p. 122.

> employment in the consumption industries is advancing *pari passu* with employment in the capital-good industries with the multiplier operating near its normal figure.[10]

In Section 1 of my last Lecture I quoted from an article published by Keynes in 1933 in which, using my figures, he demonstrated how short the income-expenditure time lag is: 'seven- eighths of the total effects [of a change] come from the primary expenditure and the first two repercussions',[11] so that if between the payment and expenditure of wages the average time-lag is a week, seven-eighths of the full effect of a change in payments are experienced in three weeks.

As late as February 1935 Dennis Robertson was still pleading for recognition of the time element,[12] a tribute to Robertson's persistence and to Keynes' patience. Had Keynes given way he would have had largely to rewrite the book, which was in fact completed nine months later. Lack of interest by Keynes in time-lags accounted in part for Robertson's failure to accept Keynes' methods.

Pigou devoted the final passage of his partial renunciation of his bitter and sarcastic review-article[13] on the *General Theory* to an account – for the most part highly acceptable to Keynesians – of the same fundamental factors which I am identifying as determining the position of the economy.

> Keynes' method could then tell us, not merely what employment, investment and so on tend to be at the two dates, but what they actually will be. But it could not tell us what happens to employment, investment and so on while the system is in *course of movement* from one of these equilibrium positions to the other; what they will be on the intervening days or months or years of this disequilibrium. Thus even in the most favourable circumstances that analysis is a staccato one, adapted to provide, not a moving picture, but only a succession of stills.
>
> These are very serious limitations – limitations of which it is specially proper to remind ourselves when attempts are made to apply Keynes' apparatus directly to the solution of practical problems. This is in no sense to 'attack' Keynes or to decry his achievement. When a man has devised a new

[10] *Ibid.*, pp. 124–5.

[11] Keynes, vol. ix, p. 343.

[12] *Letter* from Dennis H. Robertson, *3 February 1935*; published in Keynes, vol. xiii, pp. 496–506.

[13] Arthur C. Pigou, 'Mr. J.M. Keynes' General Theory of Employment, Interest and Money', *Economica*, May 1936, pp. 115–32.

> way of tackling an unclimbed mountain, we may, indeed, regret that this way has not led him to the top. But for the effort which has advanced him *towards* the top nothing is due but praise.[14]

Pigou was a great mountaineer, like, but better than, so many economists.

## The money-wage

Of the factors on which in the *General Theory* the position of the whole structure depends I begin with the money-wage. It is the fulcrum which supports the price-structure – all prices, incomes of every kind, and all money values. A lower level of money-wages means that everything expressed in terms of money is lower in the same proportion. The one important exception is the quantity of money. If it is held constant, its real value rises, and a lower money-wage means that in real value – in terms of its purchasing power over labour and goods – the quantity of money is higher. The important influence on the real state of the economy of a lower money-wage takes the form of the lower rates of interest, and the general relaxation of credit, which result from an increase in the value of the quantity of money expressed in real terms.

In addition, all incomes and debts fixed contractually in terms of money are larger in real value as a result of the money-wage being lower.

For the present-day reader it is ridiculous to write of lower, and falling money-wages. But I am lecturing about Keynes and, until shortly before the outbreak of the Second World War, the questions were why wages did not fall and whether employment would not be increased if they were cut. This was the great issue dividing Keynes from Pigou, Robertson and many other of the leading economists of the day.

The implications of rising money-wages can be presented by simply reversing the sign. But when money-wages rise as fast as in recent years, the mechanism is thrown out by time-lags and the character of expectations.

The basis of the fundamental role of the money-wage in determining all prices, money-incomes, and money-values is that money-wages not only form part of costs of production but, because they are to a large extent spent, they form part of total purchasing power expressed in terms of money. The costs resulting from a higher level of money-wages are met by

[14] Arthur C. Pigou, *Keynes's General Theory*. London: Macmillan, 1950, pp. 64–5.

the resultant raising of demand in terms of money; even if in real terms demand is unaltered.

Of course this theorem applies only in the aggregate. If money-wages rose more than the average in one part of the economy, real wages are there raised, and are lowered everywhere else, so that the aggregate real wage is unchanged.

This statement about the role of the money-wage is not to be regarded as absolutely watertight. It implies that no change in the distribution of income results from a reduction in money-wages. But I have already admitted a redistribution to those whose incomes are contractually fixed in terms of money.

If we abstract from the possible effect of a higher level of effective demand, the assumption that the distribution of income is unchanged when money-wages are lower is consistent with the findings of Kenneth Coutts, Wynne Godley and William Nordhaus over that part of the economy which they have studied.[15] The *normal price hypothesis* which they confirm by econometric methods is that

> the firm calculates the level of costs at a normal level of output, and sets prices as a mark up on normal costs without reference to temporary variations in demand.[16]

(The proportional amount of the mark-up has been found to fall over time.)

Although this provides econometric confirmation of Keynes' view for a particular level of effective demand, it is inconsistent with Keynes' view and the view of many present-day economists, including myself, of the relation between the real wage and the level of effective demand when demand is so high as to bring output sharply against the constraint of limited physical capacity.

In the *Treatise*, Keynes had switched from the Quantity Theory of Money to the flow of money-income. The important role played by the money-wage in the *General Theory* arises from its determining the money-value of everything else – profits, and other income, and prices. By this I

[15] Chemical and allied industries, mechanical engineering, electrical engineering, textiles, clothing and footwear.

[16] Kenneth Coutts, Wynne Godley and William Nordhaus, *Industrial Pricing in the United Kingdom*. Cambridge: Cambridge University Press. 1978, pp. 1–2.

do not of course mean that the magnitude of the money-wage determines real values. That would be absurd. But it takes the place of the Quantity Theory.

The fact that the quantity of money is an exception is, of course, the basis of discussion of monetary influences.

The 'wage-theorem', as Professor Sir John Hicks has conveniently called it, is to be regarded as somewhat rough-and-ready in character. At a time of rapid changes, values in terms of money-wages will display temporary variations, partly determined by expectations of the behaviour of money-wages. Of considerable significance is the recent experience of advanced industrial countries of the small movements in real-wages in the face of high, and rapidly changing, rates of wage-inflation in the years since 1973. (I do not apply the same doctrine to cases of high rates of demand inflation.)

I was surprised by Hicks' statement that:

> All expositors of Keynes (including myself) have found this procedure [working in terms of wage-units] a difficulty [...] We had to find some way of breaking the circle. The obvious way of doing so was to begin by setting out the rest (multiplier, liquidity preference and so on) on the assumptions of *fixed* money wages.[17]

The result, as Hicks points out, is the false impression that Keynes assumed wages to be constant at any level of employment short of full employment.

Hicks' procedure is completely unnecessary. Keynes, in many contexts, emphasised the 'stickiness' of wages. But that was not the reason for the use of the money-wage as a unit. There is not a word in Chapter 4 (on 'The Choice of Units') to suggest that it was.

I have, however, little doubt that Keynes' concern, over a great part of his working life, with the behaviour of wages in practice, did lead him on to his choice of unit.

Already in 1925 in the *Economic Consequences of Mr Churchill* (the return of sterling to the pre-war parity in April 1925), Keynes emphasised the unwillingness of wages to fall under the pressure of heavy unemployment. To avoid subjecting the unsheltered industries to an intolerable

[17] John R. Hicks, *The Crisis in Keynesian Economics*. Yriö Jahnsson Lectures. Oxford: Basil Blackwell, 1974, p. 60.

reduction in real wages, money-wages would have to be pushed down in the sheltered industries as well. This would necessitate the extension of heavy unemployment to the sheltered industries, involving an extremely large total of unemployment, to avoid grossly increasing inequalities of wages between the sheltered and unsheltered industries.[18]

On the Macmillan Committee (which reported in June 1931) a reduction of money-wages was discussed as a means of improving the country's competitive position.[19] Keynes' influence is clear. In the main Report itself it was recognised that, if it was to be relevant, 'a substantial general change, amounting, to (say) 10 per cent, or more, in the level of money costs and incomes', would be called for, that as a matter of equity such a reduction 'should apply to every category of income alike, including those protected by contract'; and that such a 'great social change' would require 'general consent'. It could not, therefore, 'be left to natural economic forces'.[20]

Furthermore, for 'country after country to feel compelled to resort to competition in wage-cutting' would be a counsel of despair: it would help nobody. But if 'the downward race' began (later on called a 'beggar-my-neighbour' method), 'no one can afford to lag far behind under penalty of losing all his trade'.[21]

In the important Addendum to the Macmillan Report, Keynes' influence is shown in a short passage in which the effect on employment of a reduction of wages is discussed quite apart from any consequent improvement in the country's competitive position.

> It is impossible to calculate in advance what increase of employment could be expected from a given average reduction of wages. But the relation of the one to the other might disappoint the expectations of many people, inasmuch as a false analogy is often drawn from the obvious great advantages to an individual employer of a reduction of the wages which he has to pay. For each employer perceives quite clearly the advantages he would gain if the wages which he himself pays were to be reduced, but not so clearly the disadvantages he will suffer if the money-incomes of his customers are reduced. Just as it is to the advantage of each producer that every product should be

[18] KEYNES, vol. IX, p. 215.

[19] MACMILLAN COMMITTEE ON FINANCE AND INDUSTRY, *Report.* Presented to Parliament by the Financial Secretary to the Treasury, June 1931. Cmd 3897. London: His Majesty's Stationery Office, 1931, pp. 196–9. (The Committee was appointed on 5 November 1929.)

[20] *Ibid.*, pp. 198–9.

[21] *Ibid.*, pp. 196–7.

> cheap except his own, similarly it is to his advantage that all costs and wages should be high except those which he himself incurs – since the demand for his product comes from the incomes which are paid out as costs by other producers.[22]

In the *General Theory*, Keynes dealt with the 'crude conclusion' that a reduction in money-wages would increase employment by two different methods.

The simplest method is adopted late in the book. Let us

> follow up the course of events on the hypothesis most favourable to this view, namely that at the outset entrepreneurs *expect* the reduction in money-wages to have this effect. It is indeed not unlikely that the individual entrepreneur, seeing his own costs reduced, will overlook at the outset the repercussions on the demand for his product and will act on the assumption that he will be able to sell at a profit a larger output than before. If, then, entrepreneurs generally act on this expectation, will they in fact succeed in increasing their profits? Only if the community's marginal propensity to consume is equal to unity, so that there is no gap between the increment of income and the increment of consumption [...] [otherwise] the proceeds realised from the increased output will disappoint the entrepreneurs and employment will fall back again to its previous figure.[23]

Very early in the book Keynes disputed

> the assumption that the general level of real wages is directly determined by the character of the wage bargain. In assuming that the wage bargain determines the real wage the classical school have slipt in an illicit assumption [...] There may exist no expedient by which labour as a whole can reduce its *real* wage to a given figure by making revised *money* bargains with the entrepreneurs. This will be our contention. We shall endeavour to show that primarily it is certain other forces which determine the general level of real wages.[24]

Keynes of course agreed that

[22] Macmillan Committee on Finance and Industry, *Report*, p. 194; reprinted in Keynes, vol. xx, p. 289.

[23] Keynes, vol. vii, p. 261.

[24] *Ibid.*, p. 13.

> any individual or group of individuals, who consent to a reduction of money-wages relatively to others, will suffer a *relative* reduction in real wages, which is a sufficient justification for them to resist it [...].
>
> In other words, the struggle about money-wages primarily affects the *distribution* of the aggregate real wage between different labour-groups, and not its average amount per unit of employment, which depends, as we shall see, on a different set of forces. The effect of combination on the part of a group of workers is to protect their *relative* real wage. The *general* level of real wages depends on the other forces of the economic system.[25]

If for the words 'consent to a reduction of money-wages' are substituted the words 'agree to accept a wage increase which will prove to be less than the average for the country as a whole', these words of Keynes present a very important element in the present-day problem of trying to resist wage-inflation. A patriotic response to an appeal from the Government, and perhaps the Trades Union Congress, confined to limited sectors of the labour force, penalises them. In an extreme case it is possible that, not merely do real wages lag behind, but actually suffer an absolute fall.

Keynes did not have to assume that individual unemployed workers did not on occasion secure jobs by slightly under-cutting the money-wage. The Keynesian contention is that no additional net employment would result. Workers hitherto employed would be dismissed, so that the total number employed remained constant.

In discussing the various effects of falling wages, Keynes stressed the influence of expectations.

> If the reduction of money-wages is expected to be a *reduction relatively to money-wages in the future*, the change will be favourable to investment, because [...] it will increase the marginal efficiency of capital [expected money profits in relation to the current costs of capital assets]; whilst for the same reason it may be favourable to consumption. If, on the other hand, the reduction leads to the expectation, or even to the serious possibility, of a further wage-reduction in prospect, it will have precisely the opposite effect. For it will diminish the marginal efficiency of capital and will lead to the postponement both of investment anti of consumption.
>
> [...] the depressing influence on entrepreneurs of their greater burden of debt may partly offset any cheerful reactions from the reduction of wages.

[25] *Ibid.*, p. 14.

> Indeed if the fall of wages and prices goes far, the embarrassment of those entrepreneurs who are heavily indebted may soon reach the point of insolvency, – with severely adverse effects on investment. Moreover the effect of the lower price-level on the real burden of the national debt and hence on taxation is likely to prove very adverse to business confidence.[26]

About the time when Keynes started work on the *General Theory*, a very severe fall in prices had resulted in a series of banking crises – starting in Austria and Germany in July 1931.

To quote Keynes:

> all this nervousness, and hysteria and panic, which is making a farce of out currency arrangements and bringing the world's financial machine to a standstill, is only superficially traceable, though it has all happened suddenly, to quite recent events. It has its roots in the slow and steady sapping of the real resources of the banks as a result of the progressive collapse of money values over the past two years.

This is a quotation from the article which this critical state of affairs had led Keynes to write, entitled *The Consequences to the Banks of the Collapse of Money Values.* It was published originally in an American popular monthly magazine (*Vanity Fair*) in August 1931 (revised version in October).[27]

After setting out the facts he concluded:

> Fortunately our own domestic British banks arc probably at present – for various reasons – among the strongest. But there is a degree of deflation which no bank can stand. And over a great part of the world, and not least in the United States, the position of the banks, though partly concealed from the public eye, may be in fact the weakest element in the whole situation. It is obvious that the present trend of events cannot go much further without something breaking. If nothing is done, it will be amongst the world's banks that the really critical breakages will occur.
>
> Modern capitalism is faced, in my belief, with the choice between finding some way to increase money values towards their former figure, or seeing widespread insolvencies and defaults and the collapse of a large part of the financial structure.[28]

[26] Keynes, vol. vii, pp. 263–4.
[27] Reprinted in Keynes, vol. ix, pp. 150–8. The passage is on p. 151.
[28] *Ibid.*, p. 157.

He added that 'The present signs suggest that the bankers of the world are bent on suicide'.[29]

Keynes was prophetic. In February 1933 all the American banks had to close for a short period. I remember this well because I was just about to travel by train from Harvard to New York, and therefore armed myself with an ample supply of bank notes. The result was that all the way from Boston to New York I was the only occupant of a whole Pullman coach: nobody else possessed enough cash to buy a ticket.

## The propensity to consume

In essence the 'propensity to consume' is a simple concept and I do not need to say much about it. It has of course been developed tremendously – both conceptually and econometrically. Professor Duesenberry wrote in 1949:

> By now [...] Hicks and others have shown that the Keynesian consumption function is a special case of the general theory of consumer behavior and can be deduced from it by making certain assumptions.[30]

Keynes attempted only a superficial treatment. He pointed to the fundamental psychological law that at higher levels of income the rate of saving was also higher (but not necessarily the ratio of saving to income).[31] In other words the marginal propensity to consume is less than unity. This Keynes regarded as the 'key to our practical problem', in his basic chapter on 'The Principle of Effective Demand'. It meant that, with a given propensity to consume, employment cannot increase except as a result of an increase in the rate of investment.[32] The treatment suffers from the defect that no distinction is drawn between saving out of profits and out of wages.

Being a psychological 'law' of behaviour, Keynes recognised that its quantitative operation depended on the character of the change under review, and the length of time which had elapsed since it occurred.

[29] *Ibid.*

[30] James S. Duesenberry, *Income, Saving, and the Theory of Consumer Behavior*. First published as Harvard Economic Study, Number 87. Cambridge, Mass.: Harvard University Press, 1949, p. 1.

[31] Keynes, vol. vii, p. 96.

[32] *Ibid.*, pp. 29–30.

The extent to which a man will adjust his standard of life to a rise in his income depends on the length of time which has elapsed since the rise has occurred and the confidence with which it can be felt that it will not be reversed.

Keynes was concerned with the behaviour of the economy as a whole: mainly with the relation between income and saving as income reacted to a change in a given short-period situation. But in the concluding chapter there is some discussion of the longer-term future.

Keynes did not in any systematic way consider the effect of wealth per head on the propensity to consume. A clue is provided in a short and unsatisfactory passage on *windfall changes in capital values.*

> These are of much more importance in modifying the propensity to consume, since they will bear no stable or regular relationship to the amount of income.[33]

Don Patinkin has pointed out that Keynes was here thinking purely of the *temporary* effects on consumption of windfall gains or losses.[34] Keynes left the effects of income on consumption to proxy for the effect of wealth on consumption – not a satisfactory treatment.

Don Patinkin has pointed to one exceptional passage – in Keynes' profound Chapter 16 on 'Sundry Observations on the Nature of Capital'. Here Keynes contemplated

> an amount of wealth sufficiently great to satiate to the full the aggregate desire on the part of the public to make provision for the future, even with full employment, in circumstances where no bonus is obtainable in the form of interest.[35]

In Chapter 19, on 'Changes in Money-Wages', which appears late in the *General Theory* and from which I have already quoted, Keynes does not mention the Real Balance Effect. Mention of it would have served to reinforce arguments which are already very strong.

Keynes mentioned several favourable influences of falling money-wages although the unfavourable ones are overwhelming.

[33] *Ibid.*, p. 92.

[34] Don Patinkin, *Keynes' Monetary Thought. A Study of its Development.* Durham, North Carolina: Duke University Press, 1976, p. 111.

[35] Keynes, vol. vii, p. 218. Patinkin refers to this passage on p. 110 of his book.

One exception is the case in which 'money-wages are believed to have touched bottom, so that further changes are expected to be in the upward direction'.[36]

Keynes had on the previous page mentioned the rise in the real burden of the National Debt and taxation. This was in addition to the heavier burden of debt on entrepreneurs, whose 'embarrassment [...] may soon reach the point of insolvency'.[37]

Keynes summed up with the passage:

> We can, therefore, theoretically at least, produce precisely the same effects on the rate of interest by reducing wages, whilst leaving the quantity of money unchanged, that we can produce by increasing the quantity of money whilst leaving the level of wages unchanged.[38]

## Liquidity preference

### *Introduction*

It seems to me logical to have a look at Chapter 13 on 'The General Theory of the Rate of Interest'[39] and Chapter 15 on 'The Psychological and Business Incentives to Liquidity'[40] before launching out on the section on 'The Inducement to Invest' (which appears earlier in the book) so as to make a synthesis possible at the end of 'The Inducement to Invest'.

The origins of the liquidity preference theory of the rate of interest go back to Marshall, as I explained in Section 5 of Lecture II, and even earlier.

In a primitive, but extremely interesting form, the theory is to be found in a Section of the *Treatise* entitled 'Factors Determining the Volume of the financial Circulation'.[41]

### *Basic concept*

The basic concept is simple, and so familiar that I need not devote much space to it. Later in the *General Theory* Keynes put it thus:

[36] *Ibid.*, p. 265.
[37] Keynes, vol. vii, p. 264.
[38] *Ibid.*, p. 266.
[39] Keynes, vol. vii, pp. 165–74.
[40] *Ibid.*, pp. 194–209.
[41] Keynes, vol. v, pp. 222–30.

> the current rate of interest depends, as we have seen, not on the strength of the desire to hold wealth, but on the strengths of the desires to hold it in liquid and in illiquid forms respectively, coupled with the amount of the supply of wealth in the one form relatively to the supply of it in the other.[42]

The question is what are the motives which induce the holding of the excess of the total quantity of money over that part needed for the purpose of transactions, to bridge the gap between receipts and expenditure. If everybody foresaw with complete conviction the complete future pattern of risk-free interest rates, money would be held only to satisfy the transactions motive.

Keynes did not confine his treatment to money in the ordinary sense but was prepared to include such instruments as three-month treasury bills. Towards the end of my treatment of 'The Inducement to Invest', I shall be suggesting a much more extensive generalisation – covering, e.g., overdraft facilities and prospective marketability of a firm's equities and bonds.

Apart from the *transactions motive* for holding money, Keynes dealt with

> the precautionary-motive, i.e. the desire for security as to the future cash equivalent of a certain proportion of total resources; and [...] the speculative-motive, i.e. the object of securing profit from knowing better than the market what the future will bring forth.[43]

The distinction between these two motives is not entirely watertight. This will become very clear when, in Section II, I bring in to the discussion the concept of 'finance', introduced by Keynes in the course of the immediately post-*General Theory* controversies in the *Economic Journal*. A firm may cover its prospective investment programme – at least in part – by holding cash or short-term securities; this Keynes called finance. This is 'precautionary'. The question is why it does not hold a portfolio of fixed-interest securities maturing at the dates on which payments for the investment will become due, and meanwhile secure higher rates of interest. This is 'speculative'. The firm holds cash to the extent that it is afraid that interest-rates may rise, in which case the prices of the longer-term securities would fall.

[42] Keynes, vol. vii, p. 213.
[43] Keynes, vol. vii, p. 170.

In a published article I have tried to deal with the difficulties of distinguishing between the precautionary and speculative motives, the distinction between which is very blurred:

> in principle the precautionary motive can be said to operate in so far as some persons think that the rate of interest is likely to move; the speculative motive in so far as some prisons think that on balance it is likely to move one way rather than the other.[44]

Under the influence of the precautionary motive the firm makes provision for financing its investment programme; but only in the form of cash unless the influence of the so-called speculative motive operates.

Keynes gives the impression, when he discusses the speculative motive, that he is thinking mainly of the management of portfolios by financiers, ranging from private individuals to large investment trusts and insurance companies. But industrial companies also play an important part.

In so far as the precautionary and speculative motives can be distinguished Keynes pointed out that the quantity of cash held under the influence of the precautionary motive 'is not very sensitive to changes in the rate of interest'.[45]

The elasticity of response of the rate of interest to the excess of the total quantity of money over that absorbed by the transactions motive is largely derived from the speculative motive.

The magnitude of this elasticity varies greatly between one time and one situation and another. It is not an easy subject to elucidate. In the same published article I tried to show that the elasticity is greater, the greater the density of the population around the margin between 'bulls' and 'bears' of long-term bonds. (There is not only an extensive margin. There is also an intensive margin inside the head of any individual who is doubtful – who is not a completely convinced bull or bear.)

As Keynes put it, 'Public opinion can be fairly rapidly accustomed to a modest fall in the rate of interest and the conventional expectation of the future may be modified accordingly'.[46] A few pages earlier Keynes wrote:

[44] RICHARD KAHN, 'Some Notes on Liquidity Preference', *Manchester School of Economic and Social Studies*, September 1954, p. 239; reprinted in *Selected Essays on Employment and Growth*. Cambridge: Cambridge University Press, 1972, p. 81.

[45] KEYNES, vol. VII, p. 171.

[46] *Ibid.*, p. 204.

It is evident, then, that the rate of interest is a highly psychological phenomenon.[47]

And:

It might be more accurate, perhaps, to say that the rate of interest is a highly conventional, rather than a highly psychological, phenomenon. For its actual value is largely governed by the prevailing view as to what its value is expected to be. *Any* level of interest which is accepted with sufficient conviction as *likely* to be durable *will* be durable.[48]

### *Exclusion of assets other than fixed-interest securities*

It is strange that in the first passage from the *General Theory* quoted in this section Keynes contemplated no liquid forms of wealth other than cash and fixed-interest securities. There is an appreciable elasticity of substitution between money and equities; and also between money and houses, and between money and commodities which are dealt with in organised produce markets. And of course there are elasticities of substitution between every pair of these assets. It is not only the price-level of fixed-interest securities which is related to the excess of the quantity of money over that absorbed by the transactions-motive. There is an infinite number of combinations of the prices of these various assets each of which is compatible with any particular such excess of the quantity of money.

In fact what Keynes needed was a simple form of portfolio analysis. After the publication of the *General Theory* he ventured into this field, with rather unsatisfactory results.[49]

In the *Treatise on Money,* Keynes presented a primitive form of liquidity preference theory.[50] The securities which Keynes had in mind were equities. But the ambiguity of the word 'investment' caused considerable confusion. Before long the price of an equity becomes the price of the underlying capital-good. For example:

[47] *Ibid.*, p. 202.

[48] KEYNES, vol. VII, p. 203.

[49] JOHN MAYNARD KEYNES, 'The Theory of the Rate of Interest', in ARTHUR D. GAYER (ed.), *The Lessons of Monetary Experience. Essays in Honor of Irving Fisher.* London: George Allen and Unwin, 1937, pp. 145–52; reprinted in KEYNES, vol. XIV, pp. 101–8.

[50] KEYNES, vol. V, pp. 127–31.

> The price level of investments as a whole, *and hence of new investments*, is that price level at which the desire of the public to hold savings deposits is equal to the amount of savings deposits which the banking system is willing and able to create.[51] [My italics.]

Keynes, in the *General Theory*, recalled his treatment in the *Treatise*. He objected to it because 'bearishness' (the *Treatise* equivalent of liquidity preference) was there defined as the relationship

> not between the rate of interest (or price of debts [i.e. fixed-interest securities]) and the quantity of money, but between the price of assets and debts, taken together, and the quantity of money. This treatment, however, involved a confusion between results due to a change in the rate of interest and those due to a change in the schedule of the marginal efficiency of capital [the inducement to invest], which I hope I have here avoided.[52]

## THE INDUCEMENT TO INVEST: FOREWORD

The determination of the rate of investment is the subject to which, for obvious reasons, the bulk of the *General Theory* is devoted. It presents far greater difficulties of abstraction – and therefore of exposition – than the propensity to consume, which basically is a matter of common-sense. The major achievement of the *General Theory* is twofold. First, there is the conception of Effective Demand which, given the conditions of supply, determines the level of output and employment. Second, there is the determination of the rate of investment. While lower than the rate of consumption, this is the constituent of Effective Demand which is mainly responsible for fluctuations, and also for demand being often chronically unduly low – as well as, on occasion, unduly high.

In the causal processes involved in the determination of investment, expectations play a dominating part. If it is conceded to Keynes that in the world as we know it expectations are subject to a high degree of risk and of uncertainty, the case for a revolution of thought is overwhelming.

I shall find it convenient to bring within the orbit of discussion of the *General Theory* two contributions made by Keynes after its publication. One is the reply to Professor Viner in the *Quarterly Journal of Economics*

[51] *Ibid.*, p. 129.
[52] KEYNES, vol. VII, pp. 173–4.

of February 1937.[53] The other, to which I shall be referring later, is a series of articles which appeared in the *Economic Journal* from June 1937 to June 1938 and included important additions to his thought, made in the course of controversy, on the subject of 'finance'.

In the course of his reply to Viner, Keynes explained the character of his innovation on the subject of expectations subject to risk. I quote a few passages:

> these more recent writers [Edgeworth, Pigou and other later and contemporary writers] like their predecessors were still dealing with a system in which the amount of the factors employed was given and the other relevant facts were known more or less for certain. This does not mean that they were dealing with a system in which change was ruled out, or even one in which the disappointment of expectation was ruled out. But at any given time facts and expectations were assumed to be given in a definite and calculable form; and risks, of which, though admitted, not much notice was taken, were supposed to be capable, of an exact actuarial computation. The calculus of probability, though mention of it was kept in the background, was supposed to be capable of reducing uncertainty to the same calculable status as that of certainty itself.
>
> [...] the fact that our knowledge of the future is fluctuating, vague and uncertain, renders wealth a peculiarly unsuitable subject for the methods of the classical economic theory [...] [The theory], requires, I suggest, considerable amendment if it is to be applied to a world in which the accumulation of wealth for an indefinitely postponed future is an important factor; and the greater the proportionate part played by such wealth accumulation the more essential does such amendment become.
>
> By 'uncertain' knowledge, let me explain, I do not mean merely to distinguish what is known for certain from what is only probable. The game of roulette is not subject, in this sense, to uncertainty; nor is the prospect of a Victory bond being drawn. Or, again, the expectation of life is only slightly uncertain. Even the weather is only moderately uncertain. The sense in which I am using the term is that in which the prospect of a European war is uncertain, or the price of copper and the rate of interest twenty years hence, or the obsolescence of a new invention, or the position of private wealth owners in the social system in 1970. About these matters there is no

[53] JOHN MAYNARD KEYNES, 'The General Theory of Employment', *Quarterly Journal of Economics*, February 1937, pp. 209–23. See footnote 4 of this Lecture, for references to Viner's article and Keynes' reply; and also KEYNES, vol. XIV, pp. 109–123.

scientific basis on which to form any calculable probability whatever. We simply do not know. Nevertheless, the necessity for action and for decision compels us as practical men to do our best to overlook this awkward fact and to behave exactly as we should if we had behind us a good Benthamite calculation of a series of prospective advantages and disadvantages, each multiplied by its appropriate probability, waiting to be summed.

How do we manage in such circumstances to behave in a manner which saves our faces as rational economic men? We have devised for the purpose a variety of techniques [...].

Now a practical theory of the future based on these [techniques] has certain marked characteristics. In particular, being based on so flimsy a foundation, it is subject to sudden and violent changes. The practice of calmness and immobility, of certainty and security, suddenly breaks down. New fears and hopes will, without warning, take charge, of human conduct. The forces of disillusion may suddenly impose a new conventional basis of valuation. All these pretty, polite techniques, made for a well-panelled board room and a nicely regulated market, are liable to collapse. At all times the vague panic fears and equally vague and unreasoned hopes are not really lulled, and lie but a little way below the surface.[54]

## The Inducement to Invest: Keynes' Basic Chapter

### *Introduction*

Keynes' basic chapter on the determination of the rate of investment is Chapter 11 on 'The Marginal Efficiency of Capital'.[55] The subject is the most important one in the *General Theory*. But this chapter is one of the most confused.

The chapter opens:

When a man buys an investment or capital-asset, he purchases the right to the series of prospective returns, which he expects to obtain from selling its output, after deducting the running expenses of obtaining that output, during the life of the asset [...].

I define the marginal efficiency of capital as being equal to that rate of discount which would make the present value of the series of annuities given by the returns expected from the capital-asset during its life just equal to its supply price. This gives us the marginal *efficiencies* of particular types of

[54] Keynes, vol. xiv, pp. 112–15.
[55] Keynes, vol. vii, pp. 135–46.

capital-assets. The greatest of these marginal efficiencies can then be regarded as the marginal efficiency of capital in general [...].

Now it is obvious that the actual rate of current investment will be pushed to the point where there is no longer any class of capital-asset of which the marginal efficiency exceeds the current rate of interest. In other words, the rate of investment will be pushed to the point on the investment demand-schedule where the marginal efficiency of capital in general is equal to the market rate of interest.[56]

One clear statement is that the rate of investment 'will be pushed to the point where there is no longer any class of capital-asset of which the marginal efficiency exceeds the current rate of interest'.

Keynes proceeded to express this in a short algebraic passage:

If $Q_r$ is the prospective yield from an asset at time $r$, and $d_r$ is the present value of £1 deferred $r$ years *at the current rate of interest*, $\Sigma\ Q_r\ d_r$ is the demand price of the investment; and investment will be carried to the point, where $\Sigma\ Q_r\ d_r$ becomes equal to the supply price of the investment as defined above.[57]

It is clear that by *rate of interest* Keynes meant the risk-free rate of interest.

Keynes emphasised that he was basing his treatment on the *prospective* yield of capital and not on its *current* yield. Even to-day the confusion to which Keynes referred between three meanings of the terms 'profit' and 'rate of profit' prevails.

i. *Prospective.* Except in the absence of uncertainty, this is subjective, and varies between different individuals. Even for one individual it is not, at any particular date, in the future, one definite amount, and, with the normal association of uncertainty with risk, cannot even be represented by a probability distribution.
ii. *Current.* This is the sense in which the terms are used in theories of the determination of profit and the rate of profit.
iii. *Past.* This is objective and a matter of history, but attempts at theoretical explanation are legitimate.

[56] *Ibid.*, pp. 135–7.
[57] *Ibid.*, p. 137.

### *Risk and uncertainty*

Keynes identified his 'marginal efficiency of capital' with Irving Fisher's 'rate of return over cost', defined in his *Theory of Interest* as

> that rate which, employed in computing the present worth of all the costs and the present worth of all the returns, will make these two equal.[58]

This to-day is the familiar concept of the internal rate of return. To induce new investment Fisher wrote that '*the rate of return over cost must exceed the rate of interest*'.[59]

Keynes wrote in 1937 that the concept implied by his 'marginal efficiency of capital'

> was first introduced into economic theory by Irving Fisher in his *Theory of Interest* (1930), under the designation 'the rate of return over cost'. This conception of his is, I think, the most important and fruitful of his recent original suggestions.[60]

The important fact that Keynes failed to mention is that in 106 pages[61] Fisher completely ruled out risk and uncertainty.

When Keynes wrote that investment is

> pushed to the point where there is no longer any class of capital-asset of which the marginal efficiency exceeds the current rate of interest[62]

he was emphatically not assuming the absence of risk and uncertainty only the rate of interest was risk-free.

With the prevalence of risk and uncertainty, a prospective rate of return as low as the risk-free rate of interest would be entirely unacceptable. And it is impossible to calculate a substitute for the rate of interest which takes account of risk and uncertainty. The return for risk and uncertainty can be

[58] Irving Fisher, *The Theory of Interest.* New York: Macmillan, 1930 (First Edition), p. 168; quoted in Keynes, vol. vii, p. 140.

[59] *Ibid.*, p. 159; quoted in Keynes, vol. vii, pp. 140–1.

[60] John Maynard Keynes, 'The Theory of the Rate of Interest', in Arthur D. Gayer, *The Lessons of Monetary Experience. Essays in Honor of Irving Fisher*; reprinted in Keynes, vol. xiv, p. 101, note 2.

[61] Irving Fisher, *The Theory of Interest*, pp. 99–205.

[62] Keynes, vol. vii, p. 136.

imputed only from the excess of the prospective rate of return which is sufficiently high to encourage the investment over the risk-free rate of interest. Keynes' treatment involves circular argument.

Later in the same chapter, Keynes did discuss the excess, on account of risk, over the rate of interest, 'to give the minimum prospective yield which will induce the investment'[63] but he was of course unable to suggest how it could be computed otherwise than by empirical observations.

On die previous page two types of risk are discussed as affecting the volume of investment: 'entrepreneur's or borrower's risk' and, 'where a system of borrowing and lending exists', the risk to the lender of voluntary or involuntary default by the borrowers. The 'first type of risk [unlike the second] is, in a sense, a real social cost, though susceptible to diminution by averaging.'[64]

Some idea of the order of magnitude which Keynes had in mind is provided by a discussion of the difficulty of 'bringing the effective rate of interest below a certain figure [...] in an era of low interest rates'.[65] He had taken the view that 'a long-term rate of interest of (say) 2 per cent leaves more to fear [by way of a future rise] than to hope' [by way of a further fall].[66]

This passage suggests a very low allowance for risk, especially as Keynes had lender's risk in mind.

The *General Theory* was published early in 1936. It is curious that in a 1934 draft of the third page of what was to be Chapter 11 (on 'The Marginal Efficiency of Capital'), the phrases 'after allowance for risk', 'with equal risk', and 'with an allowance for risk' all appear.[67] Why these phrases came to be dropped is completely obscure.

Keynes can be justifiably criticised for exaggerating the importance – compared with other factors – of the risk-free rate of interest as an influence on the rate of investment. Among the other factors are risk and uncertainty, depreciation and obsolescence. In the following Section I cite Keynes as a very strong advocate against the predominance of the rate of

[63] *Ibid.*, p. 145.
[64] *Ibid.*, p. 144.
[65] KEYNES, vol. VII, p. 208.
[66] *Ibid.*, p. 202.
[67] KEYNES, vol. XIII, p. 452.

interest, compared with other factors, the most important of which can be covered by the portmanteau phrase 'state of finance'.[68]

At the same time, as of course Keynes was well aware, a considerable proportion of a country's investment is in durable assets such as dwellings, public utilities, roads and railways. Here there is usually little risk and annual depreciation is low. The rate of interest is an important influence.

This is why the level of rates of interest has some bearing on the activity of the economy as a whole, investment in durable undertakings being an important part of effective demand.

Of course, as the quotation from his reply to Viner indicates, Keynes' thinking was dominated by the prevalence of risk – especially when combined with uncertainty. This makes it difficult to refer to the prospect of a definite rate of return which will just induce investment by a firm in a particular class of capital-goods at a specified rate. But the symbol $Q_r$ was clearly intended by Keynes to serve as a proxy for the state of mind of entrepreneurs as to the prospects of profits on a particular line of investment at time *r*. The legitimacy of this simplifying procedure becomes less with an increase in the degree of uncertainty attaching to the risk.

## Keynes' chapter on investment in real life

### *Introduction*

Having ridden on a tight rein in Chapter 11 on 'The Marginal Efficiency of Capital', Keynes seems to have become bored – perhaps dissatisfied – and in Chapter 12 on 'The State of Long-Term Expectations' allows himself the pleasure of a full gallop. The contrast is astonishing. There is little similarity to the scholastic treatment of Chapter 11.

### *The role of equity prices*

Both in the *Treatise* and in the *General Theory* the treatment of equities, as opposed to fixed-interest securities, is limited in scope and hesitant as to

[68] Among the many investigations conducted in this field by questioning industrialists may be mentioned the relevant sections of *Oxford Studies in the Price Mechanism* (edited by Tom Wilson and P.W.S. Andrews. Oxford: Clarendon Press, 1951, pp. 1–74). Hubert Henderson (pp. 16–27) supported the view put forward in my text. Some of the Oxford economists were surprised by the replies they received. (I reviewed the book in the *Economic Journal*, March 1952, pp. 119–30).

the importance of the behaviour of equities as an influence on real investment. Keynes attached more importance to the influence on consumption. There was no lack of familiarity with the subject – as First Bursar of his College, a Director of two Investment Trusts, and on his own personal account, he look a lively and practical interest in equity markets. It does not, of course, follow that he believed that the behaviour of equity markets constituted a real influence on the economy. Some of the passages which I quote from Chapter 12 suggest that he did believe that it was. But there is considerable ambivalence.

Ambivalence on this issue has prevailed among economists up to the present day. In the following section I venture to give an indication of my own views.

Considerable confusion is caused – Keynes was not immune to this confusion – by the ambiguity of the word 'investment', which is used to mean both real investment and the purchase of Stock Exchange securities.

This is one of the occasions on which the French vocabulary is richer than the English. For over twenty years Joan Robinson, acting on a hint from Hicks, has avoided the confusion by borrowing from France the word *placement* to mean the purchase of securities.[69]

In the *Treatise*, equities play an important role as constituents of portfolios and they are discussed at a number of points in the text. Their price-levels are rarely, however, mentioned as an influence on the rate of investment. In one exceptional passage Keynes alluded to the fact that in the United States boom of 1928-29 high short-term money rates deliberately imposed by the Federal Reserve Bank were proving rather unsuccessful in achieving the desired effect of 'retarding investment and so bringing the period of business prosperity to an earlier conclusion'. Keynes' explanation was that

> the very high prices of common shares, relatively to their dividend yields, offered joint stock enterprises an exceptionally cheap method of financing themselves. Thus, whilst short-money rates were very high and bond rates somewhat high, it was cheaper than at any previous period to finance new investment by the issue of common stocks [equities]. By the spring of 1929 this was becoming the predominant method of finance. Thus easy terms were maintained for certain types of investment, in spite of the appearance of very dear short-money.[70]

[69] Joan Robinson, *The Accumulation of Capital*. London: Macmillan, 1956, p. 8.
[70] Keynes, vol. vi, pp. 174–5.

By the time he came to the *General Theory*, Keynes did not accept this form of explanation. This seems very odd. Referring back to this passage in a footnote, he stated that his interpretation would now be that 'a high quotation for existing equities involves an increase in the marginal efficiency of the corresponding type of capital'.[71]

This footnote appears in the very chapter which I am now discussing, in which the behaviour of the prices of equities, in some passages but not in others, has an important influence on real investment. It has to be regarded as an aberration.

### *Extracts from Chapter 12 which do not suggest influences on real investment*

I have tried, in quoting some extracts from the chapter, to pick out, in the first place, those which do *not* suggest that the behaviour of equity markets is an influence on the level of activity of the economy.

> A conventional valuation which is established as the outcome of the mass psychology of a large number of ignorant individuals is liable to change violently as the result of a sudden fluctuation of opinion due to factors which do not really make much difference to the prospective yield; since there will be no strong roots of conviction to hold it steady.
>
> [...] It might have been supposed that competition between expert professionals, possessing judgment and knowledge beyond that of the average private investor, would correct the vagaries of the ignorant individual left to himself. It happens, however, that the energies and skill of the professional investor and speculator are mainly occupied otherwise. For most of these persons are, in fact, largely concerned, not with making superior long-term forecasts of the probable yield of an investment over its whole life, but with foreseeing changes in the conventional basis of valuation a short time ahead of the general public. They are concerned, not with what an investment is really worth to a man who buys it 'for keeps', but with what the market will value it at, under the influence of mass psychology, three months or a year hence. Moreover, this behaviour is not the outcome of a wrong-headed propensity. It is an inevitable result of an investment market organised along the lines described. For it is not sensible to pay 25 for an investment of which you believe the prospective yield to justify a value of 30, if you also believe that the market will value it at 20 three months hence.

[71] Keynes, vol. vii, p. 15.1, note 1.

Thus the professional investor is forced to concern himself with the anticipation of impending changes, in the news or in the atmosphere, of the kind by which experience shows that the mass psychology of the market is most influenced. [....] The social object of skilled investment should be to defeat the dark forces of time and ignorance which envelop our future. The actual, private object of the most skilled investment to-day is 'to beat the gun', as the Americans so well express it, to outwit the crowd, and to pass the bad, or depreciating, half-crown to the other fellow.

This battle of wits to anticipate the basis of conventional valuation a few months hence, rather than the prospective yield of an investment over a long term of years, does not even require gulls amongst the public to feed the maws of the professional; – it can be played by professionals amongst themselves. Nor is it necessary that anyone should keep his simple faith in the conventional basis of valuation having any genuine long-term validity. For it is, so to speak, a game of Snap, of Old Maid, of Musical Chairs – a pastime in which he is victor who says *Snap* neither too soon nor too late, who passed the Old Maid to his neighbour before the game is over, who secures a chair for himself when the music stops. [...] Or, to change the metaphor slightly, professional investment may be likened to those newspaper competitions in which the competitors have to pick out the six prettiest faces from a hundred photographs, the prize being awarded to the competitor whose choice most nearly corresponds to the average preferences of the competitors as a whole; so that each competitor has to pick, not those faces which he himself finds prettiest, but those which he thinks likeliest to catch the fancy of the other competitors, all of whom arc looking at the problem from the same point of view [...] We have reached the third degree where we devote our intelligences to anticipating what average opinion expects the average opinion to be. And there are some, I believe, who practise the fourth, fifth and higher degrees.[72]

## *Extracts from Chapter 12 which do suggest influences on real investment*

The outstanding fact is the extreme precariousness of the basis of knowledge on which our estimates of prospective yield have to be made. Our knowledge of the factors which will govern the yield of an investment some years hence is usually very slight and often negligible. [73]

[72] Keynes, vol. vii, pp. 154–6.
[73] *Ibid.*, p. 149.

[...] Business men play a mixed game of skill and chance, the average results of which to the players are not known by those who take a hand. If human nature felt no temptation to take a chance, no satisfaction (profit apart) in constructing a factory, a railway, a mine or a farm, there might not be much investment merely as a result of cold calculation.

Decisions to invest in private business of the old-fashioned type were, however, decisions largely irrevocable, not only for the community as a whole, but also for the individual. With the separation between ownership and management which prevails to-day and with the development of organised investment markets, a new factor of great importance has entered in, which sometimes facilitates investment but sometimes adds greatly to the instability of the system. In the absence of security markets, there is no object in frequently attempting to revalue an investment to which we are committed.

[...] the daily revaluations of the Stock Exchange, though they are primarily made to facilitate transfers of old investments between one individual and another, inevitably exert a decisive influence on the rate of current investment. For there is no sense in building up a new enterprise at a cost greater than that at which a similar existing enterprise can be purchased: whilst there is an inducement to spend on a new project what may seem an extravagant sum, if it can be floated off on the Stock Exchange at an immediate profit. Thus certain classes of investment are governed by the average expectation of those who deal on the Stock Exchange as revealed in the price of shares, rather than by the genuine expectations of the professional entrepreneur.[74] How then are these highly significant daily, even hourly revaluations of existing investments carried out in practice?[75]

[...] if there exist organised investment markets and if we can rely on the maintenance of the convention, an investor can legitimately encourage himself with the idea that the only risk he runs is that of a genuine change in the news *over the near future*, as to the likelihood of which he can attempt to form his own judgment, and which is unlikely to be very large. For, assuming that the convention holds good, it is only these changes which can affect the value of his investment, and he need not lose his sleep merely because he has not any notion what his investment will be worth ten years hence. Thus investment becomes reasonably 'safe' for the individual investor over short periods, and hence over a succession of short periods however many, if he

[74] This does not apply, of course, to classes of enterprise which are not readily marketable or to which no negotiable instrument closely corresponds. The categories falling within this exception were formerly extensive. But measured as a proportion of the total value of new investment they are rapidly declining in importance.

[75] Keynes, vol. vii, pp. 150–1.

can fairly rely on there being no breakdown in the convention and on his therefore having an opportunity to revise his judgment and change his investment, before there has been time for much to happen. Investments which are 'fixed' for the community are thus made 'liquid' for the individual.

It has been, I am sure, on the basis of some such procedure as this that our leading investment markets have been developed. But it is not surprising that a convention, in an absolute view of things so arbitrary, should have its weak points. It is its precariousness which creates no small part of our contemporary problem of securing sufficient investment.[76]

[...] Investment based on genuine long-term expectation is so difficult to-day as to be scarcely practicable. He who attempts it must surely lead much more laborious days and run greater risks than he who tries to guess better than the crowd how the crowd will behave; and, given equal intelligence, he may make more disastrous mistakes. There is no clear evidence from experience that the investment policy which is socially advantageous coincides with that which is most profitable. It needs *more* intelligence to defeat the forces of time and our ignorance of the future than to beat the gun.

[...] it is the long-term investor, he who most promotes the public interest, who will in practice come in for most criticism, wherever investment funds are managed by committees or boards or banks. For it is in the essence of his behaviour that he should be eccentric, unconventional and rash in the eyes of average opinion. If he is successful, that will only confirm the general belief in his rashness; and if in the short run he is unsuccessful, which is very likely, he will not receive much mercy. Worldly wisdom teaches that it is better for reputation to fail conventionally than to succeed unconventionally [...].

A collapse in the price of equities, which has had disastrous reactions on the marginal efficiency of capital, may have been due to the weakening either of speculative confidence or of the state of credit. But whereas the weakening of either is enough to cause a collapse, recovery requires the revival of *both*. For whilst the weakening of credit is sufficient to bring about a collapse, its strengthening, though a necessary condition of recovery, is not a sufficient condition.

These considerations should not lie beyond the purview of the economist. But they must be relegated to their right perspective. If I may be allowed to appropriate the term *speculation* for the activity of forecasting the psychology of the market, and the term *enterprise* for the activity of forecasting the prospective yield of assets over their whole life, it is by no means always the case that speculation predominates over enterprise. As the organ-

[76] *Ibid.*, pp. 152–3.

isation of investment markets improves the risk of the predominance of speculation does, however, increase. In one of the greatest investment markets in the world, namely, New York, the influence of speculation (in the above sense) is enormous. [...] Speculators may do no harm as bubbles on a steady stream of enterprise. But the position is serious when enterprise becomes the bubble on a whirlpool of speculation. When the capital development of a country becomes a by-product of the activities of a casino, the job is likely to be ill-done. The measure of success attained by Wall Street, regarded as an institution of which the proper social purpose is to direct new investment into the most profitable channels in terms of future yield, cannot be claimed as one of the outstanding triumphs of *laissez-faire* capitalism – which is not surprising, if I am right in thinking that the best brains of Wall Street have been in fact directed towards a different object [...].[77]

Even apart from the instability due to speculation, there is the instability due to the characteristic of human nature that a large proportion of our positive activities depend on spontaneous optimism rather than on a mathematical expectation, whether moral or hedonistic or economic. Most, probably, of our decisions to do something positive, the full consequences of which will be drawn out over many days to come, can only be taken as a result of animal spirits – of a spontaneous urge to action rather than inaction, and not as the outcome of a weighted average of quantitative benefits multiplied by quantitative probabilities. Enterprise only pretends to itself to be mainly actuated by the statements in its own prospectus, however candid and sincere. Only a little more than an expedition to the South Pole, is it based on an exact calculation of benefits to come. Thus if the animal spirits are dimmed and the spontaneous optimism falters, leaving us to depend on nothing but a mathematical expectation, enterprise will fade and die; – though fears of loss may have a basis no more reasonable than hopes of profit had before.[78]

[...] it is our innate urge to activity which makes the wheels go round, our rational selves choosing between the alternatives as best we are able, calculating where we can, but often falling back for our motive on whim or sentiment or chance [...][79]

For my own part I am now somewhat sceptical of the success of a merely monetary policy directed towards influencing the rate of interest. I expect to see the State, which is in a position to calculate the marginal efficiency of capital-goods on long views and on the basis of the general social advantage, taking an ever greater responsibility for directly organising investment; since

[77] KEYNES, vol. VII, pp. 157–9.
[78] *Ibid.*, pp. 161–2.
[79] *Ibid.*, p. 163.

it seems likely that the fluctuations in the market estimation of the marginal efficiency of different types of capital, calculated on the principles I have described above, will be too great to be offset by any practicable changes in the rate of interest.[80]

## Limitations of the 'General Theory'

### *Misconceptions about the General Theory*

Keynes made it clear in his Preface that the book's 'main purpose is to deal with difficult questions of theory, and only in the second place with the applications of this theory to practice'.[81] This is often overlooked. For example:

1) The book contains almost no references to international trade and the problem of reconciling an acceptable balance of payments with a high level of activity. And yet in Keynes' more practical writings this problem was uppermost in his mind. Very often it took the form of regarding excessive overseas lending as part of the cause of the country's troubles, both because, if in excess of the current account balance of payments, it resulted in a loss of monetary reserves, and because, to avoid this, the necessary rise in rates of interest had a discouraging effect on domestic investment and so caused unemployment.

   Keynes did develop this theme in 'Notes on Mercantilism', his penultimate chapter on a number of historical topics.[82] At the very end of the book he wrote that 'if nations can learn to provide themselves with full employment by their domestic policy [...] there need be no important economic forces calculated to set the interest of one country against that of its neighbours',[83] each country's exports benefiting from the other countries' high level of activity.

   The world still has to accept this simple lesson taught by Keynes.

[80] *Ibid.*, p. 164.

[81] Keynes. vol. vii, p. xxi.

[82] *Ibid.*, Chapter 23: 'Notes on Mercantilism, the Usury Laws, Stamped Money and Theories of Under-Consumption', pp. 333–71.

[83] *Ibid.*, p. 382.

2) Only in one passage did Keynes advocate the policy with which his name still is so closely associated – largely as a result of *Can Lloyd George Do It?* – 'loan expenditure' by public authorities as a means of sustaining employment if other means fail.

'wasteful' loan expenditure .may [...] enrich the community on balance. Pyramid-building, earthquakes, even wars may serve to increase wealth, if the education of our statesmen on the principles of the classical economics stands in the way of anything better.[84]

3) Many of the passages in the book are not easy to read, and some of the chapters are profound, and therefore especially difficult – namely Chapter 16 on 'Sundry Observations on the Nature of Capital', Chapter 17 on 'The Essential Properties of Interest and Money', and the final Chapter 24 on 'Concluding Notes on the Social Philosophy'. Nevertheless, it was Keynes' object, in presenting his basic propositions, to avoid the qualifications and complications which were called for by a comprehensive treatment. In his burning anxiety to convince, he did enormously over-simplify.

This statement will be ill-received by those who find the book difficult and believe that the essence of it can be presented by some simple geometry or algebra.

That is the great tragedy. The behaviour of the economy is an immensely complicated subject. The diagrams and bits of algebra in the text-books up to the present day have often led to the difficulties being submerged, and incidentally to Keynes being discredited.

For example, both in his exposition of the liquidity preference theory of the rate of interest and in his exposition of the inducement to invest, Keynes made use of schedules – simple relationships between two parameters, one the rate of interest in both cases – which could be represented by a curve or by a piece of algebra of the type $y = f(x)$. And yet Keynes' insistence on the overwhelming importance of expectations, highly subject to risk and uncertainty, was one of his biggest contributions. This completely undermines the prevalent idea – for which Keynes' attempt at simplification is responsible – that such schedules can be regarded as stable relationships handed down from heaven.

[84] *Ibid.*, pp. 128–9.

Keynes' letter of 31 March 1937 to John R. Hicks about Hicks' article on 'Mr Keynes and the Classics' (1937)[85] is friendly in tone but contains one criticism:

> At one time I tried the equations, as you have done, with *I* [income] in all of them. The objection to this is that it over-emphasises current income. In the case of the inducement to invest, expected income for the period of the investment is the relevant variable. This I have attempted to take account of in the definition of the marginal efficiency of capital [...] whilst it may be true that entrepreneurs are over-influenced by present income, far too much stress is laid on this psychological influence, if present income is brought into such prominence.[86]

Keynes' rebuke was too mild. It left Hicks unrepentant. In the course of his reply of 9 April, he wrote:

> Of course I agree that it is expected income that logically matters; but the influence of current events on expectations (admittedly a loose and unreliable connection) seems to me potentially so important, that I feel much happier if it is put in and marked unreliable.[87]

The result has been that the elementary teaching of Keynesian economics has been the victim of *IS-LM* and related diagrams and algebra. It is tragic that Keynes made no public protest when they began to appear.

As Joan Robinson has recently put it:

> modern teaching has been confused by J. R. Hicks' attempt to reduce the General Theory to a version of static equilibrium with the formula IS/LM. Hicks has now repented and changed his name from J. R. to John, but it will take a long time for the effects of his teaching to wear off.[88]

As recently as 1977 Hicks was still insisting about his *IS-LM* diagram:

[85] JOHN R. HICKS, 'Mr. Keynes and the "Classics": A Suggested Interpretation', *Econometrica*, April 1937, pp. 147–59; reproduced in JOHN R. HICKS, *Critical Essays in Monetary Theory*. Oxford: Clarendon Press, 1967, pp. 126–42.

[86] *Letter* to John R. Hicks, *31 March 1937*; published in KEYNES, vol. xiv, pp. 79–81.

[87] *Letter* from John R. Hicks, *9 April 1937*; published *ibid.*, pp. 81–3.

[88] JOAN ROBINSON, *Contributions to Modern Economics*. Oxford: Basil Blackwell, 1978, p. xiv.

> There is indeed much more in the *General Theory* of Keynes than this formal model [...] I am nevertheless convinced that those later writers (so many later writers!) who have taken their Keynes from the *ISLM* diagram have indeed taken over what is one of the elements in what Keynes said.[89]

It is comforting to read in an article included in the same book, but published four years earlier, that

> the *General Theory* [...] provides a model on which academic economists can comfortably perform their accustomed tricks. Haven't they just? With *ISLM* I myself fell into the trap.[90]

### *Keynes' provocative tone*

It is widely held that Keynes was mistaken in adopting a provocative tone in his comments on the classical economists, especially on his friend and colleague, Pigou.

About the drafts of Chapter 14 on 'The Classical Theory of the Rate of Interest', Harrod remonstrated with Keynes for being unduly provocative.[91] A short extract from a reply from Keynes will suffice:

> I expect a great deal of what I write to be water off a duck's back. I am certain that it will be water off a duck's back unless I am sufficiently strong in my criticism to force the classicals to make rejoinders. I *want*, so to speak, to raise a dust; because it is only out of the controversy that will arise that what I am saying will gel understood.[92]

In his Preface Keynes wrote:

> Those, who arc strongly wedded to what I shall call 'the classical theory', will fluctuate, I expect, between a belief that I am quite wrong and a belief that I am saying nothing new [...] My controversial passages are aimed at providing some material for an answer.[93]

[89] John R. Hicks, *Economic Perspectives*. Oxford: Clarendon Press, 1977, p. viii.

[90] *Ibid.*, pp. 147–8, reprinted from John R. Hicks, 'Recollections and Documents', *Economica*, February 1973, p. 11.

[91] *Letter* from Ralph F. Harrod, *21 August 1935*; published in Keynes, vol. xiii, pp. 544–6.

[92] *Ibid.*, p. 548.

[93] Keynes, vol. vii, p. xxi.

Sir Austin Robinson touched on this issue in his Biography:

> Keynes had meant to shock. An ordinary book, wooing with sweet reason, would not have fulfilled his purpose. The ideas that happened to be congenial might have been accepted, the others discarded according to taste.[94]

## The post 'General Theory' Keynes on 'finance'

### *Keynes and finance*

Keynes' thinking developed after the publication of the *General Theory*. Every number of the *Economic Journal* from March 1937 to June 1938 devoted at least one article or note to discussions and controversy with Professor Bertil Ohlin, the Swedish economist, Dennis Robertson and Ralph Hawtrey. These are outside the scope of this book.

But Keynes' exposition of the concept of 'finance' is an important qualification of the *General Theory* exposition of the determination of the rate of investment. It is discussed in the June 1937, December 1937 and June 1938 issues of the *Journal*.

It is a factor in the determination of the rate of investment additional to expectations of future profitability, the physical capacity of the industries producing the capital goods in question, and 'animal spirits'. It provides an answer to all those who are doubtful about the strength of the risk-free rate of interest when set off against expectations of profits, highly subject to risk and uncertainty.

Keynes now brought in the availability of funds as a more important restraint, irrespective of the rate of interest.

It is not necessary to regard Keynes' treatment as entirely satisfactory, to appreciate the great importance of the concept.

Keynes' basic statement was

> the fact (which may deserve more emphasis than I have given it previously) that an investment *decision* [...] may sometimes involve a temporary demand for money before it is carried out, quite distinct from the demand for active balances which will arise as a result of the investment activity whilst it is going on.
>
> [...] There has, therefore, to be a technique to bridge this gap [...].

[94] Austin Robinson, 'John Maynard Keynes, 1883–1946', *Economic Journal*, March 1947, p. 40.

> This service may be provided either by the new issue market or by the banks; – which it is, makes no difference.[95]

Either there will be increased pressure on the limited facilities which the market is prepared to provide (the new issue market or the banks) or the entrepreneurs will accumulate extra cash balances. Finance Keynes 'regarded as lying half-way, so to speak, between the active and the inactive balances'.

> If investment is proceeding at a steady rate, the finance (or the commitments to finance) required can be supplied from a revolving fund of a more or less constant amount, one entrepreneur having his finance replenished [...] as another exhausts his [...] But if decisions to invest are (*e. g.*) increasing, the extra finance involved will constitute an additional demand for money.[96]

(Keynes should have added 'or overdraft facilities or new issue market facilities'.)

> [...] lack of finance may prove an important obstacle to more than a certain amount of investment decisions being on the tapis at the same time.[97]

In a footnote to the first page of his following article in the December 1937 issue of the *Economic Journal* – which I am coming on to – Keynes conceded:

> In what follows I use the term 'finance' to mean the credit required in the interval between planning and execution.[98]

Nevertheless, I do not feel that I am being captious in taking exception to Keynes' contention that 'It is, so to speak, as though a particular piece of saving had to be earmarked against a particular piece of investment before either has occurred'.[99] (But in the December 1937 issue of the

[95] JOHN MAYNARD KEYNES, 'Alternative Theories of the Rate of Interest', *Economic Journal*, June 1937, p. 246; reprinted in KEYNES, vol. XIV, pp. 207–8.

[96] *Ibid.*, p. 247; reprinted in KEYNES, vol. XIV, p. 209.

[97] *Ibid.*

[98] JOHN MAYNARD KEYNES, 'The "Ex-Ante" Theory of the Rate of Interest', *Economic Journal*, December 1937, p. 663, note 2; reprinted in KEYNES, vol. XIV, p. 216, note 1.

[99] JOHN MAYNARD KEYNES, 'Alternative Theories of the Rate of Interest', p. 246; reprinted in KEYNES, vol. XIV, pp. 207–8.

*Economic Journal* Keynes conceded that the two are not necessarily equal.[100]) The basic concept was:

> a heavy demand for investment can exhaust the market and be held up by lack of financial facilities on reasonable terms.[101]

Part of the trouble is that the character of the funds required for the finance of investment does not match the character of the saving which flows with the investment. The economy would operate far more smoothly if the only form of investment was house-building financed by building societies and the only possible home for saving was deposits with building societies.

Later in the same article in the December 1937 issue of the *Economic Journal:*

> the banks hold the key position in the transition from a lower to a higher scale of activity. If they refuse to relax, the growing congestion of the short-term loan market or of the new issue market, as the case may be, will inhibit the improvement [...] On the other hand, there will always be *exactly* enough ex-post saving to take up the ex-post investment.[102]

### *The crowding-out effect in some quarters to-day*

In some quarters this 'growing congestion' has been regarded as evidence that Keynes, late in his life, had come in effect to accept the 'crowding-out' effect believed in by many economists and financiers at the present day. It is a question of degree. The 'crowding-out' effect is absolute: any increase in the rate of investment in one field – at any rate if it is public investment financed by the banking system – is said to involve an equal reduction in some other field. It is our old friend 'the Treasury view'. Keynes' 'growing congestion' means that the rate of total investment will rise, in response to improving prospects of the future, but only to a limited extent unless the provision of 'finance' improves. The word 'finance' is a

[100] John Maynard Keynes, 'The "Ex-Ante" Theory of the Rate of Interest', pp. 663–4; reprinted in Keynes, vol. xiv, p. 216.

[101] John Maynard Keynes, 'Alternative Theories of the Rate of Interest', p. 248; reprinted in Keynes, vol. xiv, p. 210.

[102] John Maynard Keynes, 'The "Ex-Ante" Theory of the Rate of Interest', pp. 668–9; reprinted in Keynes, vol. xiv, p. 222.

portmanteau word, incapable of quantitative definition, indicating the degree of confidence of entrepreneurs about the case – in terms both of sacrifice and availability – with which funds will be made available for paying for the investment as it takes place.

Keynes pointed out, incidentally, that there was no reason for confining the restrictive influence of shortage of finance to the production of capital goods: it applied equally to the much narrower case of that of production of consumption-goods, which has to be planned ahead.[103]

### *The inducement to invest in real life*

Keynes' concept of finance brings his theory of the inducement to invest into much closer line with modern practice – especially of large firms providing a wide range of products.

The period into the future for which the management plans depends on the character of the products and of the markets in which they are sold. They usually operate on the basis of a moving horizon.

They estimate the funds which might be made available over the period – from the firm's own liquid assets, from its undistributed profits, from banks, and from new issues, so far as they can be estimated.

The management try to obtain estimates of the prospective internal rates of return on capital invested to be derived from the various projects brought to their notice. Such estimates are notoriously unreliable, partly as a result of uncertainty, and partly as a result of the Napoleonic instincts of the experts in each particular field. Some pruning of the estimates is usual.

It then becomes a delicate and difficult problem of distributing the available finance between the various projects. Account is taken of the estimated internal rates of return, their reliability, of the amount of surplus capacity in each line of production, of the speed with which this capacity could be expanded, of technical innovations – actual and prospective – of the probable policies of competitors, and of the availability of labour – especially of the labour endowed with the particular skills required.

The estimate of the funds prospectively available is flexible. At a time when the profitability of the relevant future looks especially hopeful the various sources will be stretched; when it looks gloomy, funds – actual and borrowing powers – will be conserved for better times.

[103] *Ibid.*, p. 667; reprinted in Keynes, vol. xiv, pp. 220–1.

There is usually a minimum qualifying cut-off rate of the estimated internal rates of return – again dependent on the state of confidence about the future.

The part played by the equity varies enormously between countries. I write only about the United Kingdom. Even here it is the subject of controversy.

A very vague but diverse relationship exists between the state of confidence about the future on the Stock Exchange and the state of confidence about future profitability entertained by industrialists. It is a two-way relationship and neither state of mind can be described as horse rather than cart. Some of my cynical quotations from Keynes' Chapter 12, presented in Section 9 of this Lecture, bear on this issue.

I turn to less vague issues. Many of my economist colleagues argue that in our country aggregate retained profits are so great and, as a result of various Government concessions, Corporation Tax so low, that the industrial and commercial sector, taken as a whole, is self-financing.

But those who argue on this line overlook the wide polarisation between companies, at one extreme, which rely heavily on new issues of equities and those, at the other extreme, which accumulate financial assets and make successful take-over bids for other companies. The financial position would be much eased if the companies at the latter extreme bought the shares of the companies at the former extreme. But – apart from take-over bids – they do not.

However, my argument does not rest mainly on the quantitative importance of new issues of equities. It raises the much-debated question of the extent to which the management of a company is influenced by a sense of loyalty to its shareholders and how it is expressed.

Except in the cases in which some of the directors own personally, and on behalf of members of their families, considerable holdings of their shares, I accept the general view that the strong motive is to grow, under the influence of Keynes' 'animal spirits', and to finance growth as far as possible from retained profits.

It very well suits wealthy shareholders, subject to high marginal rates of tax on unearned income (as especially in the United Kingdom), to obtain their return in the form of a rising price of the shares rather than dividends.

But frequently the large shareholders are institutions – pension funds, insurance companies and investment trusts – whose clients are not wealthy and want income. There is always hanging over the management of a company the threat of a group of dissident institutions ganging up together and threatening gradually to change the composition of the Board of Directors if a higher proportion of profits is not distributed.

Another very real danger to the management arises if the price of the share is seriously below the value per share of the real underlying assets. The danger is that of a successful take-over bid, which may result in the directors being displaced.

Another factor is the pride of the management in presenting an annual report which is well received.

Finally, the value placed on a share by the Stock Exchange is partly determined by its earnings yield (more than by its dividend yield). The rate of capital appreciation depends on the rate of increase of earnings per share.

For these various reasons the management are subject to strong pressure to avoid growing so fast as seriously to prejudice the rate of growth of earnings and the price of the shares.

The result is that, indirectly if not directly, pressure is exercised on them to take account of their shareholders' interests. The prospective earnings yield per share, both on the real assets of the company (the internal rate of return) and on its shares, must not fall below the rate generally prevailing in the country. This factor acts as a restraint on the rate of growth of the company rather than Keynes' rate of interest. This is why the price of a company's shares matters to its management even if there is no question of making an issue of shares.

We have come quite a long way in this Lecture from Section 7 – the first section on the inducement to investment – to this final subsection dealing with real life. The long intervening discussion has not radically undermined Keynes' theory. I am not, of course, suggesting that the behaviour of entrepreneurs – as opposed to that of all those who try to manage economies – is influenced by Keynes' teaching. What I am saying is that Keynes was a great pioneer – in the sense that he evolved the theory of how things happen in real life which no economist before him had succeeded in evolving.

PART III

# International Money and Trade

CHAPTER 8

# International Regulation of Trade and Exchanges

*Richard F. Kahn*

My theme is the edifice which in the last few years of the war was erected at various international conferences concerned with commercial policy and regulation of currencies. I want to discuss the concept which was in the minds of those who planned the edifice, the reasons why the concept has not been fully realised, and the question whether it is ever likely to be fully realised in the foreseeable future, or, indeed, whether it is desirable that it should be. It was, of course, appreciated that there would have to be a period of years after the war to permit the necessary transition to peace-time conditions before the new ideas could become thoroughly effective. Meanwhile, the edifice was erected—the International Monetary Fund, and, perhaps more important than the Fund itself, its Articles of Agreement; and although the Charter for an International Trade Organisation, which I will refer to as I.T.O., has never been ratified, largely

Originally publ. in: Kahn, R. F. (1952) In *Banking and Foreign Trade* (pp. 1–18), Lectures delivered at the Fifth International Banking Summer School, Oxford, July. London: Europa Publications for the Institute of Bankers.
Reprint by Springer International Publishing 2022 with kind permission

R. F. Kahn



M. C. Marcuzzo, P. Paesani (eds.), *Richard F. Kahn*, Palgrave Studies in the History of Economic Thought, https://doi.org/10.1007/978-3-030-98588-2_8

because of the unlikelihood that the United States Congress would accept it, there is the General Agreement on Tariffs and Trade, into which a great deal of the Charter has been written—I will refer to it as G.A.T.T. There is much in the Articles of Agreement of the International Monetary Fund and in G.A.T.T. which is actually in operation, but much is still in suspense.

The testing time has now arrived and governments are having to ask themselves whether it is any longer a matter of transition from war to peace or whether there are more deep-seated and less transient reasons why the provisions which are temporarily in suspense, together with some of those which are actually in operation, may not in their essence be unacceptable, at any rate without radical revision. And whether one agrees or not with those who take issue on these matters with the idealists, it is profitable to inquire what has gone wrong with the basic concept, and why it is that those who from the outset were sceptical appear now to have much justification for their scepticism.

The basic idea was, of course, free trade. But completely free trade was too much to hope for, even for the idealists of those latter war years. The abject was to reduce barriers to trade rather than to eliminate them. And since it was recognised that considerable barriers would still survive any such process, two subsidiary objectives were also relevant—one was to provide mechanism for triangular trade, so as to enable a country which exports to one country to use the proceeds to buy from some other country, and secondly there was the subsidiary objective of non-discrimination in the incidence of such barriers as might still persist.

Before 1931 liberal ideas about commercial policy were linked to the gold standard. But as a basis for free trade the gold standard was not satisfactory. It is true that it provided very well the mechanism for triangular trade. That was taken note of in these discussions of the latter war years—it was felt that here was something which must be preserved, and in one sense it is the main justification for the Articles of Agreement of the International Monetary Fund that they provide a smooth mechanism for triangular trade. In general, however, so far from promoting free trade, the gold standard positively militated against it. The maintenance of parity of exchanges has often necessitated drastic credit restriction. Under the influence of Keynes it had, in the pre-war decade, become recognised that in such a case the process of adjustment to a new free-trade equilibrium depends upon the effect of widespread unemployment in enforcing a reduction of money wages, and that until this painful adjustment had been completed the unemployment would itself maintain a spurious equilibrium by diminishing the country's need for imports. The idea that unemployment might have to play a crucial part in the mechanism of adjustment had become anathema by the time when these new ideas which I am discussing were being formulated. Today there is in some quarters a reaction the other way, but in those days it was felt that the gold standard—or, to put it another way, fixed exchange rates—must go if the free-trade idea was to be fostered. What seemed good in the gold standard it was felt important to retain—the mechanism facilitating triangular trade and the day-to-day or, if you like, month-to-month or year-to-year stability of exchange rates. What was abandoned was the idea of irrevocable stability of exchanges, and what was provided in its place was machinery for the orderly adjustment of exchange rates from time to time. The idea was that if a country's imports chronically exceeded its exports, that meant that its costs were relatively too high compared with other countries. It was—to quote from the Articles of Agreement of the International Monetary Fund—a case of fundamental disequilibrium. Instead of being forced to get its costs down through the generation, by credit restriction, of enough unemployment sufficiently long to overcome trade-union resistance against a downward movement of wages, under the new scheme of things a country would be allowed to devalue to the necessary degree. What was heresy in 1931 has already become financially orthodox. In this way the country could continue to enjoy the advantages of free trade, or such partial free trade as it had previously enjoyed.

At this point we must obviously ask ourselves what are these advantages of free trade. It may be helpful if I begin by saying what they are not—what they are not from the point of view of the fundamental case for free trade. From this fundamental point of view it is not a question, when you advocate free trade for a particular country, of asking it to make sacrifices in the interests of other countries, so that if most countries in the world respond to such a plea everybody will be better off, but if only a few countries respond they will be worse off and the others will benefit. This is not the classical case for free trade. We shall see in a moment that such a presentation has a part to play, but it is subsidiary and not fundamental. Nor is it right to say that the classical case for free trade means that free trade is the best policy for a country provided that the rest of the world has free trade too. The classical case is that free trade is the best policy whatever the rest of the world may be doing, from the selfish point of view of any individual country taken in isolation. This is really just an extension of the idea that in a closed system the free play of market prices will give you the best possible distribution of resources between different industries. Equally, if you have a country whose domestic prices faithfully reflect the prices which that country has to pay for its imports and is paid for its exports, you will have the best possible distribution of resources as between catering directly for the needs of the consumer and indirectly by the production of exports for which imports are received in exchange. Protection means that a country fails to take full advantage of the possibilities of the international division of labour.

On the level of thought which is here appropriate, it is not an argument against free trade to say that a country may be involved in balance of payment difficulties if it forgoes restrictions on its imports. That is an important point to recognise. If a country has an adverse balance of payments, then in accordance with the classical case for free trade the proper course for that country, even if we look at it purely from the point of view of its own selfish interests, is to get its costs down relatively to costs elsewhere in such a way that the restoration of equilibrium takes place without bias, the pressure being applied all along the front—both in increasing exports and in diminishing imports, instead of getting the economy distorted by an attack, on a limited part of the front, confined to imports. There are two ways, as I see it, of getting such a country's costs down. So long as you say to the country, as I regret that some of my colleagues do, 'Your proper course is to go through a painful restriction of credit and heavy unemployment in order to get wages down,' the country will say, 'We would rather lose some of the advantages of the international division of labour than go through that horror.' But the International Monetary Fund, by offering the possibility of an orderly adjustment of exchange rates, puts free trade back into the realm of practical politics. Regular adjustment can take place without all that painful business of unemployment and attacks on the wage level.

However, having very briefly put the fundamental case for free trade, I must now mention some of the qualifications. In the first place, there is a group of qualifications which I will mention only for the sake of completeness and which I am not going to discuss. There is the military argument for self-sufficiency; there is the argument for building up infant industries; there is sometimes an argument concerned with the possibility of a better internal distribution of income. Secondly, it can reasonably be maintained that in a world which is subject to fluctuations, particularly fluctuations of an unpredictable kind, the painfulness of adjustment and the waste involved in adjustment are so great that it is better to sacrifice some of the possibilities of the international division of labour for the sake of greater stability, obtained as a result of partial insulation from world disturbances. Of course, if all countries took that line, then they might all be worse off, but it is rather a strong argument when you are considering the formation of a trading group of countries operating in a discriminatory fashion against the rest of the world, provided the governments of those countries can conscientiously maintain that they are more likely to maintain stability within their own frontiers than are the countries which are left outside.

In fact, in the instruments built up for post-war use some provision has been made for temporary disturbances of this kind. G.A.T.T., which here follows, as it follows elsewhere, the Charter of I.T.O., contains a very important escape clause which permits quantitative restriction of imports, if required by a country "to safeguard its external financial position and balance of payments".[1] To continue the quotation, such safeguard is permitted only "to the extent necessary (i) to forestall the imminent threat of, or to stop, a serious decline in its monetary reserves, or (ii) in the case of a contracting party with very low monetary reserves, to achieve a reasonable rate of increase in its reserves." That is reinforced by the following very important provision, the significance of which I think is now sometimes forgotten. Its drafting was the occasion of a great deal of discussion and I think that it is important to draw attention to it. It reads as follows: "The contracting parties recognise that, as a result of domestic policies directed towards the achievement and maintenance of full and productive employment and large and steadily growing demand or towards the reconstruction or development of industrial and other economic resources and the raising of standards of productivity, such a contracting party may experience a high level of demand for imports."

The International Monetary Fund, which supplements the monetary reserves of the member countries, was also aimed to provide for a breathing space to enable countries to get over temporary disturbances. The only question here, but I have not the time to go into it, is whether that provision, in terms of orders of magnitude, is at all adequate to the need, and whether the interest charges are not too high.

Thirdly, one has to recognise that you may have a disturbance affecting part of a country's trade which is not so widespread as seriously to upset its balance of payments. Here it is relevant to remind ourselves that tariffs are the only form of protection allowed under the I.T.O. Charter and under G.A.T.T., apart from the special escape clause aimed at balance of payment difficulties and a special provision for dealing with agricultural marketing schemes. Quantitative regulation of imports is, with these exceptions, forbidden. Now, obviously, if you have an industry which is faced with additional overseas competition in the home market, the impact is going to be very much heavier if protection simply takes the form of a tariff of a given height than if there is a definite limitation on the amount of imports that can come in. This adds to the importance of the other

[1] Cmd. 8048, p. 29.

famous escape clause which I am going to read to you, introduced to match the corresponding provision in the American Reciprocal Agreements Act. It reads as follows—I quote again from G.A.T.T.—"If, as a result of unforeseen developments and of the effect of the obligations incurred by a contracting party under this Agreement, including tariff concessions, any product is being imported into the territory of that contracting party in such increased quantities and under such conditions as to cause or threaten serious injury to domestic producers in that territory of like or directly competitive products, the contracting party shall be free, in respect of such product, and to the extent and for such time as may be necessary to prevent or remedy such injury, to suspend the obligation in whole or in part or to withdraw or modify the concession."[2] As you know, the United States have come under a good deal of criticism for taking action under that escape clause, which was specifically designed to enable such action to be taken by them, and for threats of such further action. Action has actually been taken on the tariff on hats, caps and bonnets. As a result of protests, a Working Party was set up under G.A.T.T. I will read one important extract from the preface of the Working Party's Report. The Working Party "pointed out, however, that in their opinion action under Article XIX is essentially of an emergency character and a government taking such action should keep the position under review and be prepared to reconsider the matter as soon as the action was no longer necessary to prevent or remedy serious injury."[3]

Now I come to the next qualification to the fundamental case for free trade, and that arises from the possible existence within a country's territory of unemployment. By protection, or by adding to protection, a country can reduce unemployment, but it does so, of course, only by increasing unemployment in other countries whose industries suffer in consequence of its exclusion of imports. It is one of those beggar-your-neighbour remedies for unemployment. And here I think we have to remind ourselves that there is an important reference to the responsibility for maintenance of full employment in the I.T.O. Charter: "The Members recognize that the avoidance of unemployment or under-employment, through the achievement and maintenance in each country of useful employment opportunities for those able and willing to work and of a large and steadily

[2] Cmd. 8048, p. 29.

[3] "Report on the Withdrawal by the United States of a Tariff Concession", Geneva, November 1951.

growing volume of production and effective demand for goods and services, is not of domestic concern alone, but is also a necessary condition for the achievement of the general purpose and the objectives set forth in Article I," where the general purpose and the objectives of the Charter are mentioned. Furthermore, "each Member shall take action designed to achieve and maintain full and productive employment. …"[4]

The next qualification to which I come is one to which I want to draw particular attention. Its importance is very often overlooked, and it was overlooked by the architects of the edifice which I am discussing. In this oversight lies the main reason, I think, for the failure of these instruments to carry out everything that was hoped for, and until its full implications are recognised we shall not succeed in getting world trade on to a healthy basis. I refer to the effect of protection on a country's terms of trade.

That you may get such an effect has long been recognised by economists, but until recently the whole thing was regarded as a sort of plaything, suitable only for the economic classroom. The point at issue is rather obvious. Let me go back to my original exposition of the fundamental case for free trade. If the domestic prices of imported goods are above world prices, that means—I am now putting the case slightly differently—that the country can make a gain by diverting resources from the protected industries to the exporting countries, the extra amounts there produced being exchanged for additional imports, which, it is easy to see, will be worth more than the loss of production of the protected industries. Now that argument is valid only if you can take world prices as given. If the country's exports or imports or both play a significant part in world markets, that assumption is invalid. A country in moving towards free trade has to push more exports on to the world market, and if the country is an important one it can do that only by an appreciable reduction of the prices that it charges for its exports on world markets. Secondly, though usually much less important, as its demand for imports rises it bids more heavily on world markets for the goods that it imports, and it will put up prices against itself. This is what is meant when we talk about the effect of protection on a country's terms of trade. Protection means that a country's international trade is reduced; it does not have to export so much, it does not try to import so much, and therefore it can get better prices than it could if it exported and imported more. And it is easy to show that as a country moves towards the completely free-trade position there will come

[4] Cmd. 7375, pp. 9, 10.

a point short of that position at which any further move towards it will involve a greater loss, in economic terms, on these terms of trade than the gain which, if the terms of trade did not turn against it, would be secured by greater participation in the international specialisation of labour. And so for such a country, which is sufficiently important for the volume of its trade to have some effect on the prices of the goods in which it trades, free trade is not the best policy. Of course, the gain which such a country can secure by being protectionist in a modest way is made at the expense of the rest of the world. It is like the gain which monopolists make at the expense of the rest of society by raising the prices of their products above the competitive level. Economists have traditionally taken the line that even to contemplate taking such action would be anti-social conduct on the part of a country. For example, John Stuart Mill in his *Principles of Political Economy* dismissed the matter as follows: "The justice or expediency of destroying one of two gains in order to secure a rather larger share of the other does not require much discussion."

This matter has certainly not, until recently, received the attention which it deserves. It lies at the root of a great deal that has to be explained about the world as we know it. Of course, economists have been inclined to take as the basis of their discussion, not the world as we know it, but an ideal world in which all countries are already free-trade, and they have discussed the effect of a deviation from that ideal position. If that is the way in which the discussion is handled, it is fairly easy to exploit the argument based on morality and point out to a country how wrong it would be to deviate from this ideal position and to secure a gain which would be secured at the expense of other countries. It is easy, too, to demonstrate that if such a country did deviate from free trade it would probably provoke retaliation and in consequence all countries would be worse off, including itself.

But instead of starting with this ideal world, suppose we start with the real world as we know it, in which most countries, in fact all countries, have restrictions on their imports. Then it is very different. The moral argument is not very convincing: "If only you become a free-trade country, or move towards free trade, it is true you will lose"—I am assuming that the tariffs are sufficiently low to permit the gain on the terms of trade to outweigh the loss on the international division of labour—"but your loss will be other countries' gain, and it is immoral to deprive other countries of that gain merely because you do not want to make a loss yourself?" The argument based on retaliation is also very weak. One country by lowering its barriers will not get other countries to lower theirs unless it is part of an international attempt to reduce restrictions on trade. Neither argument will be convincing, even if all countries were alike in terms of standards of living. It is more convincing if you address it to a relatively rich country; it is extremely unconvincing if you address it to a poor country.

Now, as I have put the argument so far, I have not been altogether fair to the free-trade case. A free trader would claim that it is all very well but this loss which a country may suffer from becoming free-trade, because it is a loss on the terms of trade, will be outweighed by the gain conferred on other countries. If the issue is put in that form and is addressed to a relatively wealthy country, it is a fair argument to use. You might persuade such a country that it could afford to suffer a loss for the sake of a bigger gain elsewhere, the world as a whole being better off as a result of greater international specialisation. But if, as is common nowadays, the argument is addressed to relatively poor countries, then obviously the whole idea of a net gain to the world as a whole—a loss to some countries which is less than the gain to others—is not a very useful one. What you are really saying is that the poor should become poorer in order to make the rich richer. By failing to take account of inequality in the international sphere in the distribution of incomes, the free-trade economists have done a grave disservice to the cause which they aim to serve.

Now let us try to get down to brass tacks and see what this business about terms of trade boils down to. Let us take a country in the sort of world with which we have to deal, with restrictions on its imports maintained in order to avoid a balance of payments deficit. It is suggested, let us suppose, that it ought to make a move towards free trade. If it docs that, its balance of payments will be upset. However, even if you leave the painful method of adjustment, involving heavy unemployment, associated with the gold standard, for the fundamental ideas of which some economists still seem to have a *penchant,* what we say is, in accordance with the Articles of Agreement of the International Monetary Fund, devalue, or depreciate the value of your currency. Here we have to be careful. Devaluation by itself will raise domestic prices, as we know only too well. But what we are dealing with here is devaluation combined with a lowering of the barriers to imports. If the barriers to trade take the form of a uniform *ad valorem* tariff, the lowering of the tariff will exceed the devaluation, since the additional exports resulting from devaluation mean that the domestic consumer can be allowed to buy additional imports. In other words, the domestic prices of imported goods will fall. Against this benefit has to be set the loss of revenue from the tariff, which has to be made up in other ways. This loss of revenue will usually outweigh the fall in prices.

In practice, import restrictions do not take the form of a uniform *ad valorem* tariff. They fall less heavily on essentials—such as raw materials and foodstuffs. While the movement towards free trade may result in lower prices for the less essential imports, the prices of the more essential imports, and of commodities made out of imported raw materials, will rise, since here the effect of the devaluation outweighs that of the relaxation of any restriction on imports. The same is true of commodities the import of which is limited by quantitative import control if the effect of scarcity on their domestic prices is avoided by means of price control. In such cases there is a direct loss to the consumer as a result of the movement of prices. More generally, there will be such a loss if the reduction in revenue from tariffs is brought into account.

Now let us take any important country today, or any trade group, such as the Western European group or the sterling area, and imagine that we ask them to make a substantial reduction in their import restrictions, at the same time maintaining their balance of payments by sufficient devaluation. The reply which we should inevitably get is that that would involve a disastrous fall in the standard of living. Part of this fall in the standard of living is simply a matter of redistribution of income. When a country devalues, you get a redistribution in favour of those engaged in exports away from the rest of the community. But part of the fall in the standard of living—and in the case of any large country, and still more in the case of any trade group, a large part of the fall—is the effect of the adverse movement in the terms of trade which results from a country (or group) pushing more exports on to the world market and buying more imports in return. That is the main reason why in the world today it is unthinkable that import restrictions should be removed, with reliance on devaluation or depreciation as a countervailing means of preserving balance-of-payments equilibrium. When we say that it is unthinkable, it is another way of saying that the effect on the terms of trade would be so great as considerably more than to offset any advantages which free trade would bring with it in the absence of such effect on the terms of trade. Of course, this does not mean that if other countries, or groups of countries, simultaneously lowered their barriers as well, the world, as a whole, and groups of countries in the world, would not be better off. Undoubtedly there is a good deal of import restriction, maintained for balance of payment reasons and not for protectionist reasons, which is purely beggar-your-neighbour in character in the sense that it exists in each country only because it exists elsewhere. That is a pretty severe criticism of the efforts that have been made under I.T.O. and G.A.T.T. to get barriers to trade lowered. If it is true, and I think it must be admitted that it is true, that by some kind of international agreement you could get a simultaneous lowering of import restrictions throughout the world, with every country consequently better off, then the idealists in working things out have in some sense or other failed. My contention is that underlying their failure is unawareness of the significance of the terms of trade in this whole business.

I would say that the reasons for this partial failure are as follows. First of all, the bargaining conducted under G.A.T.T. has all been in terms of tariffs. It was not realised that the world would get stuck with quantitative regulation, which it had been hoped would be only a temporary post-war legacy. Secondly, the very nature of the tariff bargaining itself under G.A.T.T. militates against its success; it is on a bilateral basis, negotiations being conducted between a major exporter and a major importer of a particular commodity. What is wanted is some initiative from the centre, as for example has been provided in the Western European sphere by OEEC in carrying out its programme of liberalisation of trade. On the other hand, a bilateral basis of negotiation would offer considerable advantages if the concessions arrived at could be confined to the two parties. The fact that any such concessions have to be extended to everybody else, on a most favoured-nation basis, has been a serious restricting influence. The world has suffered from a failure to attack the problem of trade restrictions in a generalised manner, while at the same time the advantages of a bilateral basis of negotiations have not been available either. Thirdly, the escape clauses to which I have already referred are too generous to provide a secure basis on which a country can make important concessions. Fourthly, there is the fear of instability in other countries, the fear of undue vulnerability to disturbances originating elsewhere. Finally, there have, of course, been the usual protectionist reasons for the maintenance of restrictions on imports of particular commodities.

When I say that there still persists a large amount of trade restriction of a beggar-your-neighbour character, I do not mean to imply that, even if you disregard what is purely protectionist, you have not got a considerable measure of trade restrictions which is not purely of that character. If, in spite of all the difficulties that I have mentioned, international action succeeded in getting rid of all import restrictions imposed by one country merely because other countries are imposing similar restrictions—we should still be left with a heavy residue of restrictions, mainly taking the form of discriminatory restrictions imposed by non-dollar countries against the dollar world. In other words, there is a considerable discriminatory bias in the incidence of import restrictions. My own view—I know that you are going to have different views put to you in the course of your sessions here—is that the volume of world trade today, which is considerable, owes a lot to that discriminatory bias, and that efforts should be directed to securing a harmonious operation of discriminatory policy rather than trying to outlaw it by more or less meaningless or ineffective talk about convertibility, and free exchange rates, and all the rest of it. The right course, in my opinion, is to introduce or retain a bias in such a way as to relieve the strains which are inherent in the system, and to avoid introducing fresh strains. That applies not only to the trade and financial relations between the dollar and the non-dollar world. It applies equally, for example, to trade inside Western Europe. Some of the difficulties of the European Payments Union at various stages over the position of Belgium, Germany and the United Kingdom have originated from the doctrine of non-discrimination inside Western Europe, and the partial success with which these difficulties have been dealt owes much to departure from the strict letter of that doctrine.

To go back to the relationship between the dollar and the non-dollar worlds, what are the alternatives to trade discrimination? The first alternative is the abolition of discrimination by non-dollar countries, so that their barriers to imports from the dollar world are no more effective than the barriers to imports from other parts of the world. That will mean a large dollar deficit for the non-dollar world, which will have to be covered by gifts or loans, obtained at the expense of one crisis after another and general instability.

The second alternative is the free-trade alternative of the non-dollar world devaluing, or depreciating the value of its currencies, sufficiently to get an increase of exports to the dollar world which will pay for the imports which will come from the dollar world into the non-dollar world if they are treated on a non-discriminatory basis. Clearly these exports are going to be obtained only by a very big reduction in the prices charged to the dollar world by the non-dollar countries, and that is what is meant by saying that any such movement towards free trade will involve a very heavy adverse movement in the terms of trade on the part of the non-dollar world, and a serious fall in the standard of living.

Here is it important to remind ourselves that, by and large, the non-dollar world is the poor part of the world and the dollar world is the rich part of the world. The free trade argument as applicable here is tantamount to asking the poor to become poorer in order that the rich should become richer.

But, of course, it is not practical politics to consider anything of that sort. You would have revolution at once in many of the non-dollar countries if you tried to secure non-discrimination by means of sufficient devaluation. Just think what it would mean to increase the exports of the non-dollar world as a whole to the dollar world as a whole by an amount sufficient to pay for the imports which would come into the non-dollar world from the dollar countries if they were not discriminated against.

The third alternative is that favoured by the I.T.O. idealists, who realise that a certain amount of restriction of imports is necessary but who say that such restriction should be essentially non-discriminatory—that no country should restrict imports from non-dollar countries less than it does from dollar countries. If you apply that doctrine it means the destruction of a great deal of trade between non-dollar countries which at present takes place behind the shelter of the discriminatory barriers to imports from dollar countries. Even the dollar countries would gain to an extent much less than might be expected at first sight. The American motor-car producers would certainly gain if non-dollar countries had to get their motor-cars—insofar as they could afford, under those conditions, to import cars at all—from the dollar countries instead of importing them from one another. But against that you have to remember that the extra dollars paid by the non-dollar world for motor-cars would be at the expense of the dollars which at present the non-dollar world is able to pay for American tobacco and cotton and such-like. The non-dollar world discriminates far more heavily against American goods which are not so necessary, or which can be produced for one another by the non-dollar countries, than it does against commodities which only the American world can produce in sufficient quantities. Against the gain to the American motor-car producers you have to set the loss to the American producers of cotton and tobacco and what-have-you. That is really another way of saying that America cannot sell to the rest of the world more than it buys from the rest of the world *plus* what it lends *plus* what it gives away.

Now, what has the I.T.O. Charter or G.A.T.T. got to say about non-discrimination ? So far as tariffs are concerned, the doctrine of non-discrimination is pre-eminent. Existing Imperial preferences were accepted, but any widening of preferential margins, even if it arises from a reduction of the preferential rate of tariff, is prohibited. On the other hand, Customs Unions and free trade areas, inside which there would be no obstacles of any kind to trade, are acceptable under the I.T.O. Charter, and the same applies to G.A.T.T. In fact they are welcome to that very school of thought to which preferences are anathema. (The utter absurdity of accepting a free-trade area but of outlawing any partial movement in that direction has recently been underlined by Professor Viner in his book on *The Customs Union Issue.*)

So much for tariffs. But I have already said that under the I.T.O. Charter and G.A.T.T. the doors are left open very wide for quantitative regulation of imports. Such regulation, however, has also to be non-discriminatory. The only exception is in relation to 'the aftermath of the war'. Here I will quote again from G.A.T.T.: "The contracting parties recognise that the aftermath of the war has brought difficult problems of economic adjustment which do not permit the immediate full achievement of non-discriminatory administration of quantitative restrictions and therefore require the exceptional transitional period arrangements set forth in this paragraph."[5] And then G.A.T.T., following the I.T.O. Charter, applies two alternative procedures for maintaining post-war discrimination. One is based on the idea of maintaining the existing pattern as it developed in the years immediately after the war. The other provides, by the famous Annex J. of G.A.T.T., an option which has been adopted by a few countries, including the United Kingdom, Canada and South Africa, and offers a rather interesting alternative. Under Annex J. a country applying import restrictions "may relax such restrictions in a manner which departs from the provisions of Article XIII to the extent necessary to obtain additional imports above the maximum total of imports which it could afford in the light of the requirements of paragraphs 2(a) and 2(b) of Article XII"—the escape clause allowing quantitative regulation of imports for balance of payment reasons—which lays down the option of non-discrimination "if its restrictions were fully consistent with the provisions of Article XIII."[6] That is interesting because it does suggest the possibility of discrimination being positively desirable as a means of achieving a bigger volume of world trade than could be secured without it.

[5] Cmd. 8048, p. 21.
[6] *Op. cit.*, p. 50.

Against the non-discriminatory elements in the Articles of Agreement of the International Monetary Fund I feel there is much less objection. Convertibility is here the issue. As laid down in the Agreement convertibility is confined to current transactions, so that restrictions on capital movements are not only allowed under those Articles of Agreement but in certain contingencies are enforced. For currency convertibility in that sense there is much to be said if the road is properly prepared. But those who today advocate it are in danger of tearing up the road. In 1947 we had a crisis as the result of adopting convertibility, and as they feel that any change must be a change for the good, many people think that now we have a crisis the solution must be convertibility. When I offer, in perhaps patronising fashion, a benevolent word in favour of convertibility, as laid down in the Articles of Agreement of the International Monetary Fund, I am only following Lord Keynes, who expressed himself as in favour of the use of powers of negotiation and of bilateral arrangements about trade, but wanted to be sure that in the upshot anything which resulted from trade negotiations was made possible by suitable exchange arrangements. This is quite different from what is intended by present-day talk about convertibility, which is something that is not dependent upon maintaining and increasing discrimination in trade, but is associated with reducing it and eventually removing it. What I should myself advocate is something very different from what lies behind the present-day irresponsible talk about convertibility—indeed it is the flat opposite. What I am saying is that if we had enough trade discrimination, harmoniously and constructively administered, we might be able to introduce convertibility of currency on current account, though I think there is the technical difficulty of distinguishing between balances arising from current transactions and balances the movement of which would really constitute withdrawal of capital. Those who talk of convertibility as a goal are really, although perhaps they do not always realise it, thinking of the re-enthronement of the doctrine of non-discrimination in international trade. That seems to me to mean the abandonment of any effort to get world trade on to a more stable and healthy basis.

CHAPTER 9

# The International Monetary System

*Richard F. Kahn*

If one single reason had to be given for the deficiencies in the operations of the international monetary mechanism in the twenty years after World War II it would be the reluctance to contemplate changes in exchange rates. At any rate in most of the leading industrial countries the parity has been regarded as sacrosanct. If this same attitude is going to be maintained in the European Economic Community (*EEC*) over the exchange rates between the currencies of the members, the Community is in for a rough passage.

Any international monetary mechanism that is to be successful must provide for exchange rate adjustments. Exchange rate adjustment involves diagnosis and prognosis of the relative competitive positions of the countries concerned. This need for diagnosis and prognosis arises whatever the method of exchange rate adjustment. It clearly arises under the Bretton Woods system of fixed parities, to be changed only to correct a "fundamental disequilibrium." Until recently changes in the exchange

Originally publ. in: Kahn, R. F. (1973). The International Monetary System. *The American Economic Review, 63*(2), 181–188. http://www.jstor.org/stable/1817072 [Copyright American Economic Association; reproduced with permission of the *American Economic Review*].
Reprint by Springer International Publishing 2022 with kind permission

R. F. Kahn



M. C. Marcuzzo, P. Paesani (eds.), *Richard F. Kahn*, Palgrave Studies in the History of Economic Thought, https://doi.org/10.1007/978-3-030-98588-2_9

rates of the leading industrial countries were rare and, when they did take place, usually large. The problem, when it did present itself to Governments, Central Banks and the International Monetary Fund (*IMF*), usually took the form of having to decide whether private operators in foreign exchange markets were justified in taking the bearish view which was resulting in downward pressure on the value of the country's currency. Decisions had to be made whether devaluation was justified and, if so, by how much.

It seems to me wrong to think that the need for diagnosis and prognosis will disappear under the reformed system, into which the *IMF* is moving, of more frequent and usually smaller exchange rate adjustments and adjustments upward as well as downward. It will be necessary for the staff and executive board of the *IMF* and for the authorities of the individual countries to maintain a continuous review of relative competitive positions, actual and prospective. The staff of the *IMF* will bear an even heavier responsibility if the function of the Fund is not merely to consider proposals put up to them—often when it is too late for anything other than acquiescence—but to a much greater extent than in the past to take the initiative in suggesting exchange rate changes.

This view will be contested by the school of thought which believes in the omniscience of operators in foreign exchange markets. The extreme members of this school would leave exchange rates to be determined entirely by the market: Central Banks would be completely passive (so that monetary reserves and the *IMF* could be dispensed with). These are the "clean floaters." The "dirty floaters" accept the desirability of some official intervention but believe that market forces will be more successful than the appreciations made by officials of the *IMF* and Governments. An even less extreme position is that adopted by the "temporary floaters." According to them, the decision of timing as to when a change in a currency parity is called for should be taken by the authorities. But they realize that it is very difficult to decide how large the change should be. They believe that if market forces are allowed to operate for a few months (though the floating need not be entirely "clean") they will steer the exchange rate to the correct level. The new parity can then be officially announced.

Those who rely on market forces fail to recognize that most foreign exchange operators are concerned with the future only over a short interval of time—very few with more than six or nine months. On the other hand, an exchange rate depreciation frequently begins by exercising a perverse influence on the basic balance of payments. The reason is that the terms of trade effects on the prices of imports and exports lead ahead of the effects on their volumes. The markets in which the producers in an industrial country sell their exports abroad and their import substitutes at home are usually more imperfect than the markets in which the country's importers buy its imports. This difference is great for countries which play a large part in international trade and for a group of countries which depreciate their exchange rates more or less simultaneously. It usually takes quite a long time for the volume effects to outweigh the price effects. In the extreme textbook case in which even the medium period elasticity of demand for a country's exports is too low to be compensated by the elasticity of its demand for imports, it is a rise rather than a fall in the value of a country's currency on the foreign exchanges which is called for to improve its basic balance of payments.

On the face of it, therefore, those who believe in the omniscience of operators on the foreign exchanges should think that when a currency which has been under downward pressure is launched on a "clean float," its value on the foreign exchanges should be raised rather than depressed. I am not suggesting that the members of this school of thought do believe any such thing. The reason is partly that they are not prepared to work out their belief to its logical conclusion. It is partly that their belief is tempered by an element of common sense. There is a third reason which is less unflattering both to the members of the school and to foreign exchange operators. Usually the decision to call off the fight to maintain a currency's parity is taken after the deficit on the basic balance of payments has grown very large. The improvement which temporarily would result from appreciation of the value of the currency would usually be insufficient to convert the deficit into a surplus.

The foreign exchange operators are therefore right to exercise a downward pressure on the value of the currency. If they are so perspicacious as to realize that, within the short span of time that concerns them, this depreciation will worsen the balance of payments, they will carry the depreciation far further than would have been called for to restore the competitive position. The danger is that the adverse effects of depreciation on the country's money wages and prices will tend to be exaggerated and that the value of its currency on the foreign exchanges called for to restore the competitive position will be lower than it would have been had the process of adjustment not been handed over to the operation of market forces. Furthermore, competing countries may feel obliged to depreciate their currencies in their turn. Competitive exchange rate depreciation may set in.

I dwell on the difficulty of giving a correct interpretation of the operation of market forces because it arises with another method of exchange rate adjustment which is now under discussion, in a more serious sense than "clean floating."

This is the method to which I have referred, and which I support myself, of adhering to the Bretton Woods system, rendered more flexible by some amendment of the Articles. The idea behind the proposal of fairly frequent and usually small changes in parities is that its adoption would lend itself to a process of trial and error and that if on occasion a mistake were made it would not seriously matter. But, because of the sluggishness of the volume effects and the misleading indications given by market forces, it is important that there should be a sufficient interval between successive changes in the exchange rate for a full development of the volume effects.

The confusion caused by operators on the foreign exchanges has become much greater than it used to be partly because of the growth of short-term funds relative to the value of international trade and partly because of the high degree of sophistication which has attended the development of different kinds of foreign exchange markets and different kinds of operations. The development of forward markets has been an outstanding feature. In a sense there is no limit to the outstanding volume of foreign exchange positions. The volume of the outstanding outright sales on forward markets in a currency which is under attack by operators is limited only by the operators' credit-worthiness with their banks and their possession of collateral, and by the cost of a bear position—that is to say, the forward discount—which depends, among other factors, on the availability of counter-parties. A Central Bank sometimes becomes committed to providing the counter-party by supporting the currency on the forward market in order to prevent the covered interest rate differential from becoming seriously adverse, and so to prevent added pressure in the spot market through the withdrawal of spot balances which would be hedged on the forward market. The Central Bank is then subsidizing the cost of maintaining bear positions in the forward markets, and the total volume of such positions may grow rapidly. I do not want it to be supposed that I am a critic of intervention by Central Banks in forward markets. I certainly am not. But the point that I am making is that under modern conditions exchange rate management is very difficult.

One lesson that many of us, certainly in my own country of Great Britain, have learned is that operators in foreign exchange markets are far more troublesome if experience has taught them that changes in exchange rates are apt to be made only as a result of the gradual building up of heavy pressure on the currency—either downward or upward—rather than of an objective enquiry by the authorities into the relative competitive position of the country, actual and prospective. If this is the lesson that is learned, it means that, as soon as it becomes clear that an attitude—either bearish or bullish—is building up in the markets, it is probable that a substantial gain will be made by joining the rest of the herd and exercising some patience. Bearishness is highly infectious. The gain is made at the expense of the Central Bank as and when, after the exchange rate adjustment has taken place, the Central Bank reverses, at a loss, the protective positions which it has taken up in spot and forward markets. It is also a gain at the expense of the country as a whole. But the two gains are not the same because some of the bear operators who make gains are nationals of the country.

Once it becomes reasonably evident to the authorities that the competitive position is becoming unduly unfavorable or favorable, it is important to act with speed before large bear or bull positions have built up. Best of all is to take the markets by surprise. Markets are very difficult to handle when considerable unanimity of view has become established—what is sometimes called "sellers only" or "buyers only." Markets exercise some stabilizing influence when there is a wide dispersion of views (what Keynes called "two views"). A small change in the exchange rate—within the permissible spread—will then bring considerable recuperative pressure into being. And if some fresh piece of news happens somewhat to strengthen bearish sentiment and weaken bullish sentiment throughout the market, the number of actual bulls who become bears will be small and vice versa.

These considerations will be highly relevant if the revised Bretton Woods system is adopted—fixed parities changed, in so far as necessary, at frequent but not too frequent intervals. The intervals should not be regular. A subsidiary aim, apart from the main objective of correcting fundamental disequilibrium, should be as often as possible to take the market by surprise. There is considerable advantage in a group of countries acting simultaneously, but only if there is no danger of a leak.

For diagnosis and prognosis of the relative competitive position of a country, its authorities normally employ two different methods. One is to try to identify a point of time in the past when the country could be said to have been in fundamental equilibrium. Estimates are then made of the movements since that date of unit money costs of production compared with those in competing countries, allowance being made for any exchange rate changes, and of the prospective relative movement of unit money costs of production over the coming years. I shall return to this method and the difficulties involved.

The other method is to make short-term and medium-term forecasts of the basic balance of payments and in particular of the balance of visible trade. This method also involves notorious difficulties and is highly unreliable. One difficulty is to detect the difference between a favorable deviation from the trend and a favorable change in the long-term trend. I can illustrate this from the recent past of the United Kingdom. Some economists, including myself, felt as early as 1963 that the time for a devaluation had come. The Labor Government notoriously missed its opportunity immediately after the General Election of October 15, 1964. Another obvious date was July 20, 1966, when the Draconian "July measures" were announced. That opportunity was also missed. By what now appears to be a sad coincidence it looked for a time as though the measures were operating. The eight months from September 1966 to April 1967 were a period of sustained recovery for sterling from the summer crisis of 1966. The visible trade account had been running at a deficit of about $750 million a year (that is $65 million a month). But in August 1966 the visible deficit was only $37 million and in September the visible account just about balanced. October provided a surplus of about $75 million and November a surplus of as much as about $200 million. But in each of the months from December 1966 to March 1967 there was a small visible deficit. By April, with a visible deficit of about $125 million, the heavily adverse trend, which had been temporarily interrupted, was resumed. However, as the monthly figures become available only some time after the beginning of the subsequent month, and as it seemed possible that April might have been a "freak" month, it was only in June, after the April figure had been confirmed by a visible deficit of about $50 million for May, that it was widely recognized that the adverse trend had been resumed and that sterling was once again coming under heavy pressure in foreign exchange markets. The period September 1966 to April 1967, which had been widely believed to mark a favorable change in the adverse medium-term trend, turned out to be a short-lived favorable deviation from the trend. This largely explains why devaluation of sterling did not take place at a much earlier date than November 18, 1967. There can be little doubt that in some quarters wishful thinking had played a part in maintaining unjustified optimism.

I refer to this episode as an example of the difficulties of forecasting the balance of payments. The other method which I mentioned presents difficulties at least as great. It involves, in the case of an industrial country, trying to forecast both the rate of increase of money earnings per man employed in manufacturing and the rate of increase of productivity in manufacturing, in the country itself and in competing countries. With money earnings rocketing as they are at present in unpredictable fashion, the task is pretty well impossible. This is one strong reason why it is so important to abandon the idea that a currency's parity is sacrosanct. Exchange rate adjustments must to some extent under present conditions be a matter of trial and error. At the same time, as I have indicated, changes in parities should not be allowed more frequently than about once in, say, three years.

So far I have been speaking almost entirely in terms of industrial countries. It is now generally recognized that a reformed international monetary system must make better provision for the needs of the developing countries. The possibility that has been under active discussion is to associate the issue of special drawing rights by the International Monetary Fund with the provision of financial aid to developing countries. There are various methods of operating what is known as the link. The most modest extreme would take the form of an undertaking by the industrial countries that, in consideration of receiving special drawing rights, they would provide untied aid to developing countries, equal to a definite proportion of the additional special drawing rights. Even if this untied aid were merely substituted for assistance that would in any case have been provided by an individual country, but in the form of tied aid, it would constitute some improvement.

I prefer to turn to the other extreme and base my discussion on the proposal that a definite proportion of newly issued drawing rights, in the case of the industrial countries, instead of being issued direct to their Central Banks, should be placed at the disposal of the International Development Association (*IDA*), the subsidiary of the World Bank (IBRD) which is specially designed to finance developing countries. *IDA* would allocate this additional finance, and the developing countries which received it would use it to place additional orders for the products of the industrial countries. The industrial countries, taken as a whole, would thus, subject to a time lag, recover their full allocations of special drawing rights, but the portion that was channeled through *IDA* would be recovered by each individual industrial country not in proportion to its *IMF* quota but in a proportion determined by its success, in competition with the other industrial countries, in securing the additional orders from developing countries resulting from the operation of the link. It should be emphasized that no individual industrial country would be worse off than it would have been if no additional special drawing rights had been issued at all. At worst, if it were completely unsuccessful in securing any of the additional orders, it would still benefit to the extent that the additional rights were issued direct to Central Banks rather than channeled through *IDA*.

If the link were operating at a substantial rate it would, purely from the point of view of the industrial countries, improve the adjustment process and help gradually to bring about a more rational distribution of monetary reserves. It is a reasonable generalization to state that the countries in which demand presses most heavily on the available productive resources—labor and equipment—are the countries which enjoy a strong balance of payments position and are adding to monetary reserves that are already quite unnecessarily large. To some extent—but this is only partially true—they are the countries the authorities of which are particularly worried about inflation. There would be a slight tendency for the producers in these countries, already heavily overwhelmed by orders, to compete least aggressively—and often not at all—for the additional orders from developing countries.

These orders would, to some extent, be secured by the countries in which productive resources were underutilized and whose producers would therefore be keen competitors. The operation of the link would alleviate their economic stagnation. Very often economic stagnation is the result of deliberate policy of the Government and the Central Bank, faced with a basic balance of payments deficit and a drain on already inadequate reserves. The link would by one and the same stroke help to relieve both the stagnation and the balance of payments deficit which was its cause. Not only would the misery and waste entailed by unemployment be alleviated, but productive investment in the industrial countries would be encouraged, and gradually a higher rate of growth of productivity and of the standard of living would result.

It may be asked why the government of a country suffering from stagnation of this kind does not provide more aid to developing countries. The aid would have to be tied. If it were untied some of the additional orders would go to competing countries. The basic balance of payments would become even more adverse, as the higher level of activity would entail higher imports, and the drain on its monetary reserves would become more rapid. But certainly additional tied aid is better than no additional aid at all. It would, however, be argued by the authorities that the object of the deliberate stagnation was to keep down the volume of imports and encourage producers to increase their commercial exports and their production of import substitutes. Additional aid, even though tied, would represent a repudiation of these objectives. The point is that although aid, if tied, reduces the visible trade deficit, it does not—quite apart from the adverse repercussions just mentioned—improve the balance of payments in the sense of reducing the drain on the monetary reserves. In formal accounting terms, the reason is that if it takes the form of free aid it represents a negative item in the current account invisible balance, and if it takes the form of loans it represents a negative item in the long-term capital account.

Where the stagnation is accidental and not deliberate, there is no case against tied aid. But it is often argued, even in such a case, that by the time the orders resulting from additional tied aid began to be implemented in additional production, there might in any case have been a recovery and the additional production resulting from the additional tied aid would then be partially at the expense of commercial exports, and so of the monetary reserves.

This would still remain true if the industrial countries suffering from adverse balances of payments and economic stagnation were to cooperate in providing additional aid, tied not to individual countries but to the group as a whole. The adverse repercussions would to a considerable extent be avoided and the advantages of more active and prospering economies would be enjoyed. But there would be no improvement in the basic balance of payments positions and the drains on reserves.

The great advantage of the link over such an arrangement is twofold. First of all, the grouping of the depressed industrial countries would not have to be organized but it would to some extent take place of its own accord. Much more important, it would mean an improvement in the behavior of the reserves, in the sense that these countries would be earning special drawing rights, in excess of the share determined by their *IMF* quotas. In formal accounting terms, aid financed by special drawing rights does not enter as a negative item either in the current account invisible balance or in the long-term capital account. It is a monetary movement and does not enter into the basic balance of payments. The monetary reserves, defined as including special drawing rights, enjoy the full benefit of the improvement in the visible trade balance resulting from the additional exports to developing countries.

This point, which in a sense is rather formal, is in fact of great importance. One of the most serious obstacles against improvement of the adjustment process is the unwillingness of even those industrial countries which have accumulated unnecessarily excessive reserves to contemplate balance of payments deficits and some loss of reserves. Aggregation of the basic balance of payments objectives of the industrial countries indicates that the group as a whole, if the objectives were realized, would enjoy a substantial surplus on its basic balance of payments and a substantial rate of growth of its monetary reserves. The United States is providing an outlet for a considerable part of this desired surplus and the Central Banks of many of the other industrial countries, together with the Euro-dollar markets, absorb the resultant dollars, balanced by the growth of the short-term liabilities of the United States.

It is widely felt that this is not a satisfactory state of affairs. The operation of the link would result in an improvement. It would result not only in a higher level of aggregate exports of the industrial countries, but also in a partial diversion of the destination of the exports of countries other than the United States to the developing countries, and in an increase of their imports from the United States. The United States deficit would be reduced, and the level of activity in the United States would be raised, while the additional growth of the reserves of the industrial countries which took the form of special drawing rights would involve the substitution of special drawing rights for dollars. In addition, of course, the United States would obtain a direct benefit from the additional orders placed with her producers by the developing countries.

My case is that the operation of the link would be vastly superior to leaving individual countries, or groups of countries, to apply their slack towards meeting the needs of developing countries. In addition to the points that I have already made in favor of the link, there is a further important consideration. There is a considerable time lag between a decision on the part of a government to increase the amount of its aid and the actual improvement in the activity of its industries that cater to the needs of developing countries. It is often argued against those who advocate an increase in aid so as to take advantage of the unintended slack that the slack, it is hoped, is only a temporary phase; and that, by the time the orders from developing countries arrived and began to be met, the slack would possibly have largely disappeared in any case. The operation of the link is more speedy. If forewarned *IDA* would act far more rapidly than an individual government because making such loans is its only business.

I would like in passing to put forward a suggestion of mine that is bound to receive an incredulous reception. So far I have relied on the normal competitive processes of the market to steer the additional orders from developing countries towards the industrial countries that need them—countries suffering from adverse balances of payments and under-utilization of productive capacity. But my audience will remember that I said that competitive forces act in this way only to a partial extent. My suggestion is that *IDA* should supplement the operation of market forces by taxing orders that are placed with the more successful industrial countries and subsidizing those placed with the less successful countries. The rates of tax and subsidy would be determined by the *IMF* and would reflect the economic position of each industrial country. Over a period the aggregate taxes would be equal to the aggregate subsidies. The rates could be altered fairly frequently so as to take account of the changing economic pattern in the industrial world. Of course the rate would not be altered on an order for which tenders had already been invited or which had already been placed. The adoption of my suggestion would arm the *IMF* with a powerful weapon for improving the adjustment process.

My proposal is that the proportion of the additional special drawing rights issued to the industrial countries which was placed at the disposal of *IDA* should be fixed year by year, even though the additional drawing rights were fixed on a quinquennial basis. The proportion would reflect the extent to which the productive capacity of the industrial countries taken as a whole was being fully utilized. This particular method of financing aid could thus be used as a stabilizing influence.

Of course the main purpose of the link would be to secure additional financial aid to developing countries. The importance of this is obvious. There would be some danger that some industrial countries would curtail other forms of aid, which would probably be tied aid, to the extent that they were providing aid through the link. It is difficult to suppose that many countries would behave in such a mean way. But in any case it would be an enormous improvement if more aid were untied. It would mean that a greater part of the competition for orders from developing countries would be competition between producers in all the industrial countries and not merely the producers in individual countries. The competition would be much keener and the developing countries would enjoy the benefit of paying lower prices.

I have been talking rather loosely of "industrial countries" and "developing countries." But of course these vague adjectives cover an enormous variety. It would seem necessary to find some method of grouping the industrial countries—say, the "highly industrialized," the "industrialized" and the "less industrialized" countries. A higher proportion of the additional drawing rights allotted to the first group might be placed at the disposal of *IDA* than of those allotted to the second group, and a higher proportion for the second group than for the third. As for the developing countries, *IDA* must in any case operate on criterions indicating relative need.

I trust that by choosing the link as the final topic of this lecture it will turn out that I am concluding on an optimistic note. Until about ten years ago many economists felt disillusioned about the and the operation of the international monetary system. It seemed that the high hopes entertained at Bretton Woods were not being realized. But a new spirit now prevails. It is not only a question of improved machinery and improved operation of the old machinery. These improvements reflect the strong desire for cooperation between the representatives of countries of every kind and the fruitfulness of this cooperation. I feel that there is good reason for being hopeful about the fairly immediate future of the international monetary system.

CHAPTER 10

# Historical Origins of the International Monetary Fund

*Richard F. Kahn*

It is a great honour to take part in the Second Keynes Seminar of Keynes College. I appreciate the opportunity of paying my first visit to the College and to the University of Kent. I look forward to the other papers which are to be presented this afternoon, and to the discussions, as well as to the opportunities which are to be provided for meeting in a less formal way members of the College and the University. I wish to express my gratitude to the Master of Keynes College, to you Professor Hagenbuch for your kind remarks, and to all those concerned with the Seminar.

As long ago as 1930, in his *Treatise on Money*, Keynes had outlined a scheme for the operation of a possible Supernational Bank.[1] I want to draw attention to-day to only two aspects of this scheme.

Originally publ. in: Kahn, R. F. (1976). Historical Origins of the International Monetary Fund. In A.P. Thirlwall (Ed.), *Keynes and International Monetary Relations* (pp. 3–35). London: Macmillan.
Reprint by Springer International Publishing 2022 with kind permission

[1] Keynes, *Treatise on Money* (London: 1930), Vol. II; Royal Economic Society edition of Keynes's *Collected Writings*. Vol. VI, pp. 358–64 (original edition, pp. 399–402).

R. F. Kahn



M. C. Marcuzzo, P. Paesani (eds.), *Richard F. Kahn*, Palgrave Studies in the History of Economic Thought,
https://doi.org/10.1007/978-3-030-98588-2_10

To assist the Supernational Bank in its task of securing stability of price-levels and of trade activity, it should have power, Keynes proposed, to conduct open-market operations in any member-country, requiring the assent of the country's Central Bank only in the case of purchases, not in the case

---

For a full record the reader is referred to *The International Monetary Fund, 1945–1965*, published by the International Monetary Fund in three volumes in 1969, especially *Volume I: Chronicle*, by J. Keith Horsefield, and *Volume III: Documents*, edited by J. Keith Horsefield. (*Volume II: Analysis*, written mainly by Margaret de Vries and edited by J. Keith Horsefield, deals with the evolution of the Fund's policies.) I have been helped very considerably by Mr Keith Horsefield's volumes, but I have tried to avoid summarising his narrative. I have also, of course, received much help from Sir Roy Harrod's *The Life of John Maynard Keynes* (London: Macmillan, 1951), and from Professor Richard Sayers' *Financial Policy 1939–45* (*Official History of the Second World War*) (London: H.M.S.O., 1956), but here again I have tried to avoid summarising their narratives.

The really serious student is referred to the *Proceedings and Documents of the United Nations Monetary and Financial Conference* at Bretton Woods, published by the U.S. Government Printing Office in two volumes in 1948.

The as yet unpublished relevant papers by Keynes, and papers related to his activities during and immediately after the Second World War, including much correspondence, were assembled for me by Dr Donald Moggridge, editor of the later volumes of the Royal Economic Society's edition of *The Collected Writings of John Maynard Keynes.* They will appear in one of the volumes to be published, it is hoped, in 1977. I wish to express my thanks to the Controller of Her Majesty's Stationery Office (Public Record Office and Crown Copyright materials). Dr Moggridge has supplied me with his draft of his extensive editorial background against which the papers will be published. This has been extremely helpful. Dr Moggridge has in other ways too been most helpful to me at every stage in the preparation of this paper, which owes much to his advice and guidance.

I have also received most valuable help from Professor L. S. Pressnell, Official Historian at the Cabinet Office, for External Economic Policy, 1945–1960. He has been most generous and skilful in drawing on his experience and knowledge.

I have tried to acknowledge in individual notes the valuable help which I have received on particular issues. For any failure in this respect I apologise.

I should mention that Dr Donald Moggridge played an important part at the First Keynes Seminar held on 10 November 1972. He contributed a paper on *Keynes: The Economist*. His edition of the proceedings was published in 1974 under the title *Keynes: Aspects of the Man and His Work.*

of sales. No such venturesome proposal was made by Keynes in the process of formulating during the War his scheme for an International Clearing Union.

On the other hand, his 1930 scheme made no provisions for adjustment of exchange-rates. At that time Keynes felt that some recompense could be gained for the agonies of returning to the Gold Standard in 1925, by a country which was an important international banker and international creditor, by striving for the maintenance of exchange-rate stability.[2]

But by March 1933 the position had been completely changed by the abandonment of the gold-standard in September 1931 by Britain, followed by a large number of other countries. With the World Economic Conference, to be held in June 1933, in mind, Keynes published *The Means to Prosperity.* I doubt whether he realised that the dollar was just about to be devalued. But he did propose an international agreement under which exchange-rates 'should be alterable, if necessary, from time to time, if circumstances were to require, just like bank rate – though by small degrees one would hope'.[3]

I turn now to Keynes's attitude towards unorthodox monetary and commercial practices, designed in an economically depressed world of *sauve qui peut*, to enable an individual country to export enough to pay for its imports. Keynes's general attitude was that if a country wished to take advantage of an international scheme designed to obviate the need for discriminatory practices, it must be prepared to abjure such practices, subject, of course, to the scheme incorporating the necessary safeguards and escape clauses. It was on that basis that, in presenting in his *Means to*

[2] See the *Report of the* [Macmillan] *Committee on Industry and Trade* (June 1931, Cmd. 3897). In the course of an Addendum Keynes and others wrote: 'For a country in the special circumstances of Great Britain the disadvantages [of devaluation] would greatly outweigh the advantages: (p. 199). Sir Thomas Allen and Ernest Bevin did not agree. See also the main Report (p. 255), and R. F. Harrod, *The Life of John Maynard Keynes* (London: Macmillan, 1951) p. 414. Of course, it was impossible for the Committee publicly to recommend devaluation, as this would have precipitated a flight from sterling. But papers of the Committee as yet unpublished indicate that this really was Keynes's view. The same line was taken by a Committee of Economists, of which Keynes was Chairman, of the Economic Advisory Council, which also reported before September 1931 (see Harrod, *Life*, p. 426).

[3] *The Means to Prosperity* (London: 1933); *Collected Writings*, Vol. IX, p. 363 (original pamphlet, p. 32).

*Prosperity*, the outline of an international monetary scheme, he laid down conditions of membership.[4]

In September 1941, together with his first draft of his *Proposals for an International Currency Union*, Keynes distributed in the Treasury a Memorandum entitled *Post-War Currency Policy.* I quote some extracts:

> Until quite recently all departures from international laissez- faire have tackled the symptoms rather than the causes.
>
> It was only in the last years, almost in the last months, before the crash, that … Dr. Schacht stumbled in desperation on something new which had in it the germs of a good technical idea.
>
> Dr. Schacht's idea was to introduce 'what amounted to barter.'
>
> In this way he was able to return to the essential character and original purpose of trade whilst discussing the apparatus which had been supposed to facilitate, but was in fact strangling it. This innovation worked well, indeed brilliantly.

Without barter,

> impoverished Germany … could scarcely have embarked on war. But, as Mr. [Hubert] Henderson remarks, the fact that this method was used in the service of evil must not blind us to its possible technical advantages in the service of a good cause. 'If Germany', he pointed out, 'had wished for butter instead of guns or aeroplanes, there is no reason to doubt that Dr. Schacht's expedients would have enabled her to obtain the butter instead of the metal from overseas.'

The alternative, Keynes suggested, to the kind of scheme set out in his International Currency Union paper, was

> not a return to the currency disorders of the epoch between the wars … but a refinement and improvement of the Schachtian device.
>
> Of the special measures which it is open to us to employ by far the most potent is to use the importance of the British market to producers of food and raw materials overseas as an inducement to them to make equivalent purchases of manufactured goods from us.
>
> This is a legitimate arrangement greatly in the interests of both parties. Without it … both countries would be condemned to unemployment and

[4] Ibid, p. 361 (original pamphlet, p. 30). See Harrod's *Life*, p. 443–4.

> impoverishment. It may be the only feasible means of maximising the value of international exchange.
>
> It would be madness on our part to deprive ourselves of the possibility of action along the above lines until we have a firm assurance of an equally satisfactory solution of a different kind. Anyone who at this stage would agree to sign away our future liberty of action would be as great a traitor to his country as if he were to sign away the British navy before he had a firm assurance of an alternative means of protection.

These preparations for peace had started, in September 1941, on Keynes's initiative, when it looked remote, as indeed it was. The Russians were being pushed back under the pressure of the German attack, the position in the Western Desert was to remain perilous for another year, and three months had still to elapse before the Japanese attack on Pearl Harbour was to bring the United States, and Japan, into the War.

Actually, preliminary talks with the Americans about post-war arrangements had begun in the early summer of 1941. The principle of Lend-Lease had been announced in January 1941 (after the re-election of President Roosevelt in November 1940), when Britain had sold out her last dollar and was in a peculiarly weak bargaining position.[5] The Lend-Lease Act was passed on 11 March. It 'called for negotiation of some "consideration", other than current payment, whereby the recipient nation was to repay the implicit debt ...' Congress left it to the President to negotiate the 'consideration',[6] i.e. the 'repayment consideration'.

On 13 June 1941 President Roosevelt was able to report to Congress that work had started. Keynes had had preliminary discussions in Washington.[7] The President entrusted them to the State Department rather than the Treasury. The Secretary of State, Cordell Hull, suffered from a 'particular bugbear – and this was in line with State Department tradition' – in the form of 'discrimination'. The Ottawa Agreements, providing for Imperial Preference, were 'particularly offensive to him'.[8]

[5] See R. S. Sayers, *Financial Policy 1939–1945 (Official History of the Second World War* (London: HMSO, 1956), pp. 18, 372–83, and 405. By August 1945, when Lend-Lease aid was abruptly and unexpectedly terminated on the surrender of Japan, the total was going to mount up to $30,000 million (ibid., p. 546).

[6] Ibid., p. 382.

[7] Ibid., p. 406.

[8] Harrod, *Life*, p. 511.

The first formal agreement took the form of the Atlantic Charter, of 14 August 1941, a Joint Declaration by the President of the U.S.A. and Winston Churchill, who met on the *Prince of Wales* off Newfoundland.[9] The fourth principle agreed to in the Charter provided for 'access, on equal terms, to the trade and to the raw materials of the world', 'by all States, great or small, victors or vanquished'. The President wished to add the words 'without discrimination and on equal terms', which, according to Cordell Hull, would have 'embodied the ideal for which the State Department had striven for the past nine years'. They would not only have meant the end of Imperial Preference, but, in the words of a senior Treasury official, quoted by Professor Richard Sayers, would have prevented any 'form of orderly regulation through the medium of exchange control, trade and payments agreements, output arrangements, and the like', which seemed essential for coping with the country's post-war difficulties in external monetary and commercial arrangements. The President gave way to Winston Churchill, and the offensive words were omitted.

The battle which resulted in this victory had been joined in the previous month between Keynes and the Americans on the instructions of the President over the drafting of what was to become Article VII of the Mutual Aid Agreement, not to be finally signed until 23 February 1942. It soon turned out that the British victory over the Atlantic Charter was not decisive.[10]

In the month before the Atlantic meeting of the two Heads of State, Keynes had, as I have indicated, been heavily engaged in Washington in the battle. He made it clear to the State Department that Britain would have to adopt Schachtian methods unless, to quote Sir Roy Harrod, 'there was a large joint Anglo-American effort to restore equilibrium of trade and thus make such measures unnecessary'. Sir Roy Harrod writes that what Keynes had mainly in mind 'was the application with American assistance of Keynesian remedies for unemployment and trade depression on a world scale', and also 'the appalling problem that Britain would face alter the war in the matter of her own trade balance'.[11]

Although that was not what the President intended, the State Department on 28 July 1941 handed Keynes a draft of Article VII which specifically provided for non-discrimination. Keynes is said to have referred

[9] Cmd. 6321 (HMSO). See Sayers, op. cit., pp. 409–10.
[10] See Sayers, op. cit., p. 410.
[11] Harrod, *Life*, pp. 512–13.

to it 'as the lunatic proposals of Mr. Hull'. He returned to London where he discussed the State Department draft just about the time of the signing of the Atlantic Chatter. He reported that Dean Acheson of the State Department had agreed that the draft, if accepted, would mean the end of Imperial Preference but that he was ambivalent on the question whether it would preclude import and exchange control.[12]

What was to prove the solution to the *impasse* was hammered out inside the State Department in the latter part of August.[13] It took the form of a provision that 'at an early convenient date conversations shall be begun between the two Governments with a view to determining ... the best means of attaining the above-stated objectives'. Meanwhile there was to be no commitment.

Nevertheless, negotiations dragged on, and not even the entry of the United States into the War as a belligerent, as a result of the attack on Pearl Harbour on 7 December 1941, brought them to an immediate head, in spite of a meeting between Roosevelt and Winston Churchill at Christmas. Finally, Roosevelt pressed for agreement and signature,[14] having successfully appealed to Churchill to forgo any accompanying exchange of Notes. The President gave his personal view 'that Article VII contains no commitment to abolish Imperial Preference'. This assurance was

[12] Sayers, op. cit., pp. 407–8.

[13] Harrod, *Life*, p. 516. See note 15.

[14] Eventually signed on 23 February 1942. For the full text of the Mutual Aid Agreement see Cmd. 6341 (HMSO). For the full text of article VII, see Sayers, op. cit., p. 413. The following are extracts:

> In the final determination of the benefits to be provided to the United States of America by the Government of the United Kingdom in return for [Lend-Lease], the terms and conditions thereof shall not be such as to burden commerce between the two countries, but to promote mutually advantageous economic relations between them and the betterment of world-wide economic relations ... provision for the expansion, by appropriate international and domestic measures, of production, employment and the exchange and consumption of goods: the elimination of all forms of discriminatory treatment in international commerce.

At an early convenient date conversations shall be begun between the two Governments with a view to determining ... the best means of attaining the above stated objectives ... and of seeking the agree action of other like-minded Governments.

eventually made public by Churchill in the House of Commons on 13 December 1945.[15]

When Attlee announced the broad terms of the Agreement to the House of Commons on 24 February 1942, he was asked about the meaning of the words 'the elimination of discriminatory treatment'. He replied that 'no commitments were undertaken by either party in advance of discussions'. As Professor Richard Sayers writes:[16]

> The 'conversations' envisaged in the concluding sentence of the Article did not in fact begin for some time – but the problem remained a continual preoccupation of those engaged in all Anglo-American discussions.

Keynes's problem had not been eased by the altitude of the Division in the Board of Trade responsible for commercial policy. Led by a well-known civil servant, R. J. Shackle – I need scarcely say not Professor George Shackle, the economist, who was also a civil servant, but a temporary war-time one – they were preparing for a liberal commercial policy after the War dependent on American co-operation, which Keynes felt would not be forthcoming.

It was about two years later, when discussions about commercial policy had been started with the Americans that Keynes was heard to remark that 'what we need is more de-Shackling and more de-Liesching' – Persivale Liesching being the Second Secretary of the Board of Trade within whose domain lay Shackle's Division. It was when they were both engaged on negotiations in Washington in October 1943 that Keynes, in the course of a note addressed to Liesching, wrote:

Americans that need is more

> As you know, I am, I am afraid, a hopeless sceptic about this return to nineteenth century *laissez-faire*, for which you and the State Department seem to have such a nostalgia.

Keynes added that he believed the future lay, *inter alia*, with 'quantitative import restrictions for non-essential manufactures'. He concluded with the words:

[15] Sayers, op. cit., p. 412.
[16] Ibid., p. 413.

Yet all these future instrumentalities for orderly economic life in the future you seek to outlaw.[17]

Sir Roy Harrod at this point in his *Life of Keynes* refers the reader forward in a footnote to the post-War commercial policy negotiations of the autumn of 1945. Sir Roy Harrod describes how, sitting in on some of the discussions, Keynes was impressed by the reasonableness and co-operation of the Americans.[18] Sir Roy Harrod refrains from reminding his readers that, in August, the Americans had abruptly terminated Lend-Lease aid immediately after the surrender of Japan – the only concession being willingness to negotiate the questions of payment for goods in the pipe-line – and that, in the course of the Loan negotiations which took place at the same time as the commercial policy negotiations, 'Keynes approached the point of exhaustion. He had to use all his resources of ingenuity and dialectic to win assent for what he conceived to be his instructions'.[19] These are Sir Roy Harrod's own words. Keynes 'had originally asked for $6,000 million as a gift'. He ended with a Loan of $3,750 million.[20] subject to the extremely onerous terms of the Financial Agreement, and in effect also subject to the *Proposals for Consideration by an International Conference on Trade and Employment, as Transmitted by the Secretary of State of the U.S.A. to His Majesty's Ambassador at Washington*,[21] on the same day – 6 December 1945 – as that on which the Financial Agreement was completed, together with a *Joint Statement* in which the British Government accepted the *Proposals* as a basis for international discussion.

According to Sir Roy Harrod, Keynes's mind 'reverted to Adam Smith and to the great truths which he preached'. The outcome was Keynes's posthumous article on *The Balance of Payments of the United States*.[22] It had its origins in an analytical telegram sent to London during the Loan negotiations. After returning to London, Keynes obtained permission to turn the telegram into an article, which at the end of January 1946 he sent to Sir Roy Harrod, who had succeeded Keynes as one of the editors of the *Economic Journal*. It was felt unwise to publish the article until the Loan had been passed by Congress, as the article could be interpreted to

[17] Harrod, *Life*, pp. 567–68.
[18] Ibid., p. 609.
[19] Ibid., p. 612.
[20] Ibid., pp. 610–11.
[21] Cmd. 6709.
[22] *Economic Journal* (London), June 1946; reprinted by Macmillan.

indicate that Britain s post-war problems of international payments would not be so overwhelming as was being contended. Keynes took advantage of the delay to improve the Statistical Tables.

After Keynes's death in April 1946, I, as one of his executors, was asked by Wilfrid Eady of the Treasury to consider whether the article could not, for the time being, be suppressed. Although it was clear that Congress would have passed the Loan by the time the article was due to be published, the Savannah Conference of the previous month, at which the International Monetary Fund was inaugurated, had in a brutal manner revealed – especially, as I shall be demonstrating, to Keynes – that the Americans were not going to prove so easy to deal with as, over a short phase of a few months, Keynes may conceivably have become lulled into believing. Keynes had been forced to accept, as a condition for the Loan, and had forced the British Government to accept. Section 8 of the Financial Agreement,[23] under which within a period of a year, unless a later date was negotiated, current account convertibility had to be introduced. Eady may have had uneasy forebodings, in the outcome justified by the convertibility crisis of August 1947. The Government had finally agreed only after taking the extraordinary step of sending Edward Bridges, Permanent Secretary to the Treasury, over to Washington to be convinced that the position was quite as hopeless as Keynes's telegrams purported it to be. As to the article, Eady and I agreed that it would be wrong for me temporarily to suppress it, and I doubt whether its publication did in the outcome aggravate our difficulties with the Americans.

Keynes commended the Articles of Agreement of the IMF to the House of Lords in a speech delivered on 23 May 1944.[24] It is true that he spoke with contempt of 'a system of bilateral and barter agreements'. But he

[23] Of 6 December 1945; Cmd. 6708. Keynes had unfortunately (as Sir Roy Harrod points out: *Life*, p. 615) resisted American pressure to insert a firm obligation on the United Kingdom to freeze the sterling balances by a certain date. But he was glad to accept, in the form of Section 10 (i), a statement of intention. Certainly Keynes assumed that the intention would be carried out before any attempt was made to introduce convertibility. But after Keynes's death little was done, and the abortive attempt to introduce convertibility was made in August 1947 under conditions which neither Keynes nor the Americans had envisaged. See Harrod, op. cit., pp. 607–8 and 615. Dr Donald Moggridge has pointed out that the problem presented by the *accumulated* sterling balances had been foreseen and that for failure to deal with it the Americans were not to blame. ('From war to peace – the sterling balances', *The Banker* (London), August 1972, pp. 1032–35.)

[24] *Official Report*, House of Lords; Seymour Harris, *The New Economics* (New York: 1948), pp. 371, 372 and 377.

admitted that 'it might make more sense' 'when all else had failed us, with this small country driven to autarchy'. On the question of commercial discrimination, he said 'there is no compulsion on us, and if we choose to come to a particular bargain in the country where we have resources, then that is entirely at our discretion'.

The question had been raised whether it was wise to become committed to an international monetary scheme before the character of other international schemes, especially in the commercial field, were known. Keynes's reply was that 'if we gain less assistance from other measures than we now hope, an agreed machinery of adjustment on the monetary side will be all the more necessary'.

In replying to a commentary on the IMF Articles which Professor Joan Robinson sent to Keynes in September 1944, Keynes wrote:

> I do not follow why the Monetary Agreement has to wait for the Commercial Policy. As regards the Commercial Policy, there are really two alternatives. The one is that we do nothing. The other is that we enter into a multilateral convention consistent with Article VII. If the Monetary Plan is itself a fairly good plan it would be required whichever of the above alternatives emerged ... You are like the investors who refuse to buy railway shares because they do not know whether the railways are going to be nationalised or not, yet nevertheless are prepared to agree that if they are nationalised the shares will be worth more, and if they are not nationalised the shares will be worth more.

In the course of her reply, Professor Joan Robinson wrote that 'your remarks about railway nationalisation leave my withers unwrung'.

In this context, account must be taken of certain dates. The Bretton Woods Conference ended on 22 July 1944. The Loan negotiations with the U.S.A., and also with Canada, a favourable outcome to which was so vital, began in September 1945. The Financial Agreement with the Americans was signed on 6 December 1945. At the same time as the Loan negotiations, commercial policy was also being negotiated in Washington, resulting in the *Proposals* of the same date for *Consideration by an International Conference.*

Both the Final Act of the Bretton Woods Conference of August 1944 and the Financial Agreement of 6 December 1945 had to be ratified by Parliament by 31 December 1945 because Congress had made participation in the IMF by other countries by that date a condition of their own membership, and wanted also to be sure about the Financial Agreement before agreeing to membership.

The first meeting of the Economic and Social Council of the United Nations was held in February 1946. At that meeting a resolution was passed condemning trade barriers and discrimination and welcoming an extension of multilateral trade. The Preparatory Committee of the United Nations Conference on Trade and Employment agreed to the text of what was to become the General Agreement on Tariffs and Trade (GATT) in November 1946.[25] The Conference itself did not meet, in Havana, until 21 November 1947 and ended on 24 March 1948.[26]

GATT does make provision for quantitative import restriction designed to safeguard a country's balance of payments position, even if its balance of payments difficulties result from 'the achievement and maintenance of full employment' or from 'reconstruction and development of its industrial and other economic resources'.[27] How very old-fashioned and out-of-date these words sound today – 'Keynesianism gone mad' would be a widely held view.

Any such import restriction has to be non-discriminatory – quite unlike the restrictions nowadays imposed by wealthy countries against textile imports from poor countries. Also there is provision for quantitative import restriction to protect particular producers who are suffering, or threatened with, serious injury from competitive imports. The fault has lain not in the Regulations, but in the reluctance of Governments to take advantage of them.

The Treaty of Rome, which governs the EEC, makes similar provision for balance of payments difficulties or the threat of such difficulties, if the mutual assistance recommended by the Commission is not granted by the council or if it is insufficient.[28] Here the protective measures which become applicable are clearly intended to discriminate against non-members of the EEC. In the case of the EEC there has been less reluctance than in that of GATT to resort to these escape clauses.

[25] *Report of the First Session of the Preparatory Committee of the United Nations Conference on Trade and Employment*, (HMSO), October 1946. (*October 1946* is the date on the outside cover, but the seminar lasted from 15 October until 26 November.)

[26] For the *Final Act* and the *Havana Charter*, see Cmd. 7375.

[27] Cmd. 7375, Articles 21, 22 and 40; also Cmd. 7258 (November 1947) and Cmd. 8048 (September 1950), Articles XII, XIII and XIX.

[28] *Treaty Establishing the European Economic Community*, Rome, 25 March 1957, Articles 108 and 109 (HMSO, 1962).

It was in preparation for the 'conversations between the two Governments', envisaged in Article VII, that on both sides of the Atlantic thought began to be devoted to the future of the international monetary system. In London it began with Keynes, who completed the first draft of his *Proposals for an International Currency Union* on 8 September 1941. Mr Keith Horsefield writes that, on the other side of the Atlantic, a scheme for stabilising exchange-rates had taken shaped in Harry White's mind by the summer of 1941.[29] But Sir Roy Harrod thinks that he was some months behind Keynes.[30] Sir Roy Harrod and Mr Horsefield agree that at that stage there was no communication between Keynes and White, although Keynes had known White since 1933 and had met him in Washington immediately before he prepared his draft.

I do not intend to give a detailed record of the various steps which led up to the signing of the Final Act at Bretton Woods on 22 July 1944. Almost three years had elapsed since Keynes and White prepared their first drafts. What I want to do is to select a limited number of key issues which were the subject of controversy, especially between the representatives of the United Kingdom and the United States. So far as possible I want to avoid the intricate technicalities which arc necessarily inherent in the subject-matter of my paper.

It should be borne in mind that I am concerned only with the actual form in which the Articles of the IMF emerged from the Bretton Woods Conference, and with the intentions of the Conference, so far as they can be identified. Developments since the setting up of the Fund are outside the scope of this paper.

For the sake of brevity and clarity, I shall refer to the *Keynes Plan* and the *White Plan*. The member countries of Keynes's *Union* bank with it and keep balances with it or run overdrafts with it. On the other hand, White's *Fund* banks with the member countries, which allow it to hold and draw on their local funds. If, under the *Keynes Plan*, a member draws on the Union, its own balance is diminished and the balances of other members are increased. If, under the *White Plan*, a member draws on the Fund, the Fund's balances with that member are increased and its balances with other members are diminished.

Before I come to the main issues which I want to discuss, a very brief history may be useful.

[29] J. Keith Horsefield, *The International Monetary Fund, 1945–1965*, Vol. I, p. 11.
[30] Harrod, *Life*, pp. 539–40.

For some months Keynes's draft aroused little comment in the Treasury, except from economists – I am this afternoon adopting the highly fictitious device of regarding the Economic Section of the Offices of the War Cabinet as part of the Treasury.

A second draft led to more comment. Lord Robbins described it as a 'real release of fresh air in this surcharged and stale atmosphere'. Dennis Robertson wrote: 'I sat up last night reading your revised "Proposals" with great excitement and a growing hope that the spirit of Burke and Adam Smith is on earth again'.[31] On the other hand, in Hubert Henderson the *Proposals* raised a feeling of 'profound aversion'.

The permanent civil servants were, on the whole, sceptical. In a letter to Richard Hopkins, the Second Secretary in charge of external finance, Keynes wrote:

> You make me feel again what I have felt so often in the last twenty-five years how fearfully and dangerously rash you cautious people are.

In July 1942 a copy of the draft White Plan arrived in the Treasury by an unorthodox route. At the end of August Keynes's fifth draft was sent to White. Keynes's immediate reaction to White's draft was that it was 'a tremendous labour to read and digest in full. It obviously won't work'. And 'seldom have I been simultaneously so much bored and so much interested'.

On 7 April 1943 the Keynes Plan was published.[32] The President was opposed at that stage to publication of the White Plan, but, as a result of a leak in the London *Financial News*, it was also published on 7 April.[33] The American press supported the White Plan, the British press the Keynes Plan. But the British support was more vigorous than the American support. Mr Horsefield has failed to find any British writer who preferred the White Plan, or any American writer who supported the Keynes Plan.

Official representatives of other countries were generally in support of the Keynes, rather than the White, Plan, but some of them were reluctant openly to take sides against the Americans. There was little noticeable opposition to the Keynes Plan in Britain, though occasional traces of

[31] Ibid., p. 331.

[32] *Proposals for an International Clearing Union* (Cmd. 6437, April 1943; Horsefield, Vol. III, pp. 19–36).

[33] *Federal Reserve Bulletin*, Vol. 29 (1943), pp. 501–21. (Mr Horsefield in his Vol. III reproduces the revised version published on 10 July 1943, pp. 83–96).

scepticism. Conservative Members of Parliament supported it, with the exception of Lord Boothby, then a member of the House of Commons, who carried his opposition to considerable lengths – and still maintains it. Keynes commended his plan to the House of Lords on 18 May 1943.[34]

British and American experts, led by Keynes and White, held formal meetings in September and October 1943. After extensive redrafting, a final version was published in April 1944, under the title *Joint Statement by Experts on the Establishment of An International Monetary Fund.*[35] It was introduced by some *Explanatory Notes by the United Kingdom Experts*, setting out some of the more important respects in which the *Joint Statement* differed from, or resembled, the Keynes Plan. At this stage, so far as the form of the Plan was concerned, Keynes had conceded victory to White.

A Debate in the House of Commons took place on 10 May 1944. Keynes, sitting in the Peers' Gallery, was 'lacerated in mind and body'. A letter from Lord Balogh, which had appeared that morning in *The Times*,[36] was commented on in the course of the Debate, and led to a second letter from Lord Balogh appearing eight days later. Keynes replied that 'since the monetary proposals are concerned only with currency, they involve no commitments about commercial arrangements'. However, Keynes went on to write that 'Schachtian minds ill consort with great Empires'. A spirited reply from Thomas Balogh was not printed. A postscript which Thomas Balogh published in his book is well worth reading.[37]

Keynes spoke in the Debate in the House of Lords on 23 May 1944.[38]

The Bretton Woods Conference opened on 1 July 1944. Lord Robbins commented at the time in a note:[39]

> At the end of the Conference Keynes capped the proceedings by one of his most felicitous speeches, and the delegates paid tribute by rising and applauding again and again. In a way, this is one of the greatest triumphs of his life. Scrupulously obedient to his instructions, battling against fatigue and weakness, he has thoroughly dominated the conference.

[34] House of Lords, *Official Report*, 18 May 1943 (Seymour Harris, op. cit., pp. 359–68).

[35] *Joint Statement by Experts on the Establishment of an International Monetary Fund* (Cmd. 6519 (April 1944); Horsefield, Vol. III, pp. 128–35).

[36] Balogh, *Unequal Partners* (Oxford: Blackwell, 1963), Vol. II, pp. 114–16).

[37] Ibid., pp. 116–20 and 125–6.

[38] House of Lords, *Official Report*, 23 May 1944 (Seymour Harris, op. cit., pp. 369–79).

[39] See also Robbins, *Autobiography*, p. 200.

I turn now to a number of specific issues. An attempt to make an appreciation of the development of Keynes's attitude presents the difficulty that while Keynes was obviously fighting a rearguard action, constantly being forced to yield ground to the Americans, he was claiming from time to time that his concessions on points to which he had attached importance were not after all of serious consequence. He was terrified of failing to secure agreement with the Americans, and, at the same time, he had to maintain the *morale* of the U.K. Delegation, of officials and Ministers in London, of the Bank of England – and of himself.

The Americans were apt, as is their habit, to use the argument that if they yielded ground, Congress would refuse to ratify. In addition the views of American bankers were frequently invoked.

I begin with the basic issue of the language in which the Articles of the new organisation should be written – Keynes language or White language. The British took the line that the Keynes language was easier to follow.

Certainly the issue of Special Drawing Rights is a reform which would have been achieved earlier if Keynes language had been adopted. It is much easier to conceive of the transferring of a credit balance from one country to another than of an overdraft facility. And the Link between the creation of Special Drawing Rights and aid to developing countries would be easier to forge in Keynes language.

Keynes was apt to jeer at the infelicities of White's language. But it was not only a matter of language. It was also a question of literary style. Keynes did not help matters by calling White's language Cherokee, and contrasting it with his own *Christian* English (my italics: Morgenthau, the Secretary of the Treasury; White, and Bernstein, also of the Treasury, who played a very prominent part, were all Jews).

However the fundamental differences between the earlier drafts of the Keynes Plan and the White Plan were not just a matter of language. In its original form the White Plan did not provide for multilateral clearing. It was too much tied up with gold. Morgenthau, on one occasion in September 1943, presiding at a luncheon party for Keynes, Lord Robbins and White, reported that Winston Churchill had said:

> There is too much gold business in the Stabilization Fund [the White Plan]. The one mistake in my life was listening to Treasury advice and going back to the gold standard.

In fact the White Plan bore some resemblance to the gold standard. For its main object was to secure stable exchange-rates. Keynes's main object was to enable exchange-rate adjustments to be made in an orderly way, and to help countries to weather balance of payments troubles. Phillips, the Treasury representative in Washington, reported that the President had turned the White Plan down because it did not provide genuine international money.

However, in a letter from Bretton Woods written to the Governor of the Bank of England, Keynes wrote: 'In the Fund we have in truth got both in substance and in phrasing all that we could reasonably hope for'.

In his speech in the House of Lords, delivered before the Bretton Woods Conference. Keynes had said:

> There were, it is true, certain features of elegance, clarity, and logic in the Clearing Union [the Keynes] plan which have disappeared. And this, by me at least, is to be much regretted.
>
> I commend the new plan to your Lordships as being, in some important respects ..., a considerable improvement on either of its parents. I like this new plan and I believe that it will work to our advantage.

Perhaps Keynes's greatest failure was over the treatment of a creditor country. In his earlier drafts it was penalised in five ways:

1. It received no interest on its credit balance with the Union (in later drafts it actually paid interest).
2. If at the end of any year its credit balance exceeded its quota, the excess was transferred to a Reserve Fund.
3. There was further provision for transfers from its credit balance to the Reserve Fund.
4. A persistent creditor was obliged to revalue.
5. It was obliged to cancel any exchange-control restrictions against the withdrawal by non-residents of balances and investments.

It was argued, on the other hand, that there was the Scarce Currency Clause in the White Plan. This I now come to.

The Scarce Currency Clause was an American invention, which first made its appearance in the draft of the White Plan of 16 December 1942.

Sir Roy Harrod writes that it 'was a very remarkable concession'.[40] Keynes, in the course of a reply to a letter about it from Sir Roy Harrod, wrote:[41]

> Perhaps I ought to have attached more importance to it. I interpreted it as a half-baked suggestion, not fully thought through, which was certain to be dropped as soon as its lull consequences were appreciated.

But the Americans, so far from withdrawing the clause, actually strengthened it.

Professor Joan Robinson, in her article on *The International Currency Proposals*,[42] drew attention to the difficulty of interpreting how the Clause would operate in practice in the light of the fifth of the six Purposes of the Fund:[43]

> To reduce the use of foreign exchange controls that interfere with world trade and the international flow of productive capital.

In July 1943, Professor Kyriacos Varvaressos, the Greek envoy in Washington, sent a Memorandum to White about the difficulties of operating the Clause. The result was to receive agreement from the Americans that:

> The declaration that a currency was scarce would operate to permit all other members temporarily to introduce exchange restrictions against the member concerned.

The Canadians had been unsuccessful in persuading United States officials to agree to this. Keynes telephoned to Professor Varvaressos, congratulating him on the acceptance of his criticism.[44]

Professor Joan Robinson also drew attention to the fact that if a creditor country, after preventing its currency from remaining scarce by making

[40] Harrod, *Life*, p. 543.

[41] Ibid., p. 547.

[42] Joan Robinson, 'The International Currency Proposals', *Economic Journal* (London), June-September 1943, pp. 167–68.

[43] *United States Proposal for a United and Associated Nations Stabilization Fund*, (Washington, 7 April 1943, reprinted by HMSO), Section I.5, p. 5.

[44] Horsefield, Vol. I, pp. 58–9.

a loan to the Fund, wants the loan to be repaid, it can be repaid 'only in currencies of which the Fund happens to have a supply'.[45]

Keynes was ambivalent on the question of how the Clause was likely to operate in practice. In his speech in the House of Lords, delivered before the Bretton Woods Conference, he had said on the Scarce Currency Clause:

> I cannot imagine that the sanction would ever be allowed to come into effect. If by no other means than by lending, the creditor country will always have to find a way to square the account on imperative grounds of its own self interest.

At that time the Scarce Currency Clause made no provision under which the creditor country could prevent its currency from becoming scarce. Keynes did not make it clear what he meant by lending. If he meant lending to other countries, well and good: a country is perfectly free to do that. But if he meant lending to the Fund, a question is raised. In the version which emerged from the Bretton Woods Conference, Article VII (which replaced the Scarce Currency Clause) is much longer. *Inter alia* it provides that 'the Fund *may*,[46] if it deems such action appropriate …, propose to the creditor country that the latter lend its currency to the Fund'. In a letter to Professor Joan Robinson of 9 September 1944, Keynes accused Professor Robinson of treating the word 'may' as though it was 'must'. 'It is only if the majority of the Fund think it advisable to borrow the scarce currency, that borrowing will occur'. In other words, Keynes had by now come to a conclusion opposite to the one presented to the House of Lords – that the Clause was unlikely to result in sanctions against the offending creditor country.

In fact, it never has – thanks to the 'General Arrangements to Borrow', credit for which is nevertheless due to the existence of the Clause.

I wish to return for a moment to the reference made by Professor Joan Robinson in her article to the fact that one of the six Purposes of the Fund, in the American version of April 1943, was to reduce the use of foreign exchange controls. The purpose referred to by Professor Robinson had, in the *Joint Statement by Experts* of April 1944, become:

[45] Joan Robinson, loc. cit., p. 168.
[46] The italics are the speaker's.

> To assist ... the elimination of foreign exchange restrictions which hamper the growth of world trade.

The reference to exchange controls which interfere 'with the international flow of productive capital' had been cut out. But these words from the *Joint Statement* did enter into the final text of the Articles of Agreement which emerged from the Bretton Woods Conference.

The elimination of the reference to interferences 'with the international flow of productive capital' was needed to avoid inconsistency with the proviso that the obligation to abandon exchange controls as soon as feasible did not apply to controls over capital movement. This proviso was already to be found in the *United States Proposal* of April 1943. It was enormously strengthened, indeed transformed in the *Joint Statement of Experts* of April 1944 by Clause V.1, under which

> a member country may not use the Fund's resources to meet a large or sustained outflow of capital and the Fund may require a member country to exercise control to prevent such use of the resources of the Fund.

In the final text of the Articles of Agreement these words in effect became part of Article VI.1(a), except that they were weakened by the substitution of the word 'request' for the word 'require'.

The Executive Directors held their first meeting on 6 May 1946. In the course of the summer Regulations were drawn up. They were based on a draft prepared in the United States Treasury. Among the draft regulations which were strongly criticised were those dealing with exchange controls. Mr Horsefield describes Sir George Bolton (the first British Executive Director) and Mr Rasminsky (the first Canadian Executive Director) as 'the most articulate critics'. 'Mr Bolton pointed out that the draft regulations appeared to be based on a comprehensive suspicion of every form of exchange control'. Sir George Bolton emphasised the inconsistency with the specified tight of a member country 'to impose exchange controls in order to manage capital movements'. 'The regulation finally adopted conformed very closely to the line which Mr Bolton had suggested'.[47] Nevertheless, Regulation H–1[48] refers to 'the progressive removal of exchange restrictions in accordance with the Funds Agreement' without

[47] Horsefield, Vol. I, pp. 152–3.
[48] Horsefield, Vol. III, p. 293.

any reservation about restriction of capital movement. It appears to have been made in blatant defiance of Article VI.1(a).

This episode provides a good illustration of the way in which many of the intentions of representatives of many countries at Bretton Woods, including the United Kingdom, have been nullified by Rules and Regulations made after the Fund had come into being by the Executive Directors, subject to review by the Board of Governors. (The Rules and Regulations in force on 31 December 1965 occupy 17 large pages and are additional to 59 pages of 'Selected Decisions'.[49]) However, I am digressing outside the scope of my paper.

There was marked disagreement on the question of location. There was a strong desire that the Fund operate in Europe. At Bretton Woods it was decided that it should operate in the member country having the largest quota, i.e. the U.S.A. The U.K. Delegation inserted a reservation at Bretton Woods to the effect that 'the location ought not to be considered without reference to the location of other international bodies'.[50] If the Fund had to operate in the United States, Keynes took it for granted that it would be in New York, rather than in Washington, where it would be subject to domination by the U.S. Administration. The American view was that in New York it would be subject to domination by the Federal Reserve Bank of New York and the large commercial banks.

One other important issue on which the British had very different views front the Americans was that of the character of the management of the Fund. Keynes could not see that it need be elaborate, as he failed to realise that the Americans had not accepted his idea that, in large measure, the Fund would play a passive role, its operation being largely determined by its Articles. He wanted considerable authority to be vested in the Managing Director. He wanted a small, highly qualified Board of Management, with expert qualifications. He complained to Brand that White's idea seems to be to have a Board largely made up of retired Indian Civil Servants rather than Deputy Governors of Central Banks. Keynes was strongly opposed to the idea that the members of the Board (the Executive Directors) should be permanently resident in the city in which the Fund operated.

[49] Horsefield, Vol. III, pp. 219–303.

[50] *Documents Supplementary to the Final Act* at Bretton Woods, Cmd. 6597 (February 1945), p. 24.

The *United States Proposal* of April 1943 provided that 'the Executive Committee shall be continuously available at the head office of the Fund'. There was no such provision in the *Joint Statement by Experts* of April 1944.

The British view was strongly supported by the Netherlands delegation, who 'contended that it was essential that the Directors shall be drawn from among the most senior officials in the member countries'. Mr Horsefield goes on to state that 'the majority of the delegations accepted as a practical compromise' a formula requiring the Directors to 'function in continuous service' at the headquarters of the Fund, and to 'meet as often as the business of the Fund may require'.[51]

I now turn to a sad topic. Personal relations between Keynes and Dennis Robertson had in the course of the War resumed some of their original warmth. They became particularly warm at Bretton Woods. Keynes wrote to his mother three days after the end of the Conference:

> Dennis Robertson is perhaps the most useful of all – absolutely first-class brains do help.[52]

In the course of a letter to Richard Hopkins, of the Treasury, on the last day of the Conference, Keynes wrote:

> Everyone in our team has played splendidly together. If anyone is picked out, I think that it would have to be Dennis, whose help has been absolutely indispensable. He alone had the intellectual subtlety and patience of mind and tenacity of character to grasp and hold on to all details and fight them through Bernstein, so that I, frequently occupied otherwise, could feel completely happy about the situation.[53]

Lord Robbins made a note at the time about the seriousness of the drafting difficulties which arose during the Conference and referred to the yeoman services of Dennis Robertson.

It is sad to relate that, only twenty months before Keynes's death, a controversy started over Robertson's interpretation of Article VIII. Robertson was the U.K. representative at Bretton Woods on the Committee concerned with the drafting of this Article.

[51] Horsefield, Vol. I, p. 107; Articles of Agreement, XII, Section 3(g).

[52] Harrod, *Life*, p. 578.

[53] Ibid., pp. 578–9.

The points at issue perhaps seemed at the time to have had a greater importance for the U.K. than has been confirmed by experience. At any rate Keynes took them seriously and for some time they remained an important unresolved issue between the British and Americans.

While there is no reason to think that the resulting controversy between Keynes and Robertson became at all bitter – indeed the written interchanges displayed some playfulness of expression – the misunderstanding detracted from Keynes's delight both over the triumphant completion of the Bretton Woods Conference and over his refreshed appreciation of Robertson's great qualities.

The character of the misunderstanding is technical. It relates primarily to Article VIII of the IMF (although the relationship of various parts of Article VIII to Article V and to Article VI.3 enters into the discussion).

Dennis Robertson, the U.K. member of the Committee which was concerned with these Articles, realised that the draft which the Americans and Canadians were pushing was ambiguous and felt very doubtful whether Keynes would be prepared to accept the ambiguity, and still less the American and Canadian interpretation, although Robertson himself felt that it would be very difficult to secure an improvement on the draft.

Keynes, exhausted at the end of each hard day at Bretton Woods, was lovingly protected from intruders by Lady Keynes, and Robertson was reluctant to impose himself. Finding, however, that Wilfrid Eady had to see Keynes anyway, Robertson explained the issue to Eady and asked him to secure a ruling from Keynes. Robertson's impression was that Keynes was content to let Robertson play the game his own way (this has been confirmed by Lord Robbins). By 25 January 1945, Eady had forgotten about the incident. Keynes writing to Lord Robbins on 19 January 1945 stated that he could remember Eady coming to talk to him but had no recollection of this particular issue being raised. If it was, 'neither of us understood it'.

Originally the Conference had been expected to last a little less than three weeks, opening on 1 July 1944 and dispersing on 19 July. One consideration was the imminence of the Democratic Convention and of President Roosevelt's renomination there due on 20 July. The termination of the Conference had to be postponed until 22 July, the delegates leaving on the following day.

The Washington Hotel was involved in considerable embarrassment with numerous guests who had booked for that week-end.[54] The completion of the Conference was conducted with unseemly haste. There was no complete text available of the Final Act when is was signed; and Keynes signed it without having seen the final version of the Article, the drafting of which became a matter of dispute.

Clearly Robertson left Bretton Woods for London in a worried state. For Keynes was still in Ottawa, where he had proceeded from Bretton Woods for some discussion with the Canadians, when he received a note from Robertson which he found disturbing. The title of Dennis Robertson's Note 'An Essay in Rabbinics' and of Keynes's reply 'An Essay in Metarabbinics' are playful allusions to a well-known remark made by Keynes on one occasion when Dr Bernstein approached him with a great sheet detailing the points of difference over drafting between the British and the Americans: 'Oh Lord, the Talmud again'. (Actually Dr Bernstein enjoyed considerable respect, including that of Keynes and Robertson, as the main force behind Harry White.)

The Bretton Woods Agreement Acts were passed by Parliament in December 1945, without attention being drawn to the dispute about Article VIII.

The first meetings of the Fund and of the Bank, of which Keynes had been appointed the first U.K. Governor, were held in Savannah from 8 March to 18 March 1945. Sir Roy Harrod describes Keynes as uncertain whether to attend but looking on it as 'just a pleasant party'.[55] However, he probably decided to attend because of his concern over the problem of location and management.

In the Treasury Memorandum, parts of which became a Cabinet Paper, which Keynes presented on 27 March on his return from the Conference he wrote:

> We had not conceived it as possible that either institution would be placed away from New York ... Passing through New York on our way to the Conference we discussed these ideas at the Federal Reserve Bank of New York, and found them in complete sympathy. No rumour had reached them of any site other than New York. No rumour reached us until a day or two before we left Washington for Savannah, when Mr. Vinson [Secretary of

[54] Horsefield, Vol. I, pp. 89–90.
[55] Harrod, *Life*, p. 625.

the Treasury and Chairman of the Conference] told me that the American Delegates had decided that both institutions [Fund and Bank] should be placed in Washington and that this was a final decision the merits of which they were not prepared to discuss. At Savannah we soon found that a majority of the other Delegates ... shared our view that this was an unfortunate, indeed a very bad, decision.

This was a blow delivered before the Conference opened. Another blow of that kind was the discovery that Harry White could not be Managing Director of the Fund because the Americans had decided to have an American President of the Bank rather than an American Managing Director of the Fund, and he was to be Harry White.

Keynes was the first speaker at the first session. His speech is reproduced by Sir Roy Harrod.[56] He called for the assistance, at the christening ceremony, of the good fairies. He expressed the hope that 'no malicious fairy, no Carabosse', would attend.

For if so the curses which that bad fairy will pronounce will, I feel sure, run as follows: – 'You two brats shall grow up politicians; your every thought and act shall have an *arrière-pensée*: everything you determine shall not be for its own sake or on its own merits but because of something else'.

Sir Roy Harrod states that 'Vinson assumed the Carabosse had been intended for himself and was extremely angry'. Sir George Bolton, who was adviser to the U.K. Delegation, sent by the Bank of England, has no doubt that the bad fairy was intended to represent the American Administration.[57]

Although the question of location had been decided by the Americans, with Presidential approval, before the Conference opened, a Committee on Site went through the motions of considering it. Keynes was supported 'with greater or less tenacity by spokesmen from London and the Western European countries'.[58] In conceding defeat he said: 'I am afraid that the arguments employed have not persuaded us that a mistake is not being made'. There is much strength in Mr Horsefields's view that, in the light

[56] Ibid., pp. 631–2.

[57] George Bolton, 'Where critics are as wrong as Keynes was', *The Banker* (London), November 1972, p. 1387.

[58] Keynes in his Treasury Memorandum of 27 March. Mr Horsefield mentions only France and India.

of experience, 'this was a battle which had not been worth fighting'.[59] Sir Roy Harrod makes the same point.[60]

Keynes in his Treasury Memorandum referred to Vinson being 'vocally supported (as became usual) by a pathetic procession of stooges … These methods, however, were felt to be distasteful by many, including several of the Americans, who sympathised with and apologised to us behind the scenes, and created for a time a disagreeable atmosphere, though the cloud gradually lifted towards the end.'

The question of the character of the Executive Directors and their relationship to the Managing Director and his staff was, debated seriously. Keynes wanted the Managing Director and his Staff to be in a dominant position. Keynes urged that the Managing Director should be consulted well in advance about prospective changes in exchange rates, and said that no country would be willing to confide in the Managing Director it the Executive Directors were to be made acquainted with everything that was going on. White's reply to this argument was that economic developments of the kind that Keynes had in mind could not be kept secret from experts.[61] It seems clear now that the Fund would have operated with far more secrecy, at any rate in relation to exchange-rate adjustment, had Keynes's view prevailed.

With the American view of the whole-time character of the duties to the Fund of an Executive Director (with an allegiance to his Government in the case of appointed Directors – those appointed by the five member countries with the largest quotas) went ideas of remuneration which to Keynes and many others appeared grotesque. In his Treasury Memorandum Keynes wrote that an 'obstacle to successful opposition lay in the fact that the majority of the individuals taking part in the salary discussion were expecting to receive their jobs. Moreover, political and financial patronage was being created of the first order of attraction for South American (and other) countries – life in Washington with no defined or onerous duties and a grand tax-free salary'. Sir Roy Harrod adds that 'almost all the nations [represented at the Conference] were prospective applicants for benefit of some kind from the United States. Rebellion was out of the

[59] Horsefield, Vol. I, p. 130.
[60] Harrod, *Life*, p. 632.
[61] Horsefield, Vol. I, p. 133.

question. The Americans were "railroading" their decisions through the Conference'.[62]

On the sub committee of six which formulated the recommendations about remuneration, Keynes was the only abstainer. When recommendations came to the Governors, Keynes on instructions from the Chancellor, dissented. 'This was the only occasion during the meeting when a negative vote was recorded'.[63]

The last letter which I received from Keynes was written from Savannah on 13 March 1946. He wrote:

> The Americans have no idea how to make these institutions into operating international concerns, and in almost every direction their ideas are bad. Yet they plainly intend to force their own conception through regardless of the rest of us.

The Americans

> think they have the right to call the tune on practically every point. If they knew the music that would not matter so much; but unfortunately they don't.

I turn to the period which began with Keynes's departure from Savannah on 18 March, just over a month before his death, and ended with his Treasury Memorandum dated 27 March, and its submission to the Chancellor two days later. The *Queen Mary*, on which Keynes returned to England, sailed at 8.00 a.m. on 21 March and docked at Southampton at 6.00 p.m. on 26 March. It is to be presumed that Keynes and Lady Keynes travelled back to London by train on the evening of 26 March.[64]

It seems clear that the Treasury Memorandum must have been in final draft form by the time the *Queen Mary* docked, eight days after departure from Savannah, apart possibly from a few last-minute alterations suggested in the Treasury on 27 March.

[62] Harrod, *Life*, p. 635.

[63] Horsefield, Vol. I, p. 135.

[64] I am grateful to Lady Lee, the widow of Frank Lee, for information derived from her diary about the voyage of the *Queen Mary*. The family had been living in Washington, and she was taking her children back to England, ahead of the return of Frank Lee, for the sake of the children's education.

Keynes travelled by night train from Savannah to Washington, arriving on the morning of 19 March.[65] Frank Lee had attended the Savannah Conference, but by 14 March (at latest) was back in Washington, where he was serving under Brand on the Treasury Delegation. Between the morning of 19 March and the evening of 20 March Keynes discussed with 'Frank Lee how to overcome the difficulties that flowed from the Savannah decisions', and in Washington 'and in New York, he was obtaining up-to-date statistics for his *Economic Journal* article'.[66]

The Treasury Memorandum runs into eight printed foolscap pages (apart from eight pages of Appendices which were clearly prepared by other members of the Delegation). As a matter of drafting, most of it is straightforward. But it contains a number of critical passages which called for skill.

It is unlikely that there was time to begin the draft either at Savannah or in the two days spent in Washington and New York. It must have been written during the six days on the *Queen Mary*. (On 3 April 1946 Keynes wrote to Brand: 'On the ship I prepared a report of the Savannah Conference'.) Under ordinary conditions there would have been nothing in the least remarkable about that.

But first of all Keynes's state of health and mind have to be considered. Although there is no record of any serious heart attack at the Savannah Conference, unlike several earlier Conferences, he was in a very bad state of health, and the frustrations and bitter disappointments of the Conference must have been a severe drain on his resources. On returning to Savannah, Frank Lee expressed concern to his wife about Keynes's condition.[67] He was in a very excitable state and apt to lose his temper. Sir George Bolton records: 'We were all aware that Keynes was a very sick man, but he was still capable of vitriolic comments'.[68]

Sir Roy Harrod states that 'at Savannah all seemed black. The place became hateful to him'.[69] There follows Sir Roy Harrod's dramatic account of the ordeal of walking the next morning from the front of the train to the breakfast car at the rear: 'the greatest agony that he had ever endured in his life'. The start of the walk back after breakfast 'was the punishment

[65] Lady Lee and her children spent the night on board the ship.
[66] Harrod, *Life*, p. 639.
[67] Lady Lee's diary.
[68] George Bolton, loc. cit., p. 1387.
[69] Harrod, *Life*, p. 637.

of the damned ... He did not have to walk for long'. He collapsed. Mr Roy Bridge, who as a young Bank of England official had attended the Conference as an Adviser, recalls helping to clear the breakfast car to enable him to lie down.

Mr Bridge also recalls that the *Queen Mary* had a rough passage. Lady Lee, in her diary, makes little of the sea conditions, apart from the fourth day of the voyage. But she makes a great deal of the filthy state of the part of the ship which was occupied by members of the British delegation. The ship had been used for the movement of the brides of American soldiers, some of them with babies. The result was that everybody went down with some form of dysentery. Keynes seemed ill before the ship sailed. The illness set in very rapidly on the second day out. Lady Lee was confined to her cabin during most of the voyage. Lady Keynes dropped in to see her from time to time. On the third day out Lady Keynes was in a most unhappy state of mind about Keynes's condition. He was very weak – had no strength.

The members of the Delegation who were on the ship were Keynes, Sir George Bolton (of the Bank of England), Ernest Rowe-Dutton (of the Treasury), and Mr Roy Bridge (who did not see Keynes on the voyage),[70] together with Lady Keynes and Lady Lee. (Brand remained in Washington as Head of the U.K. Treasury Delegation and Mr Paul Bareau returned by a different route.) The survivors today are Lady Keynes, Lady Lee, Sir George Bolton and Mr Bridge.

It is clear that Rowe-Dutton and Sir George Bolton were closely concerned with Keynes's drafting on board the ship. No trace of any draft survives until it got into print on 27 March, the day after the ship docked. It seems evident that Keynes was inclined to draft an ill-tempered document. This would probably have turned into a Cabinet paper the style and contents of which might have resulted in a revolt in favour of withdrawal by the U.K. from the IMF (led possibly by Ernest Bevin, but he was Foreign Secretary). 'Such action would automatically have frustrated the US and Canadian Loan Agreements', to quote Sir George Bolton. This was to be avoided at all costs.

*Prima facie* it may seem unlikely that Keynes was in such a bitter mood, and in such an already bad physical condition, much aggravated by

[70] Mr Bridge did meet Keynes frequently at Savannah, and appreciated Keynes's characteristic kindness to junior officials and his readiness to explain the problems which were being faced.

diarrhoea, the condition of the ship, and the state of the sea,[71] that he, presumably unwittingly, could have drafted in such a way as to imperil the Loan which, in spite of his tribulations, disappointments, and defeats sustained during three months of uncomfortable negotiations from September to December 1945, he recommended to the House of Lords on 18 December 1945 in a speech, delivered the day after he landed, which, to quote Sir Roy Harrod, 'was graceful and persuasive: it was deemed a truly great performance. He handled an embarrassing situation beautifully ... He tried to convey to the House the difference of outlook and mood on the other side of the Atlantic'.[72] The speech which he had written on the ship he had scrapped after listening to the earlier part of the Debate on the previous afternoon (17 December 1945) immediately after arriving in London from Southampton.

The evidence for what took place on the *Queen Mary* in March 1946 is an article by Sir George Bolton in *The Banker* of November 1972, together with a letter written to me by him, and Keynes's printed Treasury memorandum.

Sir George Bolton's own account[73] is that Keynes

> spent the voyage in writing an article for publication condemning American policy with extraordinary ferocity and passionately recommending H.M. Government to refuse to ratify the Fund and Bank agreement; such action would automatically have frustrated the U.S. and Canadian Loan Agreements ... The Government had to have the money and also access to the Fund resources ... So Ernest Rowe-Dutton and I spent most of the voyage trying to persuade Keynes from pursuing these proposals. Eventually he agreed to destroy the paper, which was fortunate as it was a striking example of his lack of political judgement.

(The Bretton Woods Agreement had already been ratified by the U.K. It would have been a question of withdrawing from the Fund.)

Rowe-Dutton vetted and approved almost entirely Keynes's draft Treasury Memorandum. He added (but Keynes rejected) a note on the

[71] Sir Roy Harrod is wide of the mark when he writes: 'On the boat he was able to rest; he had some pleasant talks with Professor Jacob Viner, who was travelling with him'. (*Life*, p. 639).

[72] Harrod, *Life*, p. 617.

[73] George Bolton, loc. cit., p. 1387.

closing scene of the Conference, when everybody rose to sing to him 'For he's a jolly good fellow'.

The outcome – by the time that the *Queen Mary* docked – was a sober, workmanlike and well-written Memorandum, betraying no signs of Keynes's ill-health nor of the rigours of the voyage, and only cautiously restrained indications of Keynes's sense of disappointment and disgust. It was, however, remarkably ambivalent in tone. It included no reference to the importance of ratification by Congress of the Anglo-American Financial Agreement, but obviously that could be taken as read.

The following are extracts:

> Nevertheless, the outcome, though discouraging to our previous efforts and a doubtful augury for the efficient working of the new institutions, must be viewed in its right perspective. No specifically British interest has been injured. In the judgement of the members of the British Delegation, the strength of the new institutions has been impaired, both for effective action and for unwise interference alike. The outfit of experienced whole-time Directors and Alternates was imposed by the Americans because they wanted their own representatives to be of the highest calibre and to be free to play a significant, and perhaps decisive, part in the management.
>
> By the time that the Conference was coming to an end, the Americans were becoming increasingly conscious of the force and justice of our criticisms ... They nearly all confessed, in private, to cold feet about the effect of what they had been doing on the daily efficiency of the young twins.

Keynes referred to an important constitutional development in the United States, not by way of pointing to a danger, but as 'for all of us, a step forward, the importance of which is not to be under-estimated'. Under the Bretton Woods Act, Congress had set up a National Advisory Council, to take charge of all economic and financial international affairs, and to act as 'an organ for international collaboration on economic and financial affairs which is relatively independent of Congress'.

Keynes continued:

> It is the character of the duties envisaged which explains the American determination for a team of whole-time directors and alternates of the highest calibre and correspondingly remunerated. It may have been rather stupid of us not to tumble to all this sooner. Some of our criticism and opposition may have seemed childish and a little off the point. But we were not handled in a way which made apprehension easy.

This was the document which emerged from the voyage of the *Queen Mary*. Very few changes were made in the process of its becoming a Cabinet paper. It was not in that process that, as Sir Roy Harrod suggests, the change of heart occurred, but on board the ship under the influence of Rowe-Dutton and Sir George Bolton.[74]

Keynes submitted his Memorandum to the Chancellor of the Exchequer, Hugh Dalton, on 29 March – two days after he had arrived with it from the *Queen Mary* – with a view to converting it into a Cabinet paper. He suggested that the long opening Section was 'too long and has the effect of giving a greater emphasis of discontent than I really intend ... The truth is that my own reactions to the Conference changed with further reflections'. He offered to rehash the document but Hugh Dalton did not encourage him to do so.

No real change of substance was made. Half a page proposing consequential changes in Treasury organisation was omitted, as were a number of Appendices. Apart from very minor amendments, there were only two changes of substance – both omissions.

The seven-line paragraph describing the unworthiness of the motives which explained why there was no opposition (apart presumably from the U.K. Delegation) to the excessively high salaries proposed for Executive Directors was shortened by the omission of the sentence: 'It was noticeable that the French representatives, who were thus placed expecting to be appointed to Directorships and Alternate Directorships of the Fund and the Bank, refused to take part in the discussion, but others were less delicate'.

The following paragraph was omitted:

> In spite of the bad atmosphere of the early days, which I have mentioned above, the Conference mellowed, as generally happens, towards the end. My last memory is of Dr. Harry White, with vine leaves (or were they cocktails?) in his hair, leading into the dining room a Bacchic rout of satyrs and Silenuses from Latin America, loudly chanting the strains of 'Onward Christian Soldiers'. So we must hope for the best.

Keynes, at the age of 62, died four weeks after his departure from Savannah.

[74] Harrod, *Life*, p. 639.

PART IV

# Unemployment and Inflation

CHAPTER 11

# Unemployment as seen by the Keynesians

*Richard F. Kahn*

There can be no doubt that Keynes' distinction between 'involuntary' and 'voluntary' unemployment presented in his *General Theory*[1] was the basis for his analysis of the causes of unemployment and for his formulation of

Originally publ. in: Kahn, R. F. (1976). Unemployment as seen by the Keynesians. In G.D.N. Worswick (Ed.), *The Concept and Measurement of Involuntary Unemployment* (pp. 19–33). London: Allen and Unwin. Reprint by Springer International Publishing 2022 with kind permission

Dr Donald Moggridge (who, in October 1975, became Professor at the University of Toronto), the editor of the later volumes of Keynes' writings published by the Royal Economic Society, has been of great help to me in the preparation of this paper. Those of Keynes' writings to which I refer which have not yet been published will be published in due course in the Royal Economic Society edition.

For the extract near the end of my paper from a Memorandum written by Keynes in the Treasury, I thank the Controller of Her Majesty's Stationery Office (Public Records Office and Crown Copyright materials).

[1] J. M. Keynes, *The General Theory of Employment, Interest and Money*, completed in December 1935 after five years' work (dating from the publication of *A Treatise on Money* in 1930) and published by Macmillan in 1936; republished in 1973 as Volume VII of the Royal Economic Society edition of Keynes' writings.

R. F. Kahn


M. C. Marcuzzo, P. Paesani (eds.), *Richard F. Kahn*, Palgrave Studies in the History of Economic Thought, https://doi.org/10.1007/978-3-030-98588-2_11

the remedies. The unemployment in question was 'involuntary'. Keynes' concept of 'involuntary unemployment' constituted a resounding challenge to the established school of thought. Keynes was entitled to regard Pigou's *Theory of Unemployment*[2] as representative of the classical (now often called 'neo-classical') school.

But here I am confronted by a difficulty. The first use of the term 'involuntary unemployment' of which I am aware occurs in Pigou's popular little book, *Unemployment*, published in the Home University Library series in 1914: 'Unemployment clearly does not include all the idleness of wage earners, *but only that part of it which is, from their point of view and, in their existing conditions at the time involuntary*'.[3] A few pages further on Pigou wrote: 'The amount of unemployment ... in any industry is measured by the number of hours' work ... by which the employment of the persons attached to or occupied in that industry falls short of the number of hours' work that these persons would have been willing to provide at the current rate of wages under current conditions of employment'.[4] Pigou proceeded to base his definition on the drafting of the National Insurance Act. A man is not disqualified from being treated as unemployed because 'in the district where he was last ordinarily employed' he refuses work offered 'at a rate lower, or on conditions less favourable, than those which he habitually obtained in his usual employment in that district, or would have obtained had he continued to be so employed', or if he cannot find work 'in any other district otherwise than at a rate of wage lower, or on conditions less favourable, than those generally obtained in such district by agreement between associations of employers and of workmen, or, failing any such agreement, then those generally recognised in such district by good employers'.[5]

[2] A. C. Pigou, *The Theory of Unemployment*, Macmillan, 1933. The manuscript had been read by Dennis Robertson, more pious in his attitude towards earlier economists than even Pigou, and Robertson had made very valuable suggestions for improvement. It is of interest that at the time when Dennis Robertson wrote his *A Study of Industrial Fluctuation*, published by P. S. King in 1915, his thinking was ahead of that of Keynes, who, criticising an early draft, seemed 'inclined to doubt a fall even in the monetary demand price for consumable goods, and to refer the decline in the consumptive trades to a diversion of productive energy into constructional industry' (Robertson, ibid., p. 221n). Robertson commented on this view on p. xii of his new Introduction to the reprint of his book issued by the London School of Economics in 1948.

[3] A.C. Pigou, *Unemployment*, Williams and Norgate, 1914, p. 14. (The italics are Pigou's.)

[4] Ibid., p. 16.

[5] Ibid., pp. 16, 17. Pigou referred in a footnote to the White Paper, Cd 5991, p. 3.

Excluded under this definition of unemployment are the incapacitated, the old, those who are idle from choice, including vagrants, and those on strike.

Dennis Robertson also used the term 'involuntary unemployment' in his early book.[6] To me it was a shock when, in the course of preparing this paper, I discovered that the term 'involuntary unemployment' was already in use in 1914, and that of all possible people it was used by Pigou, whom in 1936 Keynes was going rightly to denounce for publishing a book (in 1933) which was exclusively concerned with unemployment which was not involuntary.

I suffered another shock when I reread the first few pages of Pigou's 1933 book. Although Keynes was right in maintaining that the subject of Pigou's book was 'voluntary unemployment', in these opening pages Pigou implicitly denied this. Without actually using the term 'involuntary unemployment', Pigou wrote: 'A man is only unemployed when he is *both* not employed and *also* desires to be employed. ... The desire to be employed must be taken to mean desire to be employed at current rates of wages. ... A man is not unemployed because he would like to work if the current wage were £1,000 a day but does not so like when the current wage is 5s a day.'[7]

By taking the ridiculous figure of £1,000 a day, Pigou seriously obscured the argument. What about a man who would like to work if the current wage were 6s a day but does not so like when the current wage is 5s a day?

Pigou's book is, in fact, largely devoted to unemployment of that kind of man. Apart from frictional and cyclical unemployment, unemployment is due to the real wage being maintained – usually through collective bargaining or State action – at a level above that at which everybody would be employed.[8] As Keynes pointed out, the title of Pigou's book was 'something of a misnomer'. The book is not really concerned with unemployment but with the question of 'how much employment there will be ... when the conditions of full employment are satisfied'.[9]

Pigou appears to have been unaware of the inconsistency between his definition of unemployment in the first few pages of his book and the subject-matter of his book. Keynes appears to have overlooked the first few pages. And even if Pigou became aware of his inconsistency after

[6] Dennis Robertson, op. cit., p. 210.

[7] Pigou, *The Theory of Unemployment*, pp. 3, 4. (The italics are Pigou's.)

[8] Ibid., pp. 252, 253.

[9] Keynes, *General Theory*, p. 6.

reading Keynes' criticism of his book, he did not draw attention to it in his review of the *General Theory*.[10]

I come now to Keynes' own treatment in his *General Theory*. Coming back to it after a period of 38 years, I feel that Keynes made unnecessarily heavy weather of the concepts involved. He had said about as much as needed to be said in explanation of the idea of 'involuntary unemployment' in the statement that 'the population generally is seldom doing as much work as it would like to do on the basis of the current wages. ... More labour would, as a rule, be forthcoming at the existing money-wage if it were demanded.'[11] But Keynes' formal definition of 'involuntary unemployment' ran as follows:

> *Men are involuntarily unemployed if, in the event of a small rise in the price of wage-goods relatively to the money-wage, both the aggregate supply of labour willing to work for the current money-wage and the aggregate demand for it at that wage would be greater than the existing volume of employment.*[12]

I am today unable to see why it was necessary to be so complicated. The quotation which I have given from page 7 of the *General Theory* seems perfectly adequate. Or, in slightly different words, there is involuntary unemployment to the extent that, at the current money-wage and with the current price-level, the number of men desiring to work exceeds the number of men for whose labour there is a demand.

There seems to be no need to introduce into the argument the effect of a small fall in the real wage on the supply of labour. (The effect is in either direction according as the supply curve of labour is forward or backward rising.) And the fact that a fall in the real wage is associated with an increase

[10] Pigou, 'Mr J. M. Keynes' General Theory of Employment, Interest and Money', *Economica*, May 1936. In the course of this review Pigou reaffirmed his own attitude. He wrote (p. 131) that Keynes 'tacitly assumes that his full employment (above which no increase can be brought about by additions to effective money demand) is equivalent, allowance being made for frictions and so on, to maximum possible employment, i.e. to the situation at the peak of a boom. But this need not be so. Wage earners may exercise a continuous pressure directed to keep rates of real wages above what is compatible with maximum possible employment. So far as they do this, enhancements in money demand for labour will not be able to raise employment permanently to the boom level, because they will be offset by rising money wages.'

[11] Keynes, *General Theory*, p. 7.

[12] Ibid., p. 15. (The italics are Keynes'.)

in employment resulting from an increase in demand does not seem to be particularly relevant.[13]

I deliberately concluded my last paragraph but one with the words 'the number of men for whose labour there is a demand' rather than with the words 'the number of men employed'. The reason is that apart from 'involuntary unemployment' there is 'voluntary unemployment'. Furthermore, Keynes excluded 'frictional unemployment' – due to 'temporary loss of work of the 'between jobs' type' – from his definition of 'involuntary unemployment'.[14] He also excluded the effect of 'intermittent demand for highly specialised resources', and, I suppose, 'seasonal unemployment'.

Keynes did not, in so many words, refer to 'structural unemployment', but clearly he would have included it in 'involuntary unemployment'.

'Full employment' means the absence of 'involuntary unemployment', but not of 'voluntary', 'frictional', or presumably 'seasonal' unemployment. This leads to a simpler definition of 'involuntary unemployment'. It is the kind of unemployment which is non-existent when the situation is such that an increase in effective demand will fail to bring about an increase of output because it will fail to result in additional employment.[15]

'Cyclical unemployment' is, of course, included in 'involuntary unemployment'. Keynes did not use the term; in a letter to Beveridge he referred to it as 'so-called', and pointed out that 'I am mainly concerned with what you call cyclical unemployment'.[16]

In the same letter to Beveridge, Keynes referred to a kind of unemployment which is not, I think, mentioned in the *General Theory* – 'unemployment due to a lack of homogeneity in the units of labour'. Clearly he had in mind the 'unemployability' which arises when an inefficient man is either unable to accept a wage at which it would be worthwhile employing

[13]The *General Theory* is based, on the whole, on the economics of the short period. It was assumed that short-period supply curves were rising curves. Work done by J. G. Dunlop and Lorie Tarshis threw doubt on this assumption. Keynes rightly attributed his error to me and pointed out that, if in fact the real wage remains constant when the demand for labour rises, 'it would be possible to simplify considerably the more complicated version of my fundamental explanation', particularly in Chapter 2, in which the concepts of 'voluntary' and 'involuntary' unemployment are explained. And 'my practical conclusions would have, in that case, *a fortiori* force' (*Economic Journal*, March 1939, reprinted in the Royal Economic Society edition of the *General Theory*, p. 401).

[14]Keynes, *General Theory*, p. 16.

[15]Ibid., p. 26.

[16]Volume XIV of the Royal Economic Society edition, p. 56.

him because the wage system does not permit it, or is unwilling to accept such a wage, possibly because he fares better as an unemployed man. This kind of unemployment is also, of course, excluded from 'involuntary unemployment'. It is, in a sense, part of 'voluntary unemployment'.

Keynes' treatment of 'voluntary unemployment' also seems to me unsatisfactory. It is 'due to the refusal or inability of a unit of labour, as a result of legislation or social practice or of combination for collective bargaining or of slow response to change or of mere human obstinacy, to accept a reward corresponding to the value of the product attributable to its marginal productivity'.[17] That seems reasonably straightforward.

But Keynes seems to me to place too much weight on the idea that a reduction of money-wages 'would lead, through strikes or otherwise, to a withdrawal from the labour market of labour which is now employed'.[18] In criticising Pigou's *Theory of Unemployment*, Keynes stated that 'the whole of Pigou's book is written on the assumption *that any rise in the cost of living, however moderate, relatively to the money-wage will cause the withdrawal from the labour market of a number of workers greater than that of all the existing* unemployed'.[19] It is not clear why it matters whether the withdrawal would be greater or less than the number of existing unemployed. Presumably it would depend on the magnitude of the rise in the cost of living.

But the real obscurity lies in the concept of withdrawal. Presumably Keynes did not mean the withdrawal which is the manifestation of a strike. What he should have said is that the repercussions of a rise in the cost of living would result in a reduction in the demand for labour to the point at which the supply price of the amount of labour demanded is equal to the new real wage. The repercussions would take the form of a wage-price vicious spiral, which brings restraints on demand into operation, monetary and possibly fiscal, automatic as well as possibly discretionary. Keynes emphasised that organised labour is normally unwilling to accept a cut in the money-wage, whereas it often does tacitly accept a moderate fall in the real wage. This after all is the normal procedure between wage settlements, when the cost of living is constantly rising, in all those industries in which wages are governed exclusively by national settlements. But this fact does not need to be cited in order to define voluntary unemployment.

[17] Keynes, *General Theory*, p. 6.

[18] Ibid., p. 8.

[19] Ibid., p. 277 (the italics are Keynes'). See also p. 13.

At this point I have to make an apology. It was only in the process of preparing this paper that I discovered – too late for remedial action – that it is not I who should be presenting this paper. Referring to Keynes' new concept of involuntary unemployment, presented in his *General Theory*, David Worswick, in his letter of invitation to me, expressed the hope that I would give an account of how Keynes and my colleagues and I 'saw things at the time and how far this has been borne out by subsequent experience'.

As I have been asked to be personal, I am bound to say – partly in a self-defensive, and partly in a shame-faced, attitude – that the concept of 'voluntary unemployment' left me very cold and that I took no interest in the wording of Chapter 2 of the *General Theory* which I have been criticising. I began the study of economics in June 1927. Between then and the date of publication of the *General Theory* (February 1936), unemployment was always over 10 per cent (the number unemployed was always over 1,200,000) and in the early 1930s rose above 20 per cent (in 1932 unemployment was about 22 per cent – a total of 2,700,000).[20] To my young mind the important thing was to demonstrate analytically the hollowness of the arguments that were used against the adoption of the obvious remedies. I recollect feeling particularly incensed by a talk to the Marshall Society by Sir Horace Wilson, Permanent Secretary of the Ministry of Labour until 1930 and then official Industrial Adviser to the government, in which he purported to show that real unemployment did not amount to much, after you had deducted those whose names appeared on the register only because they had staked out a precautionary claim to unemployment benefit but became absorbed again into industry within a day or two, after you had deducted those changing from one job to another or suffering seasonal or cyclical unemployment, those attached to industries in which 5 per cent or less were unemployed, the 'temporarily stopped' and the 'casuals', after you had deducted those who were of doubtful employment value and were unable or unwilling to accept any alternative employment on offer, and after you had deducted women and juveniles and men over 50 years of age. I was still more incensed by the

[20] As a result of the adoption of a recommendation by an Inter-Departmental Working Party, whose Report (Cmnd 5157) was issued in November 1972, the number of those 'temporarily stopped'' is now no longer included in the published figures for the total number and for the percentage of the unemployed, but is published separately. Nowadays it is usually a small percentage of the total, but in the early 1930s it was roughly one-quarter of the total.

notorious White Paper of 1929.[21] The contribution of the Ministry of Labour was based on the assumption that the only persons who could benefit from State-aided works were those fitted for heavy manual work, excluding those highly skilled men whose skill would deteriorate as a result of being employed on heavy manual work. In the Memorandum by the Ministry of Labour it was stated that, although the total number unemployed amounted to slightly over one million, in each year the total number who had registered as unemployed was 3 to 4 million. The White Paper also included the Treasury Memorandum in which the notorious Treasury view was expounded.

It seemed clear that, however successfully the problem of unemployment was tackled, there would still remain a considerable amount of 'involuntary unemployment'. It seemed to me unimportant exactly how 'involuntary' and 'voluntary' employment were defined.

Fortunately, Roy Harrod took the matter seriously and, although he did not receive the galley proofs of the *General Theory* until June 1935, his criticisms did result in considerable improvement.[22]

In the course of his friendly review of the *General Theory* published in November 1936,[23] Jacob Viner commented on Keynes' definition and treatment of involuntary unemployment.[24] In his reply Keynes wrote that 'this part of my book is particularly open to criticism. I already feel myself in a position to make improvements'.[25]

Beveridge, in the middle of 1936, read a highly critical paper about the *General Theory* at the London School of Economics.[26] At a time when there were 1¾ million unemployed, he completely denied that there was any evidence for the existence of 'involuntary unemployment'. He did, of course, admit the existence of 'cyclical unemployment', but had failed to realise that Keynes included this in 'involuntary unemployment' and that,

[21] Cmd 3331.

[22] See Royal Economic Society edition, Volume XIII, pp. 528, 537 and 543.

[23] Jacob Viner, 'Mr Keynes on the Causes of Unemployment', *Quarterly Journal of Economics*, November 1936; reprinted in R. Lekachman (ed.), *Keynes' General Theory*, Macmillan, 1964.

[24] Lekachman, op. cit., pp. 236–8. Incidentally Jacob Viner forestalled J. G. Dunlop and Lorie Tarshis in questioning Keynes' assumption that real wages and volume of output are inversely correlated (ibid., p. 237).

[25] *Quarterly Journal of Economics*, February 1937; reprinted in Royal Economic Society edition, Volume XIV, p. 110.

[26] It was circulated privately under the title 'Employment Theory and the Facts of Unemployment'. There is a copy among the Keynes papers.

though he did not use the phrase, it was the main subject of Keynes' book. Beveridge would have preferred to call 'voluntary unemployment' 'wage unemployment'. He utterly rejected Keynes' analysis and conclusions.[27] In 1944 Beveridge published his *Full Employment in a Free Society*, with a motto on the title page – 'Misery generates hate'. He wrote that: 'A new era of economic theorising about employment and unemployment was inaugurated by the publication in 1936 of the *General Theory* – by J. M. Keynes'. And later on: 'There may be unemployment through chronic deficiency of demand for labour, as well as unemployment through fluctuation of demand and through friction'.[28]

While the *General Theory* was going through the press, Joan Robinson wrote her *Essays in the Theory of Employment*, published in 1937. In her first essay, entitled 'Full Employment',[29] she completely broke away from Keynes' definitions and classifications. Keynes read the draft and, as Joan Robinson wrote in 1972, 'it can be taken that he accepted my amendment to his definition of full employment'.[30] Keynes had written to her: 'I like very much indeed the section on full employment and I think your treatment is a considerable improvement'.[31] On the assumption of perfect mobility of labour, Joan Robinson thought it 'plausible to say, in a general way, that in any given conditions of the labour market there is a certain more or less definite level of employment at which money wages will rise, and a lower level of employment at which money wages fall. Between the two critical levels there will be a neutral range within which wages are constant'. 'The point of full employment is the point at which every impediment on the side of labour to a rise in money wages finally gives way'.[32] In her 1972 comment Joan Robinson wrote that, at the time when the essay was written, 'there had been no experience of continuous near-full employment. I certainly would not want to maintain now that there is

[27] For Keynes' comments in a letter to Beveridge, see Royal Economic Society edition, Volume XIV, pp. 56–9. For the 'mass of statistics' referred to in Beveridge's reply see *Economica*, November 1936 and February and May 1937.

[28] W. H. Beveridge, *Full Employment in a Free Society*, George Allen and Unwin, 1944, pp. 93 and 97.

[29] Reprinted in Joan Robinson, *Collected Economic Papers*, vol. 4, Basil Blackwell, 1973, pp. 176–98.

[30] Ibid., p. 174.

[31] Royal Economic Society edition, Volume XIV, p. 137.

[32] Joan Robinson, *Collected Economic Papers*, Vol. 4, pp. 178,182.

some particular level of unemployment (say, a statistical record of 3 per cent) at which money-wage rates will remain constant'.[33]

The second essay in Joan Robinson's book was on 'Mobility of Labour'. She wrote: 'No precise meaning can be given to the notion of full employment for a system within which mobility of labour is imperfect, unless it is taken to imply a state of affairs in which there is complete full employment all round, that is to say, in which no available labour is unemployed in any district or in any occupations'.[34] In the course of correspondence with Keynes about a draft of this essay, she wrote: 'I am more doubtful about the idea that the amount of employment which is full employment is increased. This seems to reintroduce the idea of voluntary unemployment, which I tried to get rid of in my other essay (on 'Full Employment'). *Individuals* may be voluntarily unemployed if they are holding out for a wage, but it is very hard to make sense of the idea of net voluntary unemployment'.[35]

Joan Robinson was doubtful also about the concept of 'frictional unemployment'. 'It is impossible to … give precision to the concept of specifically 'frictional' unemployment, because it is impossible to make a hard-and-fast distinction between unemployment which is due to frictions and unemployment which is due to a deficiency of effective demand. … It seems preferable to say that full employment, in a precise sense, can never be attained so long as frictions exist, rather than to use 'full employment' in an imprecise sense in which it can be said to be attainable, such unemployment as remains being vaguely attributable to frictions'.[36] Keynes did not entirely agree. 'I have found what you have to say about this is very helpful and stimulating, but I still consider that it is a necessary concept to which it is possible to give a useful interpretation'.[37]

David Worswick, in his letter of invitation, asked me to state whether it was conceived at the time that Keynes' new concept of involuntary unemployment 'constituted a step forward in positive economics. Or was the main implication a moral shift, in the sense that an implication of the concept is that, however much he may try, the individual unemployed man can do little to help himself?' My answer is that the concept of involuntary

[33] Ibid., p. 174.
[34] Joan Robinson, *Essays in the Theory of Employment* (2nd ed.), Macmillan, 1947, p. 41.
[35] Royal Economic Society edition, Volume XIV, p. 140. (The italics are Joan Robinson's.)
[36] Joan Robinson, *Essays in the Theory of Employment* (2nd ed.), p. 42.
[37] Royal Economic Society edition, Volume XIV, p. 142.

unemployment provided part of the basis of the Keynesian analysis of the causes of unemployment and of his exposition of the remedies. There was very little moral shift. This was partly because even a classical or 'neo-classical' economist could scarcely attach much, if any, blame to the normal unemployed individual for being unemployed.

But on the effect of an all-round rise in money-wages in a closed system Keynes did make an extremely important break-through... He was the first to demonstrate that, apart from the effect of a tightening of the state of credit resulting from the quantity of money being held constant, prices would rise in the same proportion, and neither the real wage nor the levels of output and employment would be altered, except in so far as the rise created an expectation of a further rise, in which case investment would be stimulated and, therefore, output and employment would rise.

The final question which David Worswick addressed to me was how far our feelings at the time about Keynes' concepts 'had been borne out by subsequent experience'. My own answer is that the distinction between 'voluntary' and 'involuntary' unemployment, while important conceptually as a basis for the Keynesian system of analysis, has not proved to have any practical significance, either in terms of statistical measurement or in terms of targets or objectives.

In his own popular writings, such as *Can Lloyd George Do It?*, published in 1929, and *The Means to Prosperity*, published in 1933, Keynes had not found it necessary to make the distinction. In the course of *The Means to Prosperity*, Keynes did, however, comment that 'many people are trying to solve the problem of unemployment with a theory which is based on the assumption that there is no unemployment'. In *How to Pay for the War*,[38] published in *The Times* in November 1939 and in book form in February 1940, Keynes simply stated that output could be increased by absorbing a 'considerable proportion of the 12¾ per cent of insured workers who were unemployed (in the fiscal year 1938–9), by bringing into employment ... boys, women and retired or unoccupied persons, and by more intensive work and overtime'.

In 1937 unemployment was still 1.5 million (over 10 per cent). Nevertheless, in three articles published in *The Times* on the 12th, 13th

[38] These three pamphlets are republished in *Essays in Persuasion*, Royal Economic Society edition, Volume IX.

and 14th January 1937, under the title 'How to Avoid a Slump',[39] Keynes sounded a note of caution:

> It is widely agreed that it is more important to avoid a descent into another slump than to stimulate ... still greater activity than we have. ... It is natural to interject that it is premature to abate our efforts to increase employment so long as the figures of unemployment remain so high. ... I believe that we are approaching, or have approached, the point where there is not much advantage in applying a further general stimulus at the centre. ... The economic structure is unfortunately rigid. ... The later stages of recovery require a different technique. To remedy the condition of the distressed areas, *ad hoc* measures are necessary.

Keynes was relying, not on the distinction between 'involuntary' and 'voluntary' unemployment, but – in effect, though he did hot use the term – on the concept of 'regional unemployment', which had not figured in the *General Theory.* 'We are in more need today of a rightly distributed demand than a greater aggregate demand'.

Keynes' attitude, displayed in these articles, is summarised in the following sentences: 'Three years ago it was important to use public policy to increase investment. It may soon be equally important to retard certain types of investment, so as to keep our most easily available ammunition in hand for when it is more required'.[40]

In September 1930 unemployment amounted to about 2,300,000 – above 19 per cent. In a memorandum addressed to a Committee of Economists of the Economic Advisory Council, Keynes replied to a

[39] When I prepared this paper, I was taken by surprise by these articles, which I had forgotten. Unfortunately I did not have time before delivering the paper to track down the following articles, etc. by Keynes: Chairman's annual address to the National Mutual Life Assurance Society, 24th February 1937; 'Borrowing for Defence', *The Times*, 11th March 1937; 'Borrowing by the State', *The Times*, 24th and 25th July 1939; 'Crisis Finance', *The Times*, 17th and 18th April 1939; 'Will Rearmament Cure Unemployment?', *The Listener*, 1st June 1939. These articles will be reprinted in due course in one of the volumes of the Royal Economic Society edition. This will also include relevant papers of the Economic Advisory Council, about which a book by Mrs Susan Howson and Professor Donald Winch will be published in 1976.

[40] It thus becomes clear that one of the considerations in Keynes' mind in January 1937 was the importance of retaining a reserve army of unemployed to meet the requirements of a higher rate of rearmament, which Keynes thought it impolitic to advocate until the end of the following month, by which time the government had indicated a readiness somewhat to speed up rearmament.

questionnaire which had been issued to the members. In answering the question 'how much too high are (a) real wages, (b) money wages?' Keynes wrote:

> If we put our present abnormal unemployment at 1,500,000, I should estimate (in order of magnitude) that one third of this is due to the world slump, five-ninths to the emergence of a transfer problem and one-ninth to excessive real wages. …

Thus, in the language of the *General Theory*, 'voluntary unemployment' amounted to about 165,000. Including this 'voluntary unemployment', 'normal', as opposed to 'abnormal', unemployment amounted to about 800,000 (about 6½ per cent). What Keynes meant by 'normal' unemployment was not made clear.

This order of magnitude, suggested by Keynes in 1930, was confirmed, rather remarkably, in a Memorandum written by Keynes in the Treasury in June 1942 about a draft Paper on 'National Income and Expenditure after the War'. In the course of the Memorandum Keynes wrote:

> Unemployment is due to –
>
> a. the hard core of the virtually unemployable (100,000);
> b. seasonal factors (200,000);
> c. men moving between jobs (300,000);
> d. misfits of trade or locality due to lack of mobility (200,000); and
> e. a deficiency in the aggregate effective demand for labour.
>
> Pre-war statistics are not a useful guide, because at all recent dates before the war (e) played a significant part, whereas the probable heavy demands for labour in excess of the supply indicated below suggest that the most convenient 'standard' assumption for the post-war period is the virtual absence of this factor. An attempt which was made by an official committee in 1935 to estimate the probable minimum level of unemployment, excluding factor (e), arrived at a figure of 760,000 or 6 per cent. Subsequent experience suggests that this survey may have overestimated the number of the virtual unemployables, an actual count of insured persons who have been classified as unsuitable for ordinary industrial employment made on March 16th 1942 having brought out a figure below 25,000, compared with 150,000 *plus* 50,000 casuals' unemployment assumed by the Committee. In view of this a 'standard' assumption of 800,000 men unemployed (or a somewhat larger aggregate of men and women together, 10

women reckoning as the equivalent of 7 men for the purpose of this calculation), which is about 5 per cent of the insured population, seems quite sufficient, made up as indicated above between brackets. It compares with about 120,000 equivalent men, or less than 1 per cent, unemployed at the present time, when factors (b) and (c) above are virtually inoperative. Experience after the last war shows that, apart from a brief transitional period in the spring of 1919, the above estimate would have been more than enough to cover the facts up to the end of 1920, although Professor Pigou reckons that the slump must be regarded as having commenced in the summer of 1920. This should, however, be regarded as a standard assumption rather than as a prophecy.

The argument based on an over-estimation of the number of unemployables should have led to a figure less than, rather than greater than, 760,000. If 760,000 represented an unemployment percentage of 6, a percentage of 5 would mean a figure of 635,000. It seems to me that the figure of 800,000 must have been an error, and the correct figure was 600,000.[41]

Beveridge, in his 1944 *Full Employment in a Free Society*, pointed out that between the two wars unemployment had averaged 14 per cent. In the second war unemployment had been reduced to ½ per cent or less. For five months from June to October 1937, at the top of a cyclical fluctuation, the unemployment rate in London (one of the prosperous areas of Britain) was 6 per cent or a little less. 'By this calculation a figure of about 5 per cent is sometimes reached, as the minimum reserve of labour'. Beveridge, however, arrived at 3 per cent 'as a conservative, rather than an unduly hopeful, aim to set for the average unemployment rate of the future under conditions of full employment. In numbers it means about 550,000 persons'.[42]

In December 1944 Keynes wrote to Beveridge warmly congratulating him on his book. In a postscript he mentioned a point of criticism. 'No

[41] These figures have been carefully checked against a xerox copy of the original stencilled version. The difficulty of reconciliation is enhanced if the 760,000 included women and the 800,000 was a 'male equivalent', indicating a considerably higher actual aggregate, ten women being reckoned equivalent to seven men.

[42] This figure is based on a consistently higher post-war level for the insured population than existed in the 1930s. In his official Report, *Social Insurance and Allied Services*, Cmd 6404, 1942, Beveridge had assumed an average unemployment percentage of 8½. This was partly due to caution. But in addition Beveridge had not yet appreciated the possibilities of a successful full employment policy.

harm in aiming at 3 per cent unemployment, but I shall be surprised if we succeed'.

So in September 1930 Keynes regarded 6½ per cent unemployed, or 800,000, as 'normal', as opposed to 'abnormal'. In January 1937 he took the rather curious line, defended by his fear that the authorities might run out of ammunition for combating unemployment, that with unemployment at over 10 per cent – over 1 million – only regional measures for reducing it should be adopted. In June 1942 Keynes may have argued that 5 per cent – about 600,000 – was the probable minimum. By this Keynes did not mean that it would be unwise or dangerous to bring the figure down lower, but that this figure probably indicated the maximum success which could be expected from full employment policy. Hence his statement to Beveridge that there was no harm in aiming at an average of 3 per cent but it was an optimistic objective.

I have chosen these three occasions on which Keynes faced the question what, in some sense or other, constituted a quantitatively low level of unemployment – one in 1930, one in 1937 and one in 1942 – to illustrate my contention that the development of Keynes' thinking on the distinction between voluntary and involuntary unemployment, as published in the *General Theory* in 1936, is not matched by any parallel development of his method of arriving at full employment targets in terms of actual levels of unemployment.

## Postscript

In the course of the conference I became even more convinced that the distinction between voluntary and involuntary unemployment, while very important conceptually, had not proved important in relation to statistical measurement. Some of the time of the conference was devoted to the idea that, while some people did voluntarily give up their jobs, many of these before long became involuntarily unemployed.

CHAPTER 12

# Thoughts on the Behaviour of Wages and Monetarism

*Richard F. Kahn*

## Sir John Hicks on the Causation of Inflation

I emphatically agree with Sir John Hicks, on the type of inflation which has afflicted the advanced industrial countries in recent years, that 'the crucial question concerns the behaviour of wages; it is not a matter of the working of financial markets but of the labour market'. I am also in strong agreement with his views about the mechanism of rising wages, and so of rising costs and rising prices.

Originally publ. in: Kahn, R. F. (1976). Thoughts on the Behaviour of Wages and Monetarism. *Lloyds Bank Review*, 119, 1–11.
Reprint by Springer International Publishing 2022 with kind permission

An article by Professor Michael Parkin on 'Where is Britain's Inflation Going?' was published in the July issue of this *Review* and one by Sir John Hicks on 'What is Wrong with Monetarism' in the October issue. Sir John does not comment on Professor Parkin's article explicitly but by implication he is highly critical. I am in strong agreement with Sir John Hicks's analysis, subject to a few reservations. This article is largely inspired by these two papers.

R. F. Kahn



M. C. Marcuzzo, P. Paesani (eds.), *Richard F. Kahn*, Palgrave Studies in the History of Economic Thought, https://doi.org/10.1007/978-3-030-98588-2_12

I place rather less emphasis than Sir John on the degree of dispersion of rates of growth of productivity as an influence on the rate of inflation. In his discussion of the behaviour of prices in Japan in the period 1963 to 1967 he regards this dispersion as the major influence. However, I agree that it is an important influence.

I feel that Sir John attaches too much importance to his *Real Wage Resistance.* I believe that such resistance is a very important influence in those exceptional periods in which it is 'the rise in import prices which set(s) off the general rise in prices'. Sir John points out that this has been the trouble since 1973 but that 'this sharp effect was something quite new. Nothing like it had been seen since the "Korean" boom of 1950'. Normally the lead is taken by money wages, which rise faster than the price level, because of the continuous growth of productivity, and because the rate of increase in the prices of imported goods is no greater than that of domestic costs and, therefore, makes no additional contribution to the rate of inflation. As real wages are always rising, except between wage settlements, it is difficult to believe that resistance against any absolute *fall* in real wages can play much part in the mechanism of inflation. It is only when, over a period of a couple of years or so, there is an absolute fall in real wages, as a result of the prices of imported goods rising faster than those of domestic goods, that Real Wage Resistance plays an important part.

## The Vicious Wage-Wage Spiral

Apart from one passing reference to 'pressure for "fair wages"', Sir John does not touch on what many economists regard as the major element in the mechanism of inflation – the vicious 'wage-wage spiral', often described as the 'leap-frogging effect'. It is the competitive struggle between the different labour groups which is the overwhelming influence. Each group has to struggle simply in order to keep its wage rising as fast as the wages of other groups. It is a real competitive struggle, because if any group does succeed in pushing ahead of the others, their real wage rises more than the average – at the expense of the real wages of everybody else. If any group fails to keep pace, their real wage rises less than the average. A group which tails seriously behind – so much so that its wage rises less fast than the cost of living – suffers an absolute fall in its real wage: in this very restricted sense Hicks's Real Wage Resistance certainly does operate, but the meaning of the phrase could be widened to cover the whole competitive struggle between labour groups, each anxious to prevent its real wage from rising less than the average. Indeed, each is trying to secure that its real wage rises faster than the average. This is an achievement which only one-half of the wage-earners can secure – at the expense of the other half. No wonder that the struggle is so bitter.

The contrast between the monetarist explanation and the explanation given by economists like Sir John Hicks and myself is now vividly presented. In the eyes of the monetarist the role of the trade unions is purely passive. Professor Parkin states that 'monetarists disagree substantially among themselves concerning the role of trade unions, but agree that whatever they do (desirable or undesirable) they do not and cannot cause inflation'.

The leap-frogging struggle is largely between trade unions. It also operates between different sections of the same trade union. To a serious extent within individual trade unions, and also within individual companies and establishments, there is a bitter struggle between the more skilled and belter-paid workers and the less skilled and less well-paid – the former trying to maintain their traditional differentials and the latter trying to encroach on them.

## Wage Differentials

Attempts have often been made to secure a better distribution of income inside the working class by conceding higher relative increases of pay to the badly paid than to the well paid. Experience demonstrates that such attempts never succeed. Before long, differentials are widened again and restored to their traditional magnitudes.

The government's present incomes policy (inspired by Mr Jack Jones) represent an extreme case of discrimination in favour of the less well paid. Everybody earning up to £8 500 a year gets an additional £6 a week. It is true that in *The Attack on Inflation* the government stated that the £6 is 'a maximum within which negotiations will take place; some employers may not be able to pay it'. Unfortunately, attached to the White Paper is an extract from a TUC document, 'The Development of the Social Contract', in which the General Council of the TUC 'conclude that there should be a universal application of the figure of £6 per week'. Thus, £6 is regarded as an entitlement, rather than as a maximum. Of all the wage increases so far conceded under the new income policy only 5 per cent have amounted to less than £6.

Six pounds on a wage of £24 is a rise of 25 per cent, on a wage of £90 it is one of 6¾ per cent. By August 1976 the differential between, say, a £90 man and a £24 girl will have narrowed by 14¾ per cent. That is a measure of the 're-entry problem'. The new incomes policy, to operate from August 1976, if it is to be acceptable, will have, on top of the general rise of wages conceded, probably on a uniform percentage basis, to concede for the better paid an *additional* rise to restore the original differential. If the badly-paid workers, typified by the girl who until her last rise was being paid £24 a week, then get an additional 7½ per cent – a figure probably too low to be acceptable with a cost of living rising, at best, at the rate of 10 per cent a year and having risen by over 20 per cent since the previous wage settlement – the well-paid workers, typified by the man who was being paid £90 a week, will demand a rise of 26 per cent. Even if this rise could be limited to, say, 17½ per cent, the average rise of wages as a whole would be very considerable – of the order of 15 per cent. In other words the success of this year's Jack Jones policy of a flat-rate increase is likely to prejudice the success of the new incomes policy of the following year.

Actually, I am seriously understating the magnitude of the 're-entry problem'. The narrowing of the differential by 14¾ per cent which I have, by way of example, described as the result of the Jack Jones policy is based on wages before payment of income tax. After payment of income tax, the narrowing, by August 1976, will be very considerably more than 14¾ per cent – how much more depending on the number of children of the well-paid worker.

## Why the United Kingdom is Heavily Subject to Inflation

There are a number of reasons why inflation is a more serious problem in this country than in any other advanced industrial country, apart, very temporarily, from Japan and Italy:

1. Our rate of growth of productivity is the lowest of all advanced industrial countries. The extent to which the rate of rise in the price level is less than the rate of rise in the level of wages is, therefore, smaller than in any other advanced industrial country.
2. This low rate of growth of productivity is reflected in a correspondingly low rate of rise in the standard of living. The standards of living in the countries of western Europe, which some years ago were far lower than ours, with the exception of the Scandinavian countries, have caught us up and are rapidly forging ahead of ours. This is one of the causes of the exceptional bitterness of our industrial relations and of the support given to unofficial worker leaders. Both trade-union and unofficial leaders press for large wage increases, believing

wrongly that by securing them they will improve the performance of the real wage.

3. Our central employer (CBI) and trade-union (TUC) organizations are very feeble bodies and the men who run them are sadly lacking in intelligence. They contrast very unfavourably with those of the Scandinavian countries and of Austria. In Italy, although in each industry there is a christian democrat, a socialist and a communist trade union, when it comes to wage negotiations the three trade unions work together as one, and the belief of communists in the virtues of discipline ensures a sane approach to the problems of wage negotiation.
4. One serious aspect of the astonishing stupidity of our trade-union leaders, and of our unofficial labour leaders, is their complete failure to take a long-sighted view. Their sole concern is with the level of the real wage in the immediate future, as opposed to the rate of increase in the real wage. By insisting on unduly high wage increases, they force the government and the central bank to adopt restrictive measures and they undermine the confidence of employers. One important link in the chain of causation is our chronically adverse balance of payments, caused by our failure to be competitive. The result is not only unemployment and surplus physical capacity, but a low rate of productive investment, resulting in a low rate of growth of productivity and a low rate of increase in the real wage.

Western Germany provides the best example of trade-union leaders who are long-sighted and who, as a result of modesty in the size of their claim for wage increases (in relation to the high rate of growth of productivity) have secured an economic climate conducive to productive investment and the growth of productivity. The result has been, and will continue to be, a rapid rise in the real wage and the standard of living.

In January 1975 a wage settlement was reached covering about 1½ million employees in the public service sector of Western Germany. The agreed increase was 6½ per cent. A year earlier the increase had been 12½ per cent granted after a three-day strike. Leaders of the trade union concerned described the result as a 'triumph for reason'.

5. Our trade-union structure is quite extraordinarily intricate and irrational. We have far too many trade unions. One of the laws of the jungle is that the greater the number of groups in the competitive

> struggle for each to secure bigger increases than the others, the faster will wages rise.

Our basic trouble is that trade-union leaders naturally want to be seen to be earning their salaries. This is the main reason for what otherwise would be quite unintelligible insistence on the virtues of our traditional system of collective bargaining.

It is easy to see how easily the laws of the jungle can result in an accelerating upward movement of wages. It could be checked by the CBI and the TUC exercising effective influence over their members. In default of that, it can be checked only by government intervention in a determined and forceful manner.

## Wage Inflation and Unemployment

In itself, a rapid upward movement of wages is not the cause of unemployment because it carries with it an equal rise in demand expressed in terms of money. Wages are not only paid out by employers – they are spent by employees. Unemployment is, however, likely to result for a number of reasons.

It can be readily conceded to the monetarists that an increase in the quantity of money, though not the *cause* of inflation, is a necessary condition. When the quantity of money is prevented from growing as rapidly as prices rise, credit becomes progressively tighter, stock-exchange prices fall and industrialists reduce the rate of investment in productive equipment and plant, partly because they foresee a deepening recession, resulting in surplus capacity and low profits or actual losses, and partly because of growing difficulty in financing investment.

At the same time, private house-building falls, because mortgage finance becomes progressively less available and more expensive, and. for the same reason, hire-purchase-financed expenditure falls. Personal saving rises as a proportion of GNP, not only as a result of the fall in hire-purchase-financed expenditure, but also as a precaution against the increasing risk of unemployment.

For all these reasons, output falls and unemployment grows. The downward movement into recession, and depression, is progressive – as a result of the 'feed-back mechanism'. (The progressively adverse effect on the growth of productivity, and so on the rate of improvement in the real wage and the standard of living of those employed, has already been emphasized in an earlier passage of this article.)

If unemployment is already appreciable before the check imposed by a growing shortage of credit begins to operate, there is no evidence, as Sir John Hicks points out, that growing unemployment in this country *in itself* has, since the second world war, had any marked effect in stemming the upward movement of wages. To do so, unemployment would have to grow to a level politically unacceptable, probably resulting in revolution. The Phillips curve is completely discredited.

But, as Sir John Hicks puts the point:

> It is not the rate of unemployment that is effectively governing the movement of wages. It is the fact that low unemployment generally goes with high activity: and high activity means large profits. It is the movement of profits, not shown in the Phillips statistics, which makes the Phillips relation work, *when it does* (my italics).

In the course of a cyclical movement this effect is important. In the depths of a depression which is confidently known to be temporary, trade-union leaders will be relatively modest in pressing their claims, because they look forward to a time not far distant when a recovery of profits will justify forceful presentation of large claims. And at a time of depression employers will be more stubborn in resisting claims. But, if there appears to be no prospect of recovery for a long time to come, the effect of growing unemployment on trade-union leaders is different. Operating in the adverse direction is growing resentment and the increasing threat of unofficial action, militant in character.

Whether the mechanism is thought to be the direct influence of heavy unemployment or the associated slump in profitability, recent experience in this country demonstrates the compatibility of rapidly rising wages with heavy unemployment and low profitability. In any case, what a peculiar mechanism on which to rely – involving not only the waste of low production and the misery of unemployment, but also seriously adverse effects on the rate of improvement in the standard of living of those employed! And it has to be borne in mind that, even if the mechanism did work, recovery from a deep recession is a slow process.

Nevertheless, the government and the central bank are under strong pressure to prevent the quantity of money rising as fast as the rate of inflation and, in addition, the government are under strong pressure to adopt restrictive fiscal measures.

Another reason why inflation results in growing unemployment is that, if it is faster than in competing countries and if the rate of exchange is not allowed to fall in fully compensating measure, exports fall and competitive imports rise. And the growing adverse balance of payments results in the government and the Bank of England adopting even more serious restrictive measures, both monetary and fiscal.

## Alternative Occupations for Trade-Union Officials

It would be much easier for the government to operate a successful incomes policy if forms of activity alternative to wage negotiations could be developed for trade-union officials. We are backward in this country in promoting mobility of labour, in training labour and in improving industrial relations inside the individual establishments and, in particular, on the shop floor. One of the obstacles to diverting more of the energies of trade-union officials into improvement of industrial relations is the enmity between them and shop stewards. But, one way and another, trade-union officials must be encouraged to divert their energies, so that they can be visibly seen to be earning their salaries, even though, under the operation of a successful incomes policy, there is little work to be done in the field of wage negotiations.

## Inflation before 1973

It is widely believed that present-day inflation is the result of the heavy increases in the prices of primary products, especially of oil, in 1973 and the very early months of 1974. Actually, what these rises did – and here Sir John Hicks's Real Wage Resistance was a very important influence – was greatly to accelerate an inflationary movement, caused by unduly rapidly rising wages, which had already been building up several years earlier. Professor Harry Johnson is one of the editors of a book, *The Current Inflation*, consisting of the proceedings of a conference held in February 1971. He begins his introduction with the following words:

> By the early autumn of 1970 it had become evident to economic observers and commentators in the academic world, finance and journalism that this country was experiencing an inflation unprecedented in the post-Second

World War period. The inflationary process was most obviously manifest in a sharp increase in the percentage wage increases demanded by the union movement, and won in collective with employers. This had begun towards the end of 1969, and was an issue in the General Election of June 1970.

The incomes policy of the Labour government of the second half of the 'sixties had not been very successful, and towards the end of their term of office they had in effect abandoned the attempt to operate one, first of all placing entirely unjustified reliance on the TUC and then bartering away incomes policy in an unsuccessful attempt to secure measures 'In Place of Strife'. In the year ending October 1970 average hourly wage earnings rose by 16 per cent, double that of the previous twelve months. But in each of the three twelve-month periods ending in October 1973 wage-rates rose by no more than 13 per cent. The rise in the price of oil, and also of other primary products, triggered off the inflation of the last two years. It was partly the result of the impasse with the coal-miners at the end of 1973, and the failure of the Conservative party in the general election of February 1974 to persuade enough of the electorate that the country should be ruled by the government rather than by the miners.

The inflationary movement of the late 'sixties and early 'seventies – preceding the large rises in the prices of oil and other primary products – was by no means confined to this country. On an international scale it took the form of a virus, infecting one country after another. The international wage explosion can be traced back to the Netherlands, as a result, because of the entry in 1959 of the Liberal party into the coalition government, of the breakdown in the Dutch statutory prices and incomes policy, which had operated so successfully since the end of the second world war. The Dutch wage explosion took place as long ago as 1963, when the annual rate of increase of wage-rates moved into double figures.

In France in 1968 there were the 'May events', followed by Italy's 'hot autumn' of 1969. In 1970 wage-rates in the manufacturing sector of the Italian economy rose by 21 per cent, compared with 7½ per cent in 1969. In Japan, the annual average rate of increase rose from 10 per cent in the period 1960–65 to 16½ per cent in 1969 and 17½ per cent in 1970. With the exception of the United States and Switzerland, the annual increases of wage-rates moved into double figures in 1970 in all the advanced industrial countries. But for the earlier wage explosion, the influence of the rises in the price of oil and other primary products would have been far less dramatic.

## The Public Sector Borrowing Requirement and the Behaviour of the Quantity of Money

In explaining the monetarists' beliefs, Professor Parkin regards the public sector borrowing requirement as the cause of the increase in the quantity of money. He rightly attributes to the monetarists the view that it is the growth in the quantity of money which is the cause of inflation.

Actually, the link between the size of the borrowing requirement and the growth in the quantity of money is very erratic. It depends on the size of the balance-of-payments deficit on current account, which determines the extent to which foreigners finance the borrowing requirement; it depends on the private sector's appetite for gilt-edged securities and on the policy of the government and the Bank about interest rates. In any case, with modern methods of control by the Bank of the banking system, the financing of the borrowing requirement by the banks can be largely prevented from enabling the banks to expand credit by more than is regarded as desirable.

The monetarists completely confuse two different causal influences. One is the direct impact on the economy of the public sector financial deficit, which constitutes most of the borrowing requirement. The excess of public sector expenditure over tax revenue has an effect on the level of over-all demand which can be expressed in straightforward terms of common sense. Public expenditure engrosses productive resources, in a physical sense, while taxation – to a much lesser extent, pound for pound, and to a degree and in a manner depending on the pattern of the tax system – serves to keep down the real demands of the private sector, partly, personal consumption, partly, private house-building and, partly, the physical investment of companies and of unincorporated businesses.

These direct physical effects are quite independent of the behaviour of the quantity of money. The influence of the behaviour of the quantity of money is, at its worst, far less in magnitude. The monetarists, in their pre-occupation with the quantity of money, completely overlook the far greater direct physical effects of the public sector financial deficit.

Both the direct effect of the public sector financial deficit and the indirect monetary effect of the borrowing requirement operate through their influence on the level of over-all demand. The question is: What is the relation between the level of demand and the rate of *cost* inflation resulting from an excessive rate of increase of wage-rates? It has been argued earlier in this article that the relation – depending on the influence of the level of unemployment on the behaviour of wages – is small, except at a time when unemployment is low and scarcities of labour in particular sectors of the economy exist to a marked extent.

The case for reducing the public sector deficit is not that a reduction would have much, if any, effect on the rate of inflation.

The case is two-fold:

1. So long as we fail to be really competitive with overseas suppliers, both in the domestic and overseas markets, as a result of the behaviour of wages, we have to resort deliberately to creating a slump in order to keep down the volume of imports. It is a dreadful resort to which to have to be driven. But there is a limit to the extent to which we should – or indeed can – borrow from overseas.
2. It is important that when, at long last, our exports do recover, with a recovery of world trade, such recovery (and equally the increase in the production of import substitutes) should not at some stage be held back by physical shortages of labour. A reserve army of unemployed is needed also to enable productive investment to recover, and – it is much to be hoped – to rise well above the previous peak and also, at the appropriate moment in time, to enable personal consumption not only to recover but to rise at a modest pace. This is really an argument for refusing to allow public expenditure to increase rather than for refusing to make tax concessions, which can easily be withdrawn as recovery begins to get under way.

## The Chancellor's Task

The Chancellor of the Exchequer is very clear about both these arguments for reducing the public sector deficit and, in particular, the second of the two arguments, which is really an argument for preventing any increase in public expenditure. His task is a difficult one. He has committed himself to the view that he will not actively combat unemployment (apart from very minor measures) until the new incomes policy has not only been accepted (as it has) but has actually been seen to be working. He takes this view although he believes (rightly) that 'to try to cure inflation by deliberately creating mass unemployment would cause widespread misery, industrial strife and a total degeneration of our productive capacity. The only sensible course is to exercise pay restraint and reduce our domestic inflation without sacrificing our long-term goals' (*The Attack on Inflation,* paragraph 4). But 'as the rate of inflation moderates and the upturn in our economy takes place, the expansion must be founded on adequate competitiveness of British firms' (paragraph 38). 'The policies put forward in this White Paper are designed to reduce inflation to a level where the Government can employ effectively all the weapons they have at their disposal to end the present unacceptable level of unemployment: and this the Government pledge themselves to do' (paragraph 42).

The Chancellor is faced with a delicate problem of timing. If, once the new incomes policy is seen to be working successfully, Mr Healey, irrespective of the state of the balance of payments, unduly postpones tax concessions designed substantially to reduce unemployment, he will severely prejudice the negotiation of a successful new incomes policy to operate from August 1976.

CHAPTER 13

# Inflation—A Keynesian View

*Richard F. Kahn*

Politicians, civil servants, central bankers and economists must all feel thoroughly ashamed of the state of the world today, especially of the advanced industrial countries. On their economic policies, and on their implementation, depend the welfare of the rest of the world—including the oil-producing countries, even though their welfare does not cause concern. The authorities are reluctant to stimulate the depressed economies more than very gently because of their fear that rapid recovery will be associated with a fresh bout of inflation, rising again to dangerously high rates.

A simple test can be used to differentiate between Keynesian (or neo-Keynesian) economists and monetarist and other anti-Keynesian economists. It is only necessary to enquire whether the danger, and degree, of renewed inflation depends on the character of the cause of an economic recovery.

The monetarists, and other anti-Keynesian economists, will reply that an increase in the rate of inflation will be associated with economic recovery only if the recovery is the result of an increase in public sector expenditure or a reduction in taxation, or an expansion of bank credit which

Originally publ. in: Kahn, R. F. (1976). Inflation—A Keynesian View. *Scottish Journal of Political Economy, 33*(1), 11–16.
Reprint by Springer International Publishing 2022 with kind permission

R. F. Kahn



M. C. Marcuzzo, P. Paesani (eds.), *Richard F. Kahn*, Palgrave Studies in the History of Economic Thought,
https://doi.org/10.1007/978-3-030-98588-2_13

stimulates the private sector directly by encouraging company investment, private house-building and hire-purchase financed expenditure.

The monetarists are not worried so long as the quantity of money does not rise more rapidly than the rate of growth of national output multiplied by the acceptable rate of rise in the price-level. It is the expansion of bank assets, and so of the quantity of money, at a higher rate than this to which they attribute inflation at an unacceptably high rate. If, on the other hand, the recovery is caused by a spontaneous upsurge of confidence, showing itself in high animal spirits on the part of industrialists, so that they feel inclined to invest at a more rapid rate in plant and equipment, the monetarists and other anti-Keynesians will feel quite happy.

Keynesian economists believe that in so far as there is a relation at all between the level of activity and the rate of inflation, the relation does not depend on the character of the economic forces responsible for any particular level of activity.

This statement calls for a minor qualification. Inflation, according to Keynesians, is largely—if not entirely—due to rapidly rising wages. The willingness of the leaders and members of trade unions to help the Government to curb inflation by exercising restraint over demands for wage increases depends to some extent on their attitude towards Government policy. They will be more co-operative if the Government stimulate the economy by reducing taxation which falls heavily on wage-earners than if they stimulate it by spending more on defence.

Monetarists believe that inflation 'has nothing or almost nothing to do with trade unions' (*The Banker,* July 1975; p. 773). Trade unions are just a cog in the machine, which would function in the same way independently of the behaviour of trade unions, or indeed of their existence.

Monetarists emphasise that the influence of the behaviour of the quantity of money on the rate of inflation is subject to considerable time-lags. The time-lags are rather unpredictable and difficult to estimate. Some years ago Professor A. A. Walters—perhaps the leading monetarist in this country—wrote of a time-lag of six months (Walters, 1969: p. 38). But under the influence of Professor Milton Friedman, it has usually been put at somewhere between three and seven quarters of a year.

Belief in monetarism thus necessarily results in an extreme degree of pessimism as to the length of time required for monetarist remedies for inflation to operate. As it is generally agreed that it would be dangerous to take steps to stimulate the economy until the monetary mechanism is in full operation on the restrictive tack, this means that monetarists feel morally obliged to condemn each industrial country, and therefore the world in general, to several years of deliberately self-imposed economic depression.

Professor David Laidler is another leader of the British monetarist school. In a recent article (Laidler, 1975) he stated the following view:—

> Even if we prevent the current recession turning into a major depression, and avoid over-reacting to unemployment with expansionary ('reflationary') policies that, in bringing unemployment down, set up a yet more violent burst of inflation than we have experienced, we shall nevertheless probably see an average of a million unemployed for five years or more if we are to get the inflation rate down below, say, 5 per cent by 1980.

If this *has* to be the prospect, it means a gigantic cost, not only in terms of human misery and potential output, but also a very low rate of productive investment and even lower rates of economic growth, and of improvement in the standard of living, not only during the depression but for an unlimited period after recovery has taken place. The set-back to the standard of living, and to its rate of improvement, will be very long-lived, if not permanent. At the end of the depression the quantity and quality of productive equipment will be far lower than they might have been. And industrialists, after such an experience, will remain very cautious and unenterprising in the development of the economy.

Since belief in monetarist doctrine leads to such pessimistic conclusions, it is enormously important to enquire into its validity. It would not be so bad if monetarist belief were confined to Great Britain. If we could rely on reasonably rapid recovery in the other large industrial countries, we could look forward to our being carried in their wake along the recovery path as a result of expansion of our exports. I assume that Professor Laidler, and other members of the monetarist school, would not be worried by 'export led growth'. But the influence of monetarist doctrine is much greater in the United States and in western Germany than in Great Britain. This helps to explain the lamentable state of the world economy.

The Keynesian view of monetary influences is quite different. It is agreed that rapid inflation can persist only if the increase in the quantity of money keeps pace with the increase in the value of national income. But the increase in the quantity of money is not the *cause* of the inflation. It is, however, a necessary condition.

When the quantity of money is prevented from growing as rapidly as the value of national income, credit becomes progressively tighter, stock exchange prices fall, and industrialists reduce the rate of investment in productive equipment and plant, partly because they foresee a recession, resulting in surplus capacity, and partly because of difficulty in financing investment, the availability of finance being reduced and its cost being raised. The fall in the prices of equities means that rights issues become unattractive to boards of directors, and, as the recession deepens, impossible because of the technical state of the equity market.

At the same time private house-building falls, because mortgage, and other kinds of finance, are less available and more expensive, and, for the same reason, hire-purchase financed expenditure falls. Personal saving rises as a proportion of GNP, not only as a result of the fall in hire-purchase financed expenditure, but also as a precaution against possible unemployment.

For all these reasons output falls, unemployment grows, and profits fall. The fall in profits leads to a further reduction in industrialists' investment in plant and equipment. The downward movement into recession, and depression, is progressive—as a result of the feedback mechanism. But the operation of the mechanism is slow. This explains the time-lags, which the monetarists have to accept—without much in the way of explanation—when they test their theories against the facts.

Many Keynesians, unlike monetarists, do not believe that the recession which results from applying the monetary brake will do a great deal to reduce the rate of inflation, if there already was appreciable unemployment and surplus capacity in existence before the brake was applied. To what extent the rate of inflation is reduced depends on the influence exerted on the outcomes of the processes of wage-bargaining of heavier, and growing, unemployment, lower and falling profitability, narrower, and narrowing, profit margins, and the growth of bankruptcies, both actual and threatened.

Present and recent experience demonstrates the compatibility of rapidly rising wages with heavy unemployment and low profitability. It is, of course, usually true that as a recession deepens, demands for wage increases become less pressing and, at any rate in the private sector, employers become less willing to grant large concessions. But it seems evident that reliance on heavy unemployment, and on that alone, to bring inflation down to a tolerable level would require levels of unemployment which, ever since 1939, would be politically unacceptable.

Indeed, before such levels are reached, the forces may sometimes work in the opposite direction. If an attempt is being made to operate an incomes policy, its success may be prejudiced as a result of resentment against the Government on the part of the leaders and members of trade unions, provoked by heavy unemployment. And, irrespective of any incomes policy, trade union leaders are apt to take the line that if the Government are not prepared to stimulate demand, it is their duty to their members to do so by pressing for an even more rapid rise in wages. (While there is not much in the idea that, in spite of its repercussions on the behaviour of prices, a more rapid rise of money wages means higher real wages, there is much more in the idea that acceleration of the upward movement of money-wages means higher real wages.)

At the moment in this country we are relying on the widespread acceptance of the belief that inflation causes unemployment. (This belief can be rationalised—but only partially—in various ways. Inflation does result in the Government and the Central Bank adopting restrictive measures—among them curbing the growth of credit. Inflation, if it is faster than in competing countries and if the rate of exchange is held fixed, results in growing unemployment in industries which compete with overseas suppliers, both in overseas and in the domestic markets. And price control can be deliberately operated—as it is today in Britain—so as to validate the doctrine.)

The Chancellor of the Exchequer has made it clear that he is not prepared to combat unemployment in any wholesale way until the new control of incomes can actually be seen to be succeeding. But when clearer signs of success become evident, the Government will have to decide to what extent and how rapidly to take steps to stimulate the economy. In the making of their decisions, the major consideration will be the vital importance of retaining the goodwill and the co-operation of the T.U.C. and the trade union leaders and members. There is the 're-entry problem' to be faced. And then there is the problem of what incomes policy is to replace the present one, which operates only up to 1 August 1976. Long before that date a new policy must be formulated, discussed and accepted.

In conclusion, reference is very briefly made to other difficulties presented by the doctrines of the monetarists and other anti-Keynesians.

1. The latest development of the monetarist view is the 'natural unemployment rate' 'at which the inflation rate neither accelerates nor slows down relatively to expectations' (Laidler, 1975: p. 39). Professor Laidler admits that it is extremely difficult to assess what the rate is. 'Work in progress at Manchester University suggests that it is perhaps a little less than 2 per cent in Britain'. Presumably—but I am not clear about this—a correct behaviour of the quantity of money is believed ultimately (in the absence of disturbances, such as in fact are always occurring) to result, when the system has settled

down to a smooth path, both in a tolerable behaviour of money-wages and in the establishment of the 'natural unemployment rate'. So the monetarists can no longer claim that the adoption of their policy will ultimately result in full employment. Of course, if the natural rate is as low as Professor Laidler's 2 per cent, there is no appreciable difference. But I am very doubtful whether, if it exists at all (I do not believe that it does), it is as low as 2 per cent in Britain, in which wage negotiations take place, in the absence of any effective incomes policy, in a manner reminiscent of jungle warfare.

2. The monetarists emphasise the damage attributable to a large public sector deficit. But presumably, in their view, the damage depends on the extent to which a large public sector deficit results in a rapid growth in the quantity of money. The relationship between the two varies enormously between one point of time and another. It depends on the size of the balance of payments deficit on current account (which helps to determine the extent to which the public sector deficit is financed by public sector borrowing from overseas). It depends on the appetite of the private sector for gilt-edged securities and the policy of the Government and the Bank about rates of interest. It depends also on the extent and character of control by the Bank over the operations of the banking system.

Keynesians draw a clear distinction between the direct influence of the public sector deficit as an important element in the determination of overall demand and its indirect influence, through its effect on the ability of the banks to expand credit.

3. At a time of heavy unemployment Keynesians of the Old School see no harm in a large public sector deficit, or in increasing it as a means of stimulating the economy. This view is now disputed by the New School of Cambridge (England) Keynesian (not monetarist) economists. They attribute the balance of payments deficit on current account to the public sector deficit. Unemployment should not be dealt with by increasing the public sector deficit, which should be reduced. Unemployment should be dealt with by rendering the country's industries more competitive with overseas suppliers—by exchange depreciation, tariffs and import restrictions.

The question which, so far as I know, my colleagues of the New School have failed so far to answer is how their doctrines apply at a time like the present when heavy unemployment prevails in all the industrial countries. They cannot each depreciate their currency in terms of the currencies of the others. And if each imposes tariffs and import restrictions against the others, what would be the advantage?

It would be interesting to try to apply the New School's doctrines and relationships to the O.E.C.D., regarded as one single country, with a very small balance of payments deficit on current account and a very large aggregate public sector deficit.

## References

Laidler, D. (1975). *British Commentary* appended to M. Friedman, *Unemployment versus Inflation*. Institute of Economic Affairs, London.

Walters, A. A. (1969). *Money in Boom and Slump*. Institute of Economic Affairs, London.

# List of Richard F. Kahn's Publications

## 1931

The relation of home investment to unemployment. *Economic Journal*, *41*(162), June, 173–198. Reprinted in R.F. Kahn (1972), *Selected Essays on Employment and Growth* (pp. 1–27).

## 1932

The financing of public works: a note. *Economic Journal*, *42*(167), September, 492–495.

Decreasing costs: a note on the contributions of Mr Harrod and Mr Allen. *Economic Journal*, *42*(168), December, 657–661.

## 1933

Imperfect competition and the marginal principle. Translated in Italian and published in R.F. Kahn (1999). *Concorrenza, occupazione e moneta*. Ed. by M.C. Marcuzzo. Bologna: Il Mulino. **Published as Chapter 2 in this volume.**

Public works and inflation. *Journal of the American Statistical Association*, *28*(Suppl. 181A), March, 168–173. Papers and Proceedings of the Ninety-fourth Annual Meeting of the American Statistical Association



R. F. Kahn et al., *Richard F. Kahn*, Palgrave Studies in the History of Economic Thought,
https://doi.org/10.1007/978-3-030-98588-2

(edited by Frank Alexander Ross), held at Cincinnati, Ohio, December 28–31, 1932. Reprinted in R.F. Kahn (1972), *Selected Essays on Employment and Growth* (pp. 28–34).

The elasticity of substitution and the relative share of a factor. *Review of Economic Studies*, *1*(1), October, 72–78.

Reply to J.R. Hicks, 'IV—A note on Mr Kahn's paper'. *Review of Economic Studies*, 1(1), October, 80.

## 1935

Some notes on ideal output. *Economic Journal*, *45*(177), March, 1–35.

Two applications of the concept of elasticity of substitution. *Economic Journal*, *45*(178), June, 242–245.

## 1936

Review of *Soviet Money and Finance* by L.E. Hubbard (London: Macmillan, 1936). *New Statesman and Nation*, August 29, 296.

Dr Neisser on secondary employment: a note. *Review of Economics and Statistics*, *18*(3), August, 144–147.

Mr. Paine and rationalisation: a note. *Economica*, *3*(11), August, 327–329.

Review of *Works on Prosperity and Depression*, by A.D. Gayer (London: Macmillan 1935). *Economic Journal*, *46*(183), September, 491–493.

Review of *Report of the Committee of Investigation for England on Complaints made by the Central Milk Distributive Committee and the Parliamentary Committee of the Co-operative Congress as to the Operation of the Milk Marketing Scheme* (1933). *Economic Journal*, *46*(183), September, 554–559.

English translation of K. Wicksell, *Geldzins und Guterpreise* (*Interest and Prices: A Study of the Causes Regulating the Value of Money*. London: Macmillan).

## 1937

The problem of duopoly. *Economic Journal*, *47*(185), March, 1–20. **Reprinted as Chapter 3 in this volume.**

The League of Nations enquiry into the trade cycle (review of *Prosperity and Depression: A Theoretical Analysis of Cyclical Movements*, by G. von Haberler. Geneva: League of Nations; London: Allen & Unwin, 1937). *Economic Journal*, *47*(188), December, 670–679.

## 1938

Review of *Studies in the Theory of Economic Expansion* by E. Lundberg (London: P.S. King & Son, 1938). *Economic Journal*, *48*(190), June, pp. 265–268.

A rejoinder (to some comments on Mr Kahn's Review of *Prosperity and Depression*). *Economic Journal*, *48*(190), June, 333–336.

## 1939

Review of *World Economic Survey. Seventh Year, 1937–38*, by J.E. Meade (Geneva: League of Nations; London: Allen & Unwin, 1938). *Economic Journal*, *49*(193), March, pp. 96–98.

Review of *Industrial Price Policies and Economic Progress*, by E.G. Nourse and H.B. Drury (Washington: The Brooking Institutions, 1938); Review of *Industrial Price Policies* (a summary of *Industrial Price Policies and Economic Progress*), by M.S. Stewart (New York: Public Affairs Committee, 1938). *Economic Journal*, *49*(194), June, 321–323.

## 1946

Exports and manpower. *The Economist*, December 14.

## 1947

Tariffs and the terms of trade. *Review of Economic Studies*, *15*(1), 14–19.

Trade make-believe. *The Economist*, January 4.

The saving campaign. *The Times*, August 25.

Marshall Aid and the dollar gap. *The Times*, December 30.

## 1948

Civil service examination. *The Times*, March 30.

The 1948 Budget: an economist's criticism. *The Listener*, May 6, 738–739.

The volume of exports. Need to raise the level. *The Times*, October 28.

## 1949

Our economic complacency. *The Listener*, February 3, 166–167 and 181.

Professor Meade on planning. *Economic Journal*, *59*(233), March, 1–16.

Disinflation continued?. *The Economist*, March 19.

Review of the *Third Annual Report of the International Bank for Reconstruction and Development, 1947–1948* (Washington, DC: IBRD, 1948). *Economic Journal*, *59*(235), September, 445–447.

Devaluation and sterling markets. *The Economist*, October 15.

A possible Intra-European payments scheme. *Economica*, *16*(64), November, 293–304.

## 1950

The dollar shortage and devaluation. *Economia Internazionale*, *3*(1), February, 89–113. Reprinted in R.F. Kahn (1972), *Selected Essays on Employment and Growth* (pp. 35–59).

The European Payments Union. *Economica*, *17*(67), August, 306–316.

An approach to economic development in the Middle East (review of the *Final Report of the United Nations Economic Survey Mission for the Middle East: An Approach to Economic Development in the Middle East*. London: HMSO for the United Nations, 1949). *Economic Journal*, *60*(239), September, 634–635.

Marshall Aid. *The Times*, November 11.

## 1951

The Budget. *The Economist*, May 5.

Home and export trade. *Economic Journal*, *61*(242), June, 279–289.

The balance of payments and the sterling area. *District Bank Review*, *100*, December, 3–17.

Manpower control. *The Economist*, December 15.

## 1952

Manpower control. *The Economist*, January 5.

Oxford studies in the price mechanism. *Economic Journal*, *62*(245), March, 119–130. **Reprinted as Chapter 4 in this volume.**

International regulation of trade and exchanges. In *Banking and Foreign Trade* (pp. 1–18), Lectures delivered at the Fifth International Banking Summer School, Oxford, July. London: Europa Publications for the Institute of Bankers. **Reprinted as Chapter 8 in this volume.**

Review of *The Problem of Employment Stabilization* by B. Ohlin (New York: Columbia university Press, 1949). *American Economic Review*, *42*(1), March, 180–182.

Comments (on monetary policy and the crisis). *Bulletin of the Oxford University*, *14*, April–May, 147–153.

Britain's economic position. *The Listener*, July 3, 18–22.

Monetary policy and the balance of payments. *Political Quarterly*, *23*(3), July, 250–261. Reprinted in R.F. Kahn (1972), *Selected Essays on Employment and Growth* (pp. 60–71).

Comments (on monetary policy again). *Bulletin of the Oxford University*, *14*, August, 278–280.

Investment. *The Economist,* December 6.

## 1953

Living with the Dollar. *The Economist*, January 1.

The Dollar Gap: Our Precarious Balance. *The Times*, February 23.

Living with the Dollar. *The Economist*, March 14.

Equipment for industry. *The Times*, April 20.

## 1954

The case for cheap money. *The Financial Times*, June 3–4.

The convertibility risk. *The Financial Times*, September 10.

Some notes on liquidity preference. *Manchester School of Economic and Social Studies*, *22*(3), September, 229–257. Reprinted in R.F. Kahn (1972), *Selected Essays on Employment and Growth* (pp. 72–96).

(With D.G. Champernowne). The value of invested capital: a mathematical addendum to Mrs. Robinson's article. *Review of Economic Studies*, *21*(2), 107–111. Reprinted as Appendix to J.V. Robinson. (1956). *The Accumulation of Capital.* London: Macmillan.

## 1955

Short-term business indicators in Western Europe. *Economic Bulletin for Europe*, *7*(3), November, 34–78.

## 1956

Lord Keynes and inflation. *The Listener*, May 3, 543–545.
Lord Keynes and the balance of payments. *The Listener*, May 10, 591–593.
Lord Keynes and contemporary economic problems. *The Listener*, May 3 and 10. Reprinted in R.F. Kahn (1972), *Selected Essays on Employment and Growth* (pp. 103–123).
An answer to the capital question. *Westminster Bank Review*, August, 1–26.
Full employment and British economic policy. *Nihon Keizai Shimbun*, 1956. Reprinted in R.F. Kahn (1972), *Selected Essays on Employment and Growth* (pp. 97–102).

## 1957

Doubts about the free trade area. *The Listener*, February 28, 331–333.
Doubts about the free trade area. *The Times*, March 21.
A positive contribution?. *Bulletin of the Oxford Institute of Statistics*, *19*(1), February, 63–68.

## 1958

Memorandum of evidence submitted to the Radcliffe Committee (May 27). In Radcliffe Committee on the Working of the Monetary System (1959), *Principal Memoranda of Evidence* (Vol. 3, pp. 138–146). London: HMSO. Reprinted in R.F. Kahn (1972), *Selected Essays on Employment and Growth* (pp. 124–152).
Evidence (October 23). In Radcliffe Committee on the Working of the Monetary System (1960), *Minutes of Evidence* (pp. 739–746). London: HMSO.
The pace of development. In *The Challenge of Development: A Symposium* (pp. 163–198). Lecture delivered at the Eliezer Kaplan School of Economics and Social Sciences. Jerusalem: Hebrew University of Jerusalem. Reprinted in R.F. Kahn (1972), *Selected Essays on Employment and Growth* (pp. 153–191).

## 1959

Exercises in the analysis of growth. *Oxford Economic Papers, 11*(2), June, 146–163. Reprinted in R.F. Kahn (1972), *Selected Essays on Employment and Growth* (pp. 192–207).

Sur l'analyse de la croissance. In *Colloques Economiques Franco-Britanniques: L'accumulation du capital* (pp. 51–69). Paris: ISMEA.

## 1961

Organisation for European Economic Co-operation. *The Problem of Rising Prices*, report by William Fellner, Milton Gilbert, Brent Hansen, Richard Kahn, Friedrich Lutz, Pieter de Wolff. Paris: OEEC.

The Budget I should like to see. *The Financial Times*, April 13.

A reasonable doubt: governments vies on wages policy. *The Times*, October 31.

## 1962

Policy on wage rates: annual or actual increases. *The Times*, May 16.

## 1963

Economic situation. *The Times*, January 24.

## 1964

(With R. Cohen, W.B. Reddaway, J.V. Robinson). Statement submitted to the Lloyd Jacob Committee on Resale Price Maintenance. *Oxford Bulletin of Economics and Statistics, 26*(2), May, 113–121.

## 1965

The progress of the British economy in 1965. *The Financial Times*, January 1.

The progress of the British economy in 1966. *The Financial Times*, December 31.

United Nations Conference on Trade and Development. *International Monetary Issues and the Developing Countries: Report of the Group of Experts* (R.F. Kahn was one of the members). New York: United Nations.

Un confronto fra la politica inglese e quella italiana. In G. Fuà (ed.), *Programmazione economica: confronti italo inglesi* (pp. 145–150). English translation by G. Ascarelli-Spierer. Urbino (Italy): Argalia.

## 1966

The Budget I would like to see. *The Financial Times*, April 5.

*The economic situation*. Address to the House of Lords, July 28.

*The prices and incomes policy*. Address to the House of Lords, August 3.

United Nations Conference on Trade and Development. *Payments Arrangements among the Developing Countries for Trade Expansion: Report of the Group of Experts* (chaired by R.F. Kahn). Geneva: United Nations.

United Nations Conference on Trade and Development. *Trade Expansion and Economic Co-operation among Developing Countries: Report of the Group of Experts* (R.F. Kahn was one of the members). New York: United Nations.

## 1967

*European Economic Community*. Address to the House of Lords, May 8.

## 1968

*The economic situation and public expenditure*. Address to the House of Lords, January 24.

## 1969

United Nations Conference on Trade and Development. *International Monetary Reform and Co-operation for Development* (R.F. Kahn was one of the members). New York: United Nations.

## 1971

Notes on the rate of interest and the growth of firms. In R.F. Kahn (1972), *Selected Essays on Employment and Growth* (pp. 208–232).

## 1972

*Selected Essays on Employment and Growth*. Cambridge: Cambridge University Press.

## 1973

The International Monetary System, *American Economic Review*, *63*(2), 181–188. **Reprinted as Chapter 9 in this volume**.

SDR and aid. *Lloyds Bank Review*, *28*(110), October, 1–18.

*Economic and industrial affairs*. Address to the House of Lords, November 6.

*Counter-inflation (prices and pay code) (no. 2)*. Address to the House of Lords, November 20.

*Economic policy and fuel supplies*. Address to the House of Lords, December 18.

## 1974

*Industrial and economic situation*. Address to the House of Lords, February 6.

Plans for a monetary system to replace the Bretton Woods agreement. In N.S. Fatemi (ed.), *Problems of Balance of Payments and Trade* (pp. 199–266). New Jersey: Rutherford.

(With M. Posner). Challenging the 'elegant and striking' paradoxes of the New School. *The Times*, April 17.

(With M. Posner). Theory dogged by its assumptions. *The Times*, April 18.

(With M.V. Posner). Cambridge economics and the balance of payments. *London and Cambridge Economic Bulletin*, *85*, July, 19–32.

(With M. Posner). Why an incomes policy remains essential. *The Financial Times*, August 22.

(With M.V. Posner). The effects of public expenditure on inflation and the balance of payments. In *Public Expenditure, Inflation and the Balance of Payments: Ninth Report from the Expenditure Committee* (HC328). London: HMSO.
The Mini-budget and the crisis. *Sunday Telegraph*, July 28.
*The economic position*. Address to the House of Lords, July 30.
Is a dose of Sir Keith's horrible medicine the only way to bring Britain to its senses?. *The Times*, September 16.
What Keynes really said. *Sunday Telegraph*, September 22.
On re-reading Keynes (Fourth Keynes Lecture in Economics delivered on November 6, 1974). *Proceedings of the British Academy* (vol. LX, pp. 361–392). Oxford: Oxford University Press, 1975.

## 1975

Erosion of UK competitive position. *The Times*, March 5.
Reducing the rate of inflation. *The Times*, July 4.
*The attack on inflation*. Address to the House of Lords, July 30.
Inflation and the Unions. *New Statesman*, August 1.
Oil and the crisis. In J. Hicks et al., *Crisis '75...?* (pp. 34–38). *IEA Occasional Papers Special*, no. 43. London: Institute of Economic Affairs.

## 1976

Thoughts on the behaviour of wages and monetarism. *Lloyds Bank Review*, 119, January, 1–11. **Reprinted as Chapter 12 in this volume.**
Inflation: a Keynesian view. *Scottish Journal of Political Economy*, *33*(1), February, 11–16. **Reprinted as Chapter 13 in this volume.**
Public expenditure cuts. *New Statesman*, February 2.
Political attitudes involved in teaching economics. *Oxford Review of Education*, *2*(1), 91–95.
Unemployment as seen by the Keynesians. In G.D.N. Worswick (ed.), *The Concept and Measurement of Involuntary Unemployment* (pp. 19–25). London: Allen & Unwin. **Reprinted as Chapter 11 in this volume.**
Historical origins of the International Monetary Fund. In A.P. Thirlwall (ed.), *Keynes and International Monetary Relations* (pp. 3–35). London: Macmillan. **Reprinted as Chapter 10 in this volume.**

## 1977

*The economic situation*. Address to the House of Lords, January 26.

Mr. Eltis and the Keynesians. *Lloyds Bank Review*, *32*(124), April, 1–13.

(With M.V. Posner). Inflation, unemployment and growth. *National Westminster Bank Quarterly Review*, *10*, November, 28–37.

Malinvaud on Keynes. Reviewing: Edmond Malinvaud, *The Theory of Unemployment Reconsidered* (Oxford: Basil Blackwell, 1977); three lectures delivered for the Yrjö Jahnsson Foundation. *Cambridge Journal of Economics*, *1*(4), December, 375–388.

A comment. In T.W. Hutchinson, *Keynes versus the 'Keynesians'* (pp. 48–57). London: IEA.

## 1978

Review of J. Hicks, *Economic Perspectives: Further Essays on Money and Growth* (Oxford: Oxford University Press, 1977). *Manchester School of Economic and Social Studies*, 46, March, 83–85.

Some aspects of the development of Keynes's thought. *Journal of Economic Literature*, *16*(2), June, 544–559. **Reprinted as Chapter 6 in this volume.**

## 1983

*L'economia del breve periodo*. Ed. by M. Dardi. Torino: Boringhieri (first publication, translated in Italian, of *The Economics of the Short Period*, Kahn's Fellowship dissertation, submitted to King's College, Cambridge, in December 1929).

## 1984

*The Making of Keynes's General Theory: Raffaele Mattioli Lectures*. Cambridge: Cambridge University Press.

'The General Theory of Employment, Interest and Money' (Fifth Raffaele Mattioli Lecture). In R. F. Kahn, *The Making of Keynes's General Theory* (pp. 119–168). **Reprinted as Chapter 7 in this volume.**

## 1985

The Cambridge 'Circus'. In G. Harcourt (ed.), *Keynes and His Contemporaries* (pp. 42–51). The Sixth Centennial Keynes Seminar held at the University of Kent at Canterbury, 1983. London: Macmillan. **Reprinted as Chapter 5 in this volume.**

## 1987

Rostas, L. Entry in J. Eatwell, M. Milgate and P. Newman (eds.), *The New Palgrave. A Dictionary of Economics* (vol. IV, pp. 222–223). London: Macmillan.

Shove, G.F. Entry in J. Eatwell, M. Milgate and P. Newman (eds.), *The New Palgrave: A Dictionary of Economics* (vol. IV, pp. 327–328). London: Macmillan.

## 1988

Inflation and Commodities in the Middle East during the Second World War. *Materie prime*, 8(3), 99–101.

## 1989

*The Economics of the Short Period*. London: Macmillan (Kahn's Fellowship dissertation, submitted to King's College, Cambridge, in December 1929). Italian translation previously published (1983). *L'economia del breve periodo*. Torino: Boringhieri.

# Index[1]



[1] Note: Page numbers followed by 'n' refer to notes.



R. F. Kahn et al., *Richard F. Kahn*, Palgrave Studies in the History of Economic Thought,
https://doi.org/10.1007/978-3-030-98588-2

## O



## P



## Q



## R



## S



## T

FSC
www.fsc.org
MIX
Papier | Fördert
gute Waldnutzung
FSC® C083411

Kolibri 360 GmbH
Ferdinand-Jühlke-Straße 7
99095 Erfurt, Deutschland
produktsicherheit@kolibri360.de